Public Choice

Public Choice
An Introduction

Iain McLean

Basil Blackwell

Copyright © Iain McLean 1987

First published 1987

Basil Blackwell Ltd
108 Cowley Road, Oxford, OX4 1JF, UK

Basil Blackwell Inc,
432 Park Avenue South, Suite 1503
New York, NY 10016, USA

British Library Cataloguing in Publication Data

McLean, Iain.
   Public choice: an introduction.
   1. Social choice   2. Political science
   I. Title
   320′.01′.9   JA77
   ISBN 0–631–13838–2
   ISBN 0–631–13839–0 Pbk

Library of Congress Cataloging in Publication Data

McLean, Iain.
   Public choice.

   Bibliography: p.
   Includes index.
   1. Social choice   I. Title.
   HB846.8.M38   1987   302′.13   86–18885
   ISBN 0–631–13838–2
   ISBN 0–631–13839–0 (pbk.)

Typeset in 10½ on 12 pt Sabon
by Opus, Oxford
Printed in Great Britain by Billing & Sons Ltd, Worcester

Contents

Contents

Preface and Acknowledgments

Public choice is burgeoning. It is filling the pages of the American political science journals, and increasingly those of the British ones as well. More and more books using public-choice methods are rolling off the presses. James Buchanan won the 1986 Nobel Prize in Economics in recognition of his role as a founding father of public choice. And yet it is all very alien to many students of politics or sociology – and often to their teachers. Public choice deals with the central phenomena of politics, such as voters, lobbyists, politicians; voting procedures and electoral reform; democratic theory and theories of obligation. But it was invented by economists and mathematicians, who extended their techniques to other people's subject-matter. There is nothing wrong with that: indeed intellectual advance often depends on looking at familiar topics in a new light. But until now there has been no introduction to public choice for readers with no background in economics or mathematics. There are a number of good introductory books, but all of them, unlike this one, assume that the reader has studied at least some economics. I think public choice is important and exciting; it need not, and should not, be closed to non-economists.

I could not have written this book without the help of the Economic and Social Research Council, which gave me a Personal Research Grant for 1984–5 to spend the year reading, thinking, and writing public choice. I was able to become a student again, and I am very grateful to David Soskice and my fellow economics students at this college for putting up with the cuckoo in their nest. Parts of this book were tried out at seminars at Oxford, York, Glasgow, Yale, Harvard, and George Mason Universities, and I am most grateful for all the criticism I received. Parts of the book (in some cases all of it) were read and criticised by Robert Axelrod, Bo Bjurulf, Richard Dawkins, Norman Frohlich, Allan Gibbard, W. D. Hamilton, Peter Jackson, Neil Mason, Ng Lak Chuan, Amartya Sen, David Steel, Alan Ware, Albert Weale, Mark Williams and John Wiseman. I am most grateful to all of them. Needless to say, none of them should be blamed for anything I have written, and neither should any of the participants in the American scrubber controversy who very kindly gave me their time to guide me through the maze I try to describe in the chapters that follow. My students have been ideal and uncomplaining (to me, at any rate) guinea-pigs.

Before starting to write, I tossed a coin. If it had come down 'heads', all personal pronouns intended to refer to both sexes would have been feminine. It came down 'tails', so I use 'he', 'his', etc., to include 'she', 'her', etc. Expressions printed in **bold type** are defined in the glossary, which also contains explanations of some mathematical symbols.

My greatest debt of all is to my wife Jo, who kept me calm, met me from the train, put me on the train, read and criticised great tracts of what follows – and all that while working for hours and in conditions that were outlawed many decades ago for every occupation except doctors. She has helped me to put it all in perspective.

University College
Oxford

Introduction

What is Public Choice?

You may never have heard of the term 'public choice'. But you have certainly heard of voters, parties, politicians, bureaucrats, interest groups, and voting rules. These are the basic subject-matter of political science, and they are the subject-matter of this book. Public choice is not a subject; it is a way of studying a subject. It has been defined as 'the economic study of nonmarket decisionmaking' (Mueller 1979, p. 1). It takes the tools of economics, and applies them to the material of politics. By applying logical, deductive reasoning, economists try to work out what a rational actor (a consumer, an entrepreneur, a trade unionist, and so on) would do to maximise his chances of getting what he wants. From this they can construct an elaborate picture of what an economy would look like if everybody acted **rationally**, compare it with the real-world economy, and make predictions about the effects of changes in conditions or policies.

Economists deal, mostly, in private choices. If I would like an apple, and if the government does not control the supply of apples, economic theory can explain how I get my apple, as part of a fuller explanation of how the wishes of millions of consumers and producers interact to determine the price and quantity of apples. My apple is a private good in two separate senses. First, as it happens the government has not intervened in the market for apples. (It might have done, but it has not.) Second, my decision to consume it does not impose any significant costs or benefits on anybody else except the other people involved in bringing it to market. (You may find this condition mysterious. The importance of it is explained in the discussion of 'public goods' in chapter 1.) Any choice made under other conditions is at least partly a public choice. If the government intervenes to fix the maximum price of apples, it is taking the decision away from the market and into the political arena. If it passes a clean air law, it is taking a political decision the market cannot practicably take. But non-market political decisions can perfectly well be studied using the same tools as market decisions. We can look at voters as if they were consumers, politicians as if they were entrepreneurs, parties as if they were firms, and so on. That is what Part I of this book does. Part II moves into political theory and shows what public choice can do with traditional questions such as 'why should anybody obey the government?' and 'should government obey the will of the people?'

Who is this Book for?

The reader I have mostly in mind is a student of politics or sociology who has taken one or more empirical courses in government and perhaps a course in political theory. He knows something about how different political systems are organised but he would like to arrange his information into something more systematic than a pile of unconnected facts. He has not taken any mathematics courses since school and has never studied economics.

I also hope I have something to say to two other categories of reader. One is the economics student who wants to see how, or whether, the economic theory he has learned can be extended to cope with market failure, non-market decision-making, and bargaining in non-zero-sum games. The other is the concerned citizen who wonders why politics never turns out the way anybody ever intended, and why groups of clever people can produce very stupid results. He may find that the reasons are deeper than most people realise.

Will I Understand the Arguments?

Although this is not an economics book, it uses economists' modes of reasoning, and their way of looking at the world. Students sometimes suffer intellectual and/or emotional 'blocks' at the idea of 'thinking like an economist'. The intellectual block comes from the feeling that economics is terribly technical or mathematical. To try to overcome that block, I have given myself some strict rules. There is no maths at all in the text of the book. (There is some elementary calculus in the appendix to chapter 5, but nothing else even in the appendices that should be beyond a reader without maths but with a logical mind; and the appendices are not essential to the main argument.) I have also included a glossary of technical terms, each of which is printed in **bold type** at its first mention. For the reader who would like a more formal presentation, there is no shortage of books and articles to go on to; I suggest some in the further reading section.

I suspect, however, that the emotional block causes more trouble than the intellectual block. Oscar Wilde defined a cynic as 'a man who knows the price of everything and the value of nothing'. Many people think the phrase defines an economist. They see economics as the study of selfishness: all right for studying grasping capitalists and greedy consumers, but useless, if not immoral, as a way of studying matters of political principle, to say nothing of love or altruism. This is a mistake. 'Rational' does not mean 'self-interested'. It describes means, not ends. Economists (at least good economists) do not think a selfish individual is more rational than an altruistic one. A rational individual is one who can arrange the options he faces into a coherent **order of preference** (or **indifference**) and make consistent choices among them. Economics is the study of rational decisions, whether in the market, in politics, or anywhere else.

Two things follow from this. One is that economists were drawn into looking at social choice procedures, such as voting. Especially since 1951 they have been forced to admit that it is far more difficult for 'society' to make rational choices than for an individual to do so. This is explored in the second part of chapter 1 and chapters 8 and 9 of this book. Although this work was pioneered by economists, it is centrally important to politics and sociology. The other consequence is the prominence of *marginal analysis* in the arguments of a book like this. Let me try to show what that is and why it matters by means of a fable.

The government has been using your tax revenue for ten years to develop a supersonic aircraft. The plane has always been about to be ready to fly, but has never yet flown. Every year, the researchers have said, 'Just give us another billion dollars and we will have it airborne within the year.' Every year, they have got their billion dollars. This year, the government is getting restless, but the Minister for Scientific Research says, 'If we don't spend another billion, we shall have wasted the nine billions we have spent so far. Therefore we must spend it.' So they do. The plane gets off the ground; but it never recovers its costs – not even this year's billion.

The Minister's argument was fallacious. Bygones are bygones; there is no use in crying over spilt milk. The question should have been 'Will a further (i.e. a marginal) billion dollars spent on the plane bring more benefit than a billion dollars spent on anything else?' If the answer was 'no', the government has committed what is technically known as the *Concorde fallacy*. It has made an irrational decision (unless it did it to appeal to voters who had also committed the Concorde fallacy).

Marginal analysis asks, 'Taking what has already gone into this project as given, what is the effect of putting another dollar, or another hour's work, into it?' It is the standard method economists use to analyse the private workings of the market. It can also be used to ask questions like 'Should I join the Friends of the Earth?' 'Is it worth my while to vote?' 'What is it worth to the other parties if my party offers to join them to form a governing coalition?' Hence its importance in public choice. Marginal analysis shows why many of the answers often given to questions like these are wrong.

Why is Public Choice Important?

People who propose new ways of looking at familiar problems face two opposite dispiriting objections. If the new method produces the same conclusions as common sense, they are 'obvious'; if it produces different ones, they are 'impossible'. I do not expect the public-choice approach to politics to escape this fate. But I hope the open-minded reader will persevere. I hope to offer novel explanations for some well-known facts such as the fact that poor people are less likely to take part in politics than rich ones; throw light on less well-known facts, such as the persistent tendency of democracies to redistribute neither to the poor nor to the rich, but to the middle; show how almost everybody who argues about electoral reform has failed to understand the issue; explore why anybody ever votes (a puzzle, one of the puzzling aspects of which is how few people are puzzled by it). These are only a few of the topics on which public choice has something to say which I believe to be worth saying. If you think I may be right, read on.

How this Book is Arranged

Economists make a useful distinction between 'positive' and 'normative' economics. A new economics student may be surprised to find nothing in the early chapters of his textbook about how to reduce unemployment, whether inflation or unemployment is the greater evil, or the rival merits of monetarism and Keynesianism. These are all normative matters – discussions about what *ought* to be done. Most economics texts put the discussion of what *is* the case, and what rational actors would do – 'positive economics' – first. This book follows the same plan. Chapter 1 is an initial survey of public choice. Chapers 2 to 6 discuss what politicians, voters, bureaucrats and interest groups do, and what they would do if they were fully rational and costlessly informed. Chapters 7 to 9 are normative. They do not directly put forward my political or philosophical views (though they do contain some recommendations about electoral reform, where a lot of nonsense is talked by people who do not know that they do not know what they are talking about). But they do analyse some traditional normative arguments in political theory, with the aim of seeing how they can be refined by public-choice methods.

Part 1

Practice

1

The Scope of Public Choice

1.1 Two Problems in Politics

Public choice applies economists' methods to politics, and, in particular, to two central problems: the collective action problem and the problem of aggregating preferences. The next two sections explain the problems; the rest of the book explores some of the possible answers.

Economics is all about scarcity. So is much of politics. If we all lived on an island so bountiful that every time we felt hungry we needed only go to the nearest tree and pick a ripe fruit, or if the Lord provided us with quails and manna whenever we were hungry (see Exodus chapter 16), we would not need economists and might even manage without politicians. But in the real world, there is not enough land, labour or capital to enable each person to have as much as he wants of everything without depriving somebody else. So every society must arrive at some way of allocating scarce resources. One way is fighting for them. This is not very interesting to the social scientist. A lot of it goes on, but all that can be said about it is that the strongest usually wins, and that the society which has no other way of allocating its goods will probably be short-lived as well as nasty. There are four other ways of doing it, which I label Altruism, Anarchy, the Market, and Government (see section 1.2). Economists have traditionally studied the third almost to the exclusion of the others, and most of the economic techniques used in this book were first used to explain how markets work. But there is no reason why they should be confined to the analysis of market decisions. When I go to vote I am doing something similar but not identical to what I do when I go shopping. In both cases I 'buy' what

I 'want'. These terms are more difficult than they may look, and there are obvious differences between the cases (I don't have to buy a government, but I do have to buy food; I have a variable quantity of money to spend, but a fixed number of votes). But they are similar enough for the public-choice analyst to have things worth saying about the citizen's decisions of whether and how to vote, and also about what politicians, bureaucrats and pressure groups do.

Politics is broader than economics because it is not just about material scarcity. When the Israelites got their manna from heaven they did not need to worry about the production and distribution of food; but that did not prevent them from having political arguments. Politics, the textbooks used to say, is 'the authoritative allocation of values'. In other words, politics involves making the rules about both material and non-material matters. The decision whether to allow any particular commodity to be traded in the market, for instance, is a political decision, and one that is different in each society. But the decision whether or not to allow abortion is also a political decision. It is not about material resources, but it can still be studied by public-choice methods. To the dedicated opponent of abortion, a law against abortion is a good he seeks as much as he seeks food and clothing. He may have to seek it in a different way, but it is an example of a 'public good' about which I shall have a lot to say in a moment.

The problem of aggregating preferences is a political problem which, as it happens, has mostly been studied by economists. Economics is one of the subjects which faces the awkward problem of how to add up incommensurable things (for instance my 'utility' to your 'utility' to get 'social welfare'), and two economists wrote the works which are the starting-points for all modern discussions of the problem (Arrow 1951; Black 1958). But it is a problem which has fascinated intelligent people each of the three times it has been independently discovered. Its second discoverer was none other than Lewis Carroll, who noticed that different voting procedures could lead to utterly different decisions in the Oxford college where he worked. He wrote three pamphlets making some suggestions to solve the problem (quoted in Black 1958, pp. 214–34). Unfortunately, nobody to whom he circulated the pamphlets had the least idea what he was talking about; not only did they not understand the answers, they did not understand the question. Section 1.3 poses the question; some answers are in chapter 8.

1.2 The Problem of Collective Action

Apart from fighting, then, there are only four ways to allocate scarce goods. Allocating scarce goods is a collective action. 'Scarce goods' include rules. If there is a rule to say that apples may be traded on the market, there cannot at the same time be a rule to say that they may not. If there is a law against abortion, there cannot also be one in favour of it. So the political scientist can expand the economist's interest in the distribution of scarce resources to cover the rule-making that must go on in every society. This book is almost all about the fourth way – government – but it is necessary to sketch in the other three in order to show first that they exhaust the possibilities and, second, that every society of any size needs at least some government.

1.2.1 Public Goods

Before discussing the four methods, we need to understand the key phrase **'public goods'**. Consider the view from the lip of the Grand Canyon. The air is remarkably clear, so that you can see for perhaps ninety miles. The view, and the clean air that makes it possible, are public goods. A pure public good is defined as a good requiring *indivisibility of production and consumption, non-rivalness,* and *non-excludability.* The production and consumption of clean air are indivisible. Everybody who could pollute the atmosphere must cooperate in refraining from doing so; and you cannot take away a pound of clean air from the stock and sell it on a market stall. It is non-excludable: you cannot practicably prevent anybody from enjoying it, whether they have paid to do so or not. 'Non-rival' means that it is not subject to crowding. The view I get from the lip of the Grand Canyon is of equal value to me whether I am the only person who is getting it or not. Consider, at the opposite extreme, a picture postcard of the view from the Grand Canyon. You can produce it without help from anybody else; you may sell a batch of as many or as few as you choose; and you can prevent people who have not paid for the postcards from obtaining any.

Public goods are a problem because it is difficult to make people pay for them. If you cannot be excluded from the benefits of clean air you are tempted to 'free ride' – to get them without paying. Public goods are a special case of what economists more generally call 'externalities' or 'spillovers', which are effects, negative or positive, of any trade on people who are not parties to that trade. The Union Carbide fertiliser plant in Bhopal provided a private good to people who paid for it. Yet it also produced a catastrophic negative externality in the gas leak that killed over 2000 people in December 1984. The risks of such a catastrophe were never taken into account by the mechanism which brought buyers and sellers of fertiliser together. Externalities can be positive too. If I grow roses in my front garden, everybody who passes in the street enjoys them without paying. The passers-by are free-riders, but I do not mind, because I would have grown the roses even if I were the only person who ever saw them. But it is the negative externalities, and more specifically the public goods, that cause problems. Goods may be more or less public, of course; most goods lie somewhere in between the postcard and the clean air. But the more elements of publicness they have, the more they are vulnerable to free-riding, and hence either provided in lower quantities than people would have wanted, or not provided at all. Nature provided the Grand Canyon, but mankind has to provide the clean air. On the whole, mankind has not made such a good job of it.

Rules and conventions are public goods. The anti-abortion law, if it exists at all, exists in the same measure for everybody, even if it does not have the same effects on everybody. Therefore it by no means follows that, even if most people in a society want a particular rule, it will come into existence. In the next four subsections, we look at the four different ways of providing goods, including public goods, to see which technique is efficient at producing which category of goods.

1.2.2 Altruism

You cant get blood from supermarkets and chaine stores. People them selves must come forword, sick people cant get out of bed to ask you for a pint to save thier life so I came forword in hope to help somebody who needs blood.

To me it is a form of thanking God for my own health.

My husband aged 41, collasped and died, without whom life is very lonely – so I thought my blood may help to save some-one the heart ache I've had.

1941. War. Blood needed. I had some. Why not?

In 1967 Richard Titmuss asked over 3000 British blood donors why they gave blood. These are four of the answers (Titmuss 1970, pp. 227–31). They show more vividly than any statistics that there is at least one good which can be provided through sheer altruism. Moreover, the British blood transfusion service, which relies wholly on altruistic donations (the only reward is a cup of tea), provides more and better blood than any system that relies partly or wholly on the market. Where it is possible to sell blood, the sellers are disproportionately drawn from vagrants, alcoholics, and drug addicts, among whom there are many carriers of serum hepatitis (and, more recently, AIDS), which can be lethal to recipients. An American survey of 1966, for instance, found that between 4 and 5 per cent of blood recipients aged over 40 contracted serum hepatitis (and about 0.7 per cent of them died of it), whereas no British study up to the time Titmuss wrote had found a hepatitis attack rate over 1 per cent. An American prospective study of heart patients showed a hepatitis attack rate of 53 per cent in the group which received commercially bought blood, and zero in the group which received donated blood (Titmuss 1970, pp. 145, 148, 154–5). A seller of blood who knows he is a carrier of hepatitis or AIDS has an incentive to lie; a donor has none.

Titmuss used his data as the basis for a fierce attack on market relationships in health care. In response, it was argued that it cannot be a reduction of freedom to add a market system to an altruistic one – for instance, by introducing arrangements to buy blood alongside the UK National Blood Transfusion Service. However, not only does this argument fail to deal with the problem of the poor quality of bought blood, it fails to recognise that it is the very non-existence of a market in blood which generates some of the altruism. You can't get blood from supermarkets and chain stores (see Arrow 1972; Singer 1973; McLean 1986).

Blood itself is a private good; but a blood transfusion service may be a public good. The distinction may not be immediately clear, but it is important. Blood does not require joint supply, it is divisible, and it is excludable. So it is a pure private good. It can be supplied in the market without **market failure**, even though market blood is worse than altruistic blood. However, if there is a service which provides blood to anybody who needs it, irrespective of their past contributions, it is a public good, and subject to free-riding like any other. The superiority of UK over US blood supply is partly a matter of distribution; much less blood is wasted through going out of date in Britain (Titmuss 1970, pp. 56–8). This is not, as Titmuss seems to think, a point for altruism against the market; it is a point for government against the market. The National Blood Transfusion Service is part of the National Health Service, and was set up by the government action that created the Health Service in 1948. So the public good of a transfusion service is achieved in the UK by government; in the USA it is partly achieved through the market, and, as we would expect, the market tends to underprovide it.

However, altruism can provide some public goods. The Ethiopian famine relief operation of 1984–5 was a public good. (As with blood, food for an individual is a private good, but a distribution network is a public good.) The governments of Ethiopia and of donor nations played a part in setting up the network, but the main work was done by charities whose own funds come entirely from donations.

Some altruism is 'reciprocal altruism' (cf. Trivers 1971; Axelrod 1984). It is done either in response to gifts received in the past, or in the hope of gifts to come. Some 28 per cent of Titmuss's sample had either received transfusions themselves or had had a close relative who had received blood. The husband of the widow quoted at the head of this subsection had received a transfusion before he died. Four per cent stated that they were giving blood because in the future they or a member of their family might need it (Titmuss 1970, pp. 139, 311). Reciprocal altruism is a very important kind, which we shall examine in depth in chapter 7. It is a bridge between pure altruism, done without any hope or expectation of reward, and the sort of cooperation we discuss next, in which individuals cooperate in their own self-interest, without necessarily having any feelings for each other at all.

1.2.3 Anarchy

Most people associate anarchy with lawlessness. They are literally correct – etymologically 'anarchy' means 'an absence of ruling'. But the association is misleading because 'lawless' happens to have violent connotations. However, an absence of rulers need not entail violence. Some of the commonest things that we see happening every day are examples of anarchy, even though we do not normally think of them that way. Consider a bus queue. There is no law to say that passengers must stand in line in order of arriving at the bus stop and get on to the bus in the order that they arrived. Even if there is a rule in the bus company's by-laws, there cannot be inspectors at every stop to enforce it. The rule is enforced as a social convention. The government does not punish offenders; if anybody does, public opinion does. Bus queues are an example of anarchy.

How does anarchistic cooperation come about? It overlaps with altruism, of course. Bus queues protect the elderly or the disabled who would never get on a crowded bus otherwise. But not all anarchistic cooperation is altruistic. When I was about fourteen, we had to go twice a week from school to the playing fields two miles away on the 26 bus route. The driver and conductor of the bus that arrived at the school at 3.15 used to dread the moment when forty fighting schoolboys erupted from the pavement all trying to get on at once. Though (surprisingly) nobody was ever crushed, it took a long and acrimonious time to load the bus. Before long, the crews simply sailed past the stop rather than try to cope, even if the bus was empty. It was this, and not our teachers, which persuaded us that a queue would be a better way. So we formed an orderly queue, the bus stopped for us again, and loaded more quickly than before. The old system was 'anarchy' in the everyday sense; but the new one was a better example of an anarchy. There was a self-imposed queuing rule, reached not altruistically (fourteen-year-olds are not altruists at the end of the school day) but because each person realised that the rule was in his own interest.

Another everyday piece of anarchy is the telephone. You are in the middle of a conversation and you get cut off. One of you must call the other to restart. If you both try to do so at once you will each get the engaged tone. So you must do something without being able to discuss with the other person what to do. More often than not, it is the person who initiated the call who restarts it. That is a piece of anarchy.

As before, note that the bus queue and the telephone reconnection are *private goods* affecting only the people directly involved, but a social convention which says 'Always queue for buses' or 'The original caller should always call again, unless the cut-off was obviously the fault of the equipment at the receiving end' is a public good. It benefits everybody, whether or not they have contributed to the cost of achieving and enforcing it. So in principle there are free-rider problems. In these cases, the free-rider problems are not particularly serious, because the cost of achieving and policing the good is low (the occasional bus filling up before I can get on; the slight extra cost of making the second call). Hence they can be, and

are, provided perfectly happily by anarchy and without government
intervention.

Many public goods that governments provide could actually be
provided by anarchy. Michael Laver gives a witty example.

Imagine that it was made quite clear to all and sundry that they were free to
choose which side of the road they would like to use. I am willing to make a
small bet that nothing would happen. . . . Those people who get their thrills
from driving at 70 mph the wrong way up the fast lane of a motorway
would continue to do so. If they are not deterred by the threats posed by the
oncoming traffic, they would not be deterred by the threat of prosecution
for driving on the wrong side of the road. . . . All that would be needed is the
posting of a few prominent signs at the exits to international car ferry ports
with the message: WELCOME TO BRITAIN. YOU MIGHT LIKE TO
KNOW THAT MOST PEOPLE DRIVE ON THE LEFT OVER HERE,
BUT PLEASE DON'T LET THIS CRAMP YOUR STYLE. (Laver 1983,
pp. 55–6)

Anarchy works, most of the time, to keep us on the correct side of
the road. We know that it is very much in our own interest, so there
is no need of government coercion. However, there is often a
clear-cut conflict between self-interest, especially short-run self-
interest, and society's interest. This is most acute in cases where
everybody realises that cooperation is better than selfishness, but
where each individual sees that the very best world for him is one
where everybody else cooperates but he behaves selfishly. If the
relative benefit of behaving selfishly is high, and/or if individuals
have high discount rates (see chapter 7 for an explanation),
cooperation can probably come about only through government
action. This shifts the public-goods problem to 'Why does anybody
take part in government?'

1.2.4 Markets

Altruism is, as Titmuss said, a gift relationship; and anarchy, too,
involves voluntary cooperation without recourse to a medium of
exchange such as money. In a small group, many of whose members
are blood relations, altruism and anarchy between them may cope
with all the problems of allocating scarce goods. Many
anthropologists have been fascinated by the pattern of gifts and
exchanges among certain tribes such as the !Kung bushmen of the
Kalahari and certain Polynesian communities (see e.g. Mauss 1954;

Lee 1979; Gregory 1982). The !Kung have very few material possessions – a quiver of arrows, an empty ostrich egg shell for collecting water, an old Marks & Spencers pullover – and they circulate by means of an elaborate gift ritual. If I give you a quiver, you are in honour bound to give me something else – an ostrich egg, say – after a suitable timelag, as it would be rude to return the gift straight away. If anyone cheats on the gift relationship, varying degrees of social pressure can be put on him, ranging from telling stories loudly about him in his hearing to expelling him from the group to face certain death alone in the desert.

This sort of relationship exists in complex industrial societies too. (What do you do to somebody who fails to buy his round of drinks? Or to somebody who works through a strike?) But it is not and cannot be the only sort of relationship. As the process of production becomes more complex, it can no longer depend solely on gifts and voluntary cooperation. People will not produce goods or services unless either somebody in authority tells them to do so or somebody pays them.

This last is, of course, a market relationship. 'The market' is the most controversial concept we have encountered so far. Everybody is in favour of altruism; and of anarchy too, once they understand that the word connotes voluntary cooperation, not chaos. But people violently disagree on whether market relationships are a good to be encouraged or an evil to be eliminated. This book does not aim to answer that question. But it does aim, in Part II, to clarify it sufficiently for the reader to be able to take and defend a position. Part I, which aims to be descriptive (as economists say, 'positive'), tries not to take a position at all; but merely to explore the logical consequences of having a market, and of having a government. No complex society, however determined its government may be to have a centrally planned and controlled economy, has ever succeeded in abolishing markets. (The nearest to doing so was probably the appalling Pol Pot regime in Cambodia, which abolished money at the same time as abolishing a large proportion of the population of the country. But one horrible example is not a reason for passing judgment on all government-controlled economies.) The market has a very large role in the Soviet economy. A substantial proportion of food is traded in the market rather than the government sector; and government planners can control supply but not demand. Goods which the government supplies but people do not want pile up as displays in shop windows (shop managers in

Moscow and Leningrad can produce very artistic piles of packets of sugar). Goods which people want and the government does not supply will appear, sooner or later, on the black market. The black market is just as much a market as any other and can be analysed in the same way.

The market is a residual category. Goods which people fail to produce voluntarily, through altruism or anarchy, and which the government decides not to produce, are produced, if they are produced at all, by trade. The fact that the residual category is small in some countries (such as the USSR) and large in others (such as the USA) is unimportant. Everybody understands something of how the market produces private goods; but it can also produce public goods. To see how, take as an example the sort of machine this book is being written on: a home computer.

Home computers themselves are private goods. A number of entrepreneurs saw the chance of profit in making them, and they persuaded owners of capital to lend them some in order to go into production. By the time this new good had been on the market for a couple of years or so, I decided that a home computer was a better use for the last £399 of my money than any of the other options (such as putting it in the bank to reduce my overdraft interest). I need say no more about this, as the market in private goods is fully analysed in every economics textbook; instead, I want to look at some of the public goods associated with home computers that the market has produced.

The first is innovation. Home computers did not exist in the mid-1970s. Their existence is partly a public good, because it brings benefits to people who do not own them as well as to people who do. Even before I bought one, I benefited in a few ways that I knew about and, presumably, in countless little ways that I did not; and so did everybody else. Since 1982, the rostering of volunteer drivers and firemen on the Welshpool & Llanfair Light Railway has been done on a Sinclair Spectrum by means of a program written by the railway's rostering officer. The result – a more foolproof roster which helped the railway to run more efficiently – is not the greatest public good brought about by the existence of home computers, but is one of many small ones which together mean perceptible benefits for a society, not all of whose members own Sinclair Spectrums themselves.

The market cannot always secure innovation. Like any other public good, innovation attracts free-riders. Everyone might wait for somebody else to invent the components of a home computer in order to exploit the invention without incurring any of the costs. However, one device to get round this is the patent. If an innovation is patented, the owner of the patent is allowed a monopoly in the product for a certain period of time. During this period he will make fat profits. This prospect may be enough to encourage people to set up private research laboratories. Or innovation may be a positive externality; people may want to invent things for the sheer joy of knowing that they are first. There is a benefit to society, which everybody else gets without contributing. But the inventor does not mind; in fact he is delighted to attract everybody else as a free-rider. That is part of the joy of inventing something which benefits society. Hence, although the market is not the only form of cooperation which can produce the public good of innovation, it is one of them.

The other public good is price and quality competition. When I went into the market to buy a computer, I did not have the information necessary to judge which machines were good value for money, nor which ones were of high quality. But I did know that the home computer market was fiercely competitive, and that there had been a number of failures during the two or three years it had existed before I ventured into it. Therefore I reasoned that most of the machines on sale were of reasonable quality and price, otherwise their makers would not have survived in this market. This is often a dangerous assumption to make. Many markets are highly imperfect, and in those price may be higher and quality lower than it need be. But in a market which I know to be competitive, I can let the market itself supply the public good of product quality and value-for-money.

1.2.5 Government

Just as no complex society exists without markets, so no complex society exists without government either. Even in the most market-oriented society, there are two sorts of public good that only governments can supply: rules, and compensation for market failure.

As pointed out earlier, a rule (a law or a convention) is a public good. If anybody benefits from it, everybody does. And rules are inherently scarce: if there is a law against abortion, there cannot at the same time be a law allowing it. These features make rules an excellent subject for study by public-choice methods. Some rules can be produced by anarchy, and some which are actually produced by governments (the law saying on which side of the road to drive, for instance) could theoretically have been produced by anarchy. The market cannot normally produce binding rules. It relies on government for some of the rules it runs by (for instance, the law of contract and the bankruptcy laws); and the government may decide not to allow a market in any particular good to operate at all (in which case if there is a market it will be a black market, which will probably be less efficient than a legal one).

Hence rules are a good which only anarchy or government can provide. In general, the more expensive a rule is to enforce, and/or the more each citizen is tempted to break the rule out of self-interest, the more likely it is that government will be required. In game-theory terms, rules for cooperative behaviour can be classified in three ways, as **Assurance games**, **Chicken games** and **Prisoners' Dilemma games**. The 'drive on the left' game is an Assurance game. Assurance games can be quite easily solved anarchistically. There is a class of games, called Chicken games, where a simple rule for rational self-interested players is 'Cooperate if the others defect; defect if the others cooperate'. These are harder to solve anarchistically and more likely to require government. A compulsory voting law is an example of a rule which enforces a cooperative solution to a Chicken game; so is a land drainage tax. Prisoners' Dilemmas are the hardest of all to solve without government. In Prisoners' Dilemmas, I do better by defecting than by cooperating, irrespective of how many of the others cooperate. However, the world in which everybody defects is worse than that in which everybody cooperates. National defence is an example of a Prisoners' Dilemma public good. Without a government, the only national defence provided would be the sum of individuals' altruistic gifts.

The last paragraph may be hard to understand on first reading. Do not despair; its message should become clearer as the book progresses. A reader who wishes to understand it more fully straight away should turn to chapter 7. But the basic point is a matter of common sense. In a large society, it is obviously easier to enforce driving on the right without a government than to enforce military service without a government. Rules are one category of public goods which may require a government.

The other category involves market failures. Market failure occurs when a good is unprovided or underprovided by the market because of externalities which the market cannot cope with. In both Britain and the USA, motor vehicles are mainly provided by the market. But if many motor vehicles are brought into a city, they cause some well-known negative externalities. They pollute the atmosphere and they cause traffic congestion. Everybody, including motorists, suffers from pollution and congestion; but the market cannot force motorists (or anybody else) to pay to relieve these evils. The congestion would be relieved, for instance, if enough people went to work by bus instead of by car; but there is no price at which any rational entrepreneur will provide an unsubsidised bus service (especially as the buses get caught in the congestion as well, thus increasing the operator's costs). Any motorist can help to reduce air pollution by fitting a catalytic converter to his car. But that costs him a lot of money, and the benefits are imperceptible unless everybody else voluntarily does the same. Not surprisingly, nothing was done about the petrochemical smog in Los Angeles and San Francisco (even though everybody knew it was mostly caused by car exhausts) until first California and then the Federal Administration passed laws requiring every car to have exhaust controls fitted.

Governments provide private goods as well. These may be ordinary commodities such as houses. Council houses in the UK are a government-provided private good. Or they may be what are called 'transfers'. A transfer is any payment by a government which is not in return for a good or a service. Old-age pensions, food stamps, social security benefits and interest paid on the National Debt are examples of transfers. Even a government, such as Ronald Reagan's, which is ideologically opposed to direct provision of goods and services deals in billions of dollars of transfers. Naturally, one of the most burning political questions in any place and at any time is: what is transferred from whom to whom, and why?

In a democracy, one obvious answer is that the pattern of transfers is the people's choice. The second main branch of public choice is concerned with clarifying expressions such as 'the people's choice'. In the process, it shows that committees and elections are more complicated phenomena than anybody except the Marquis de Condorcet and Lewis Carroll realised before the 1950s. Section 1.3 begins the explanation; but first, a summary of this long and complicated section.

1.2.6 The Production of Private and Public Goods: a Summary

Public goods were defined in subsection 1.2.1. Scarce goods may be allocated by fighting over them, or by processes that involve some cooperation among the rival claimants. (Political scientists prefer to talk of conflict and consensus respectively, but it comes to the same thing.) There are four ways of allocating goods that involve at least partial cooperation: altruism, anarchy, markets, and government. At least one example of a private and a public good in each category has been given. Here is a summary:

	A Private Good	*A Public Good*
Altruism	Blood	Famine relief
Anarchy	School bus queue	Queuing convention
Markets	Home computers	Innovation
Government	Council housing	National defence

1.3 The Problem of Aggregating Preferences

1.3.1 A Scoring Problem

Suppose you are judging a decathlon. The two leading athletes have tied on every event except the 1500m, the pole vault, and the javelin. In these events, their (best) performances are:

	1500m (min.)	*Pole vault (cm)*	*Javelin (m)*
Competitor A	3.36.0	485	83.0
Competitor B	3.40.0	490	84.0

Who wins? B is 4 seconds slower than A in the race; however he can pole vault 5 cm higher and throw a javelin a metre further. You cannot add seconds, centimetres and metres together; you have to express them in terms of some common measure. So you look up the actual international scoring table for the decathlon (reproduced in MacKay 1980, p. 63; I have borrowed the illustration shamelessly from him). From this you find that the athletes score as follows:

	1500m	*Pole vault*	*Javelin*
Competitor A	1043	1017	1021
Competitor B	1002	1028	1031

So A has won by 3081 to 3061 in these three events. As they tied on the other seven, A is the overall winner. Why should B accept that as a fair result? Because he knew the rules when he entered; he was not forced to enter; if he did not like the rules, he should not have entered. This argument protects decathlon scorers from charges of unfairness. But life is harder than decathlons in one respect: you did not choose to be born and you cannot normally leave if you do not like the way results are scored. If we can show that decathlon scoring is arbitrary, we will have shown that there is something worrying about the consequences of scoring the results of elections or committee decisions in a formally similar way.

How can we say that four seconds in the 1500m outweighs the combined effect of 5cm in the vault and a metre in the javelin? To do this we need to justify the way points are allocated. First, an equal number of points must be available to each event. (They are: 1200 of them.) Then the top and bottom points must be anchored in some way that is comparable in each event. This is done by giving the top score of 1200 in each event to a performance some way above the current world record for that event. A score of zero is not easy to calibrate:

For jumping and throwing events there is, as it were, a natural zero, namely, takeoff or point of origin. But there is no comparable natural zero for running or hurdles events, there being no greatest amount of time it can take to traverse a given distance in a foot race. In fact, none of the natural zero points are used, even where available. The scale bottoms are most likely set by taking some average of a sampling of worst recorded performances in the various events. One supposes that there is something to be said for doing it this way. (MacKay 1980, p. 67)

So the zero points could be controversial; but the way scores are allocated between 0 and 1200 is bound to be even more so. Do you divide the interval between best and worst into 1200 equal slices? Or do you say that more credit should be given to one second/cm/ metre at world championship standard than to one second (etc.) at a pretty ordinary level and weight the scoring accordingly? But there is an infinity of possible weightings and no way to say which is the best. The actual procedure is more arbitrary: the four running events are weighted in this way, but the other six are weighted in the *opposite* way: 'each successive increment of performance improvement is worth less than the one before' (MacKay 1980, p. 68). But even if they got rid of this particular anomaly, decathlon scorers could not possibly get a scoring system that everybody could agree in advance to be fair. Even if everybody agreed on the principle of weighting and on where to set the top and bottom points, there is no way of judging among the infinite number of different weighting systems.

As for decathlons, so for economic and political choices. Decathlon scoring is an example of a **cardinal** procedure. It uses actual numbers to compare different people. The problems just explored convinced economists that they could only use weaker, **ordinal** measures of welfare. Ordinal measurement allows one to say 'I rank option a first, b second, and c third', but not to say 'Option a is four times as good as option b.' Individuals might be able to measure their own feelings cardinally; but they cannot be added up cardinally to make a social choice. In fact most welfare economists go even further: they eschew not just cardinal comparisons between individuals' welfare, but any interpersonal comparisons at all. Conventional welfare economics is based on the narrow principle of 'Pareto-comparability'. A state of affairs A is **Pareto-superior** to B if everyone is at least as well off in A as in B, and at least one person is better off. If in A nobody can be made better off without at least one person becoming worse off, A is called '**Pareto-optimal**'. A moment's thought will show that most real-world choices are between Pareto-incomparable options: that is, options which make some people better off and others worse off. The Pareto principle is of no help when it comes to issues of distribution. Conventional welfare economics is too arid: we need to consider some ways of adding up people's ordinal preferences.

With all its faults, the Pareto principle is of some help in the analysis of market decisions. When a voluntary trade takes place, for instance when I give you money for an apple, it is a Pareto-improvement. You and I both think we are better off as a result of the trade, or else you would not have offered the apple for sale and I would not have bought it. (Note the importance of 'voluntary': it is assumed that I am not starving or hypnotised or the victim of false consciousness; and you are not forced by your creditors to sell.) However, there is no such consolation in the analysis of government decisions, which this book is about. It is rare to come across a change of policy that would leave nobody worse off and at least one person better off. Like it or not, real decision-makers have to find some way of ranking Pareto-incomparable options. In doing so, they will encounter further paradoxes, as we shall now see.

1.3.2 Two Paradoxes

A country contains thousands, often millions, of people; but there can only be one government policy on any one matter. On some matters there are only a few possible positions; on others there are infinitely many. (Consider the problem 'How is the social security budget to be divided up among unemployment benefit, sickness benefit, and pensions?' That is an analogous problem to decathlon scoring.) Somehow, therefore, every society has to get from the millions of opinions held by ordinary citizens to the one set of decisions taken by the government. That is the problem of aggregation of preferences, and it is a problem for every government which is not run by a dictator or a soothsayer. If society is run by a dictator, his preferences may run counter to everybody else's, which is not generally thought to be a good thing. If it is run by a soothsayer who tells his fellow-citizens what the Gods have ordained, the society's choices may run counter to every individual's (even the soothsayer's).

A democracy will have some system of elections, maybe supplemented by referenda, which choose the governing party and perhaps determines some of its policies. Even an oligarchy must have a procedure for taking votes in meetings of the ruling junta. It will be shown in chapter 8 that there are deep problems with all procedures of getting from many preferences to one decision. To see what sort of problems arise, consider first a dispute in Liverpool City Council in the mid-1970s. (I discussed this case in McLean 1982a, pp. 86–7.) None of the three parties (Liberal, Labour and Conservative) commanded a majority on its own, but any two could outvote the third. Hence the number of members in each party was irrelevant; each could be treated as if it were one voter. There were three options for a piece of land: preserve it as public open space, sell it for private housing, or build council houses on it. The parties ranked the options as follows:

	Lib.	*Lab.*	*Con.*
Best	x	y	z
Middle	y	z	x
Worst	z	x	y

(where x = open space, y = council housing, and z = private housing)

When the options are compared, x beats y by two votes to one, y beats z by two votes to one, and z beats x by two votes to one. Something very odd has apparently happened. There is nothing irrational about the individual orderings of the three parties (a little knowledge of Liverpool and of British party ideology is all that is needed to see how the parties arrived at the ordering they did). But none of them can win a majority against the others. Majority voting produces an 'intransitive' result, or a 'cycle'. This cycle was first discovered by the Marquis de Condorcet in 1785 (hence 'Condorcet cycle'); lost and rediscovered independently by Lewis Carroll in the 1870s; lost again and re-rediscovered by Arrow and Black in the 1950s. At first sight it may seem tiresome and quite easy to get round. It is not; there are serious problems with all the obvious ways of 'getting round' it, but a discussion will have to wait until chapter 8. (The land in question became the site of the hugely successful International Garden Festival of 1984. The Liberals clearly had better strategic advisors than the other parties.)

Furthermore, all governing bodies have to take decisions about many matters at once. I may wish the government to ban abortion, to withdraw the troops from Northern Ireland, to increase pensions and to crack down on social security scroungers. Even if there were only two possible positions on each of these issues, there would still be sixteen (2^4) possible permutations. Yet there are only three or four viable political parties. It is not at all likely that I will find one offering exactly the bundle of policies I want; I shall have to settle for some compromise. This is where our second paradox comes in, which might be called the 'paradox of logrolling'.

Suppose there are five people present at the joint meeting of the Labour Party executive and parliamentary leadership which has the job of agreeing the party manifesto. There are three propositions, each requiring a straight Yes or No; but the manifesto must arrive at a position on each. The document must be approved by majority vote of those present. The opinions of the members are shown in table 1.1. It is easy to see there is a simple majority for each proposition; but that does not mean that each proposition will be carried. Remember that the whole document has to be endorsed as a package. Therefore there must be a coalition of at least three members, at least one of whom must vote for something he does not want. One of the winning coalitions is that of voters 3, 4 and 5, who will vote for a manifesto which says No to each proposition. By a 'winning coalition' I mean here one that cannot be beaten by a more

Table 1.1 A demonstration of the paradox of logrolling

	Issue 1	*Issue 2*	*Issue 3*
Voter 1	For	For	For
Voter 2	For	For	For
Voter 3	For	Against	Against
Voter 4	Against	For	Against
Voter 5	Against	Against	For

attractive offer to at least one of its members. In the coalition of 3, 4,and 5, each has to vote against one proposition he favours. The best the excluded members, 1 and 2, can do is offer one of the other three a coalition to say Yes to two propositions and No to the third. This is no more attractive to any of 3, 4 or 5 than the existing coalition, so that none of them has any incentive to leave it. If 1 and 2 offer any more, they will be offering to vote against two of their preferred positions. Of course, they may decide that it is better to get one than to get none, and offer to sacrifice two. But this just leads to a vicious cycle as one of the now-excluded two may, by the same reasoning, offer to join a three-person coalition endorsing only one of his preferred positions. On this reasoning the outcome is indeterminate; it may depend on who offers the last package before everybody succumbs to total exhaustion (see e.g. Dummett 1984, pp. 15–28).

Cycles and logrolling are important both in political practice and in political theory. We shall return to logrolling in coalitions in chapter 6, and to cycles, electoral reform, and democratic theory in chapters 8 and 9.

2

Entrepreneurs

2.1 Politicians as Entrepreneurs: a Public-Choice Theory

We saw in section 1.2.5 that no complex society could exist without a government. Neither altruism nor anarchy can do everything on its own, and even the most market-oriented society needs a government to provide at least two things: rules, and compensation for market failure. In this section we introduce, and criticise, a theory which tries to explain how politicians – we can call them entrepreneurs – step into the breach to provide these particular public goods. Later we introduce two running examples of policy-making on which public-choice theories will be tested. They are environmental policy in the USA, and the policies of the British Labour Party.

An entrepreneur is an innovator. Sir Clive Sinclair is an entrepreneur, and so is Mr Alan Sugar, although they are very different sorts of entrepreneur. Some, like Sir Clive, have a flair for inventing new products and bringing them to market. Others, like Mr Sugar, have a flair for producing existing products more cheaply than anyone else. Both sorts of entrepreneur have a role in economic theory. You make things happen that otherwise would not, and you pay yourself a fee, or take a share of the profits, as a reward. Frohlich et al. (1971) see political entrepreneurs as analogous to economic ones. They need not be interested in the good in its own right. Brewers make beer – at least big ones do – not because they like beer but because they like profits. But how do dealers in public goods take their profits? A brewer trades in private goods: he sells beer only to those who pay enough to provide him with a profit over the cost of production. But public goods are non-excludable. People cannot be prevented from free-riding on them. Frohlich et al. suggest four ways in which political entrepreneurs may be able to take money, and thus make profits. First, people may make *voluntary donations* to the putative entrepreneur in order to get the good provided. Second, the entrepreneur may be paid by *suppliers of the factors of production*. Those who control factors of production – land, labour and/or capital – may offer to finance the politician in the hope that he will give them the contract to produce the public good. Third, the entrepreneur may levy *taxation*. Frohlich et al. see taxes as a kind of private bad. If the entrepreneur can levy taxes and punish anybody who tries to evade them, it no longer pays to free ride. Citizens will meekly pay their taxes out of self-interest, and the public good is provided. Fourth, the entrepreneur can try *extortion*. The entrepreneur tells the whole group of citizens to pay a certain amount, on pain of punishment if they do not. This shifts the burden of collecting the money and chasing reluctant payers from the entrepreneur on to the citizens: thus entrepreneurs will prefer it to taxation, but citizens will not.

This entrepreneur seems to be a monster. What is to stop him from taxing or extorting the citizens to destitution? The theory has a partial answer: competition. Just as brewers are not normally monopolists and hence cannot charge us all our income for a pint of beer, so political entrepreneurs need not be monopolists of power like Hobbes' Sovereign. The more attractive (profitable) power is, the more likely it is that rival would-be entrepreneurs will be waiting in the wings, ready to offer their services at a lower price. Thus, if there are no barriers to entry, the price of providing public goods will be brought down to the profit level applying in every other industry. In fact there are barriers to entry, such as the very high cost of election campaigning in the USA, and the Anglo-Saxon 'first-past-the-post' electoral system, which discriminates against most sorts of entrant. In those circumstance, the theory would predict that politicians make higher profits than they would under perfect competition.

This theory has been heavily criticised (see, e.g., Laver 1980, pp. 204–8), and was later modified in important respects (Frohlich and Oppenheimer 1978). Extortion, for instance, does not stand up to serious examination as a method of providing public goods. If the citizens have any choice, they will prefer being taxed to being extorted; and, if they do not have any choice, the extortionist is a tyrant who has no reason to provide public goods unless he feels like it. Voluntary donations do not seem to stand up to much examination either. People will not donate for a public good unless either they are feeling kindly or they personally stand to gain more than the donation costs; and if one of these two conditions is met, why not donate directly to the cause rather than to an intermediary? (A reply is that there is no cause until there is an entrepreneur. Live Aid presupposed Bob Geldof.) The part of the theory which stands up best is the claim that entrepreneurs are financed either by taxation or by payments from suppliers of the factors of production. Empirical studies (some summarised in McLean 1982a pp. 158–66; cf. also Malbin 1984; Sabato 1984) show that British and American politicians do indeed get most of their campaign finance from factor suppliers such as trade unions and trade associations, although the contributions do not normally pay politicians' wages as well as their campaign costs. And politicians who finance themselves by taxation have to defend themselves at each election against the opposition claim that they could provide the same services for less.

In democratic societies this fends off the Hobbesian nightmare of a sovereign who does exactly what he likes with the power he has been given for the limited purpose of securing public goods (law and order, for Hobbes). This still leaves some sorts of entrepreneur unaccounted for: for instance, those who bring a democratic or constitutionally restricted regime into being. Frohlich's original theory cannot explain why the framers of the US Constitution sacrificed their time to write it. To account for such people, who could be described as 'ideological entrepreneurs', we need to relax the assumption that politicians are not interested in the content of the policies they implement. This is not a difficult relaxation, and it is made in the 1978 presentation of the theory. Obviously, in the real world politicians *are* interested in policy. It is also necessary to broaden the framework to take account of political parties, which Frohlich and his colleagues too easily ignore. But first, some examples of political entrepreneurship which do fit in with the original theory.

2.2 When Public Goods are Cheap at the Price

In the 1960s Howard Hughes was living in Las Vegas. His favourite occupation was watching old cowboy movies all night. However, the local TV station went off the air at midnight. A Hughes aide asked if the station would extend its hours; when it refused, Hughes bought it for some $6 million, and showed cowboy movies all night (according to Hardin 1982, p. 42).

In 1887 the young trade unionist Keir Hardie had a bitter argument with the other regional leaders of the Miners' Federation of Great Britain. The Durham and Northumberland miners had negotiated an agreement with the coalowners to secure an eight-hour maximum working day for underground workers. Hardie, who led the struggling Ayrshire Miners' Union, wanted the Trades Union Congress (TUC) to lead a campaign for a *statutory* eight-hour' day. Thomas Burt and Charles Fenwick, the Northumberland leaders, who were both Liberal MPs, were appalled. 'The regulation of the hours of labour', said Fenwick, 'is a matter of organization, and the miners do not require the intervention of Parliament.' Instead of bleating to Parliament, Hardie ought to get his own feeble union properly organised, and confront the Ayrshire coalowners as Burt and Fenwick had confronted those in Northumberland. If Hardie could not even stop workers at one pit from working on when those at the next pit were on strike, he ought to learn the first principles of trade unionism before presuming to ask the TUC to do his job for him. The dispute was bitter and long-lived; when Hardie, who by this time had formed the Labour Party, actually got his statutory eight-hour day in the Coal Mines Act 1909, Burt and Fenwick voted against (see, e.g., Morgan 1975, pp. 38–9; McLean 1976, pp. 17–18, 60–1, 90).

These stories illustrate the two cases in which entrepreneurs have an incentive to provide public goods regardless of the free-rider problem. Hughes was willing to pay $6 million for the private good of all-night TV. He was indifferent to the fact that he was also providing a public good. The fact that other people could watch the station as well was simply a positive externality of Hughes' action (but if video recorders had existed in the 1960s, Hughes would presumably simply have recorded the programmes of his choice rather than bought up the station). As there are not many people like Howard Hughes, the Hardie case is of more general interest. The Eight Hours' Act was a pure public good. Its benefits were both indivisible and non-excludable. And a rule which applies to everybody and which need be made only once is far cheaper than a series of individual agreements with each separate coalowner. Hardie's production costs, viewed in isolation, might seem high. He had to form the Labour Party and persuade the ruling Liberal Party to pass the 1909 Act in order not to lose votes to his new party. But

forming the Labour Party provided the platform for a whole range
of public goods, of which the Eight Hours' Act was only one. Burt
and Fenwick faced far higher costs. They had to get the union to a
point where it could make meaningful threats before even the first
negotiation with a coalowner. Meaningful threats include the threat
to strike. It is very hard, as Hardie well knew, to persuade a worker
only just off the breadline to strike in his neighbour's interest; and
yet Burt and Fenwick's approach to trade unionism depended on it.
They also had to make separate agreements with every single
coalowner in the Durham and Northumberland coalfield.

It is not as hard to account for the existence of rules like the Eight
Hours' Act as most public-choice writers seem to believe. Not only
was it much cheaper than a series of agreements with each
employer; its value to each miner was reasonably high, and
therefore its total value to the hundreds of thousands of miners must
have been reckonable in millions of pounds. Each miner need only
give a donation equal to a tiny fraction of his valuation of the rule
to Keir Hardie for Hardie to be able to finance the early Labour
Party and get his Act. The money miners might rationally give to
political funds need only be, and indeed was and is only, a small
percentage of their union subscription. In section 2.4 we shall see
how the same argument applies to the modern American
environmental movement.

2.3 Politicians as Private-Goods Entrepreneurs

Politicians also trade in private goods. Some of the rules that they
make are so specific that they only have a small element of
publicness. Consider a change in taxation law, for instance. A tax
break for left-handed egg-haters is still a public good for this group,
so that its efforts to get the good may be frustrated by the free-riders
in its own ranks; but from the point of view of society as a whole it
is a divisible and excludable, and hence private, good. You can make
a tax law as precise as you like in order to include or exclude a group
of any size. Therefore there is every reason to expect politicians
deciding on taxation policies to fit Frohlich's model, which is the
classical model of microeconomic theory. Entrepreneurs will
provide the good at a fee equal to the normal profit rate for industry
(if politics is a competitive industry) or higher (if there are barriers to
entry).

Hardin (1982, p. 78, quoting the *Wall Street Journal* for 7 November 1975) gives an example. In 1975 the Ways and Means Committee of the US House of Representatives voted by 20 to 14 in favour of a change in the tax treatment of oil depletion allowances. It was a highly technical matter, and it would have passed unnoticed if a journalist had not revealed that the change in rules meant an enormous increase in the income of a very small number of people. One of them was a Texan oilman called Ross Perot, who stood to make $15 million from the rule change. Against that, his $27 000 contributions to the election funds of members of the Ways and Means Committee was chickenfeed. Both he and his agents were unlucky this time, as after the article in the *Wall Street Journal* the full House voted down the rule change by 379 votes to 27. But that should not deter readers who would like to become members of the House Ways and Means Committee. It can be a very comfortable living, although you may have to spend a lot and wait a long time before you get it (see, e.g., McLean 1982a, p. 164; Sabato 1984, pp. 122–40). Similar stories can be told on a grander scale about the $300 000 American milk producers paid towards Richard Nixon's re-election in 1972, which was duly rewarded by price support worth between $500 and $700 million (Hardin 1982, p. 85). Or, once again, about Howard Hughes:

Re. Kennedy, I want him for president like I want the mumps. I can think of nothing worse than 8 years under his exalted leadership. God help us!

However, lets face it. It could happen, so lets cover our bets both ways. . . . I am not in favor, at the moment, of contributing any $$ unless he *can* and will make some kind of half-assed promise to help us postpone or abort the bombing [tests in the Nevada desert]. Now, if he gets the nomination, then I think we are forced to contribute no matter what he does about the bomb. (1960)

Politicians may also enter the business for the fringe benefits such as the free postage. As an aspiring MP wrote to the Duke of Newcastle in 1764: 'As the correspondence of the shop is very great, having the draughts of the Bristol Bank, the very postage of their letters would amount to near £800 pr. ann., and it is otherwise thought to be of great service to the house to have one of the partners in Parliament' (cited, with four other similar appeals, in McLean 1982a, p. 156; from Namier 1957, pp. 57–8).

2.4 Ideological Entrepreneurs: Clean Air in the USA

The theory as presented so far leaves vast tracts of political enterprise unmapped. Most politicians who make laws do so because they believe in them, or at least because, among other things, they believe in them. So we have to drop the assumption that politicians are not interested in the contents of the laws they make. Even after dropping that assumption, however, more remains of the 'entrepreneur' model than is usually assumed. This should emerge as we go through our first case study, which is of clean air legislation in the USA. Clean air is almost a pure public good. It is obviously indivisible (nobody has ever made a living out of selling bottled air) and non-excludable. So is dirty air, assuming that personal gas-masks or oxygen cylinders are too unwieldy for general use. Hence something which makes dirty air clean – whether a law, a tax on polluters, a fee paid in return for a promise not to pollute, or voluntary restraint – produces a public good and raises the usual questions.

Voluntary restraint sometimes works at parties and on trains. Smokers pollute the atmosphere, but occasionally they refrain from doing so out of altruism, or because of an anarchistic convention, enforced by scowls or rules of etiquette. In some circles the rule 'Do not smoke at dinner until after the Loyal Toast' does the trick. However, power companies and car owners do not normally exercise voluntary restraint. Only the market or government will produce clean air in such cases, and the market will not do so unaided, but only if the structure of market rewards is altered by government action.[1] So the problem of clean air is the problem of persuading government to bring it about, which resolves in turn into the problem of getting entrepreneurs to do the work. In this section we look at the problem from the point of view of the entrepreneurs; in later chapters we will come back to look at it from the points of view of interest groups and ordinary voters.

2.4.1 Up to 1970: the Dog that Didn't Bark

In 1965, 17 per cent of American voters thought that reducing pollution should be one of the central concerns of government; in 1970, 53 per cent did (Wilson 1973, p. 339) This is a remarkable shift by any standards, especially as the amount of atmospheric pollution in the USA was probably declining at the time because people were ceasing to burn coal in domestic and factory boilers. It was no doubt largely spontaneous: people just changed their minds, other issues receded (Vietnam, Civil Rights, poverty), perhaps a 'post-bourgeois' issue replaced economic ones like inflation and unemployment as incomes and security increased (see Inglehart 1977 for this hypothesis). But it raises two questions about entrepreneurs. First, why did nobody try to bring clean air on to the national agenda earlier, when it *was* a serious health issue? Second, how did entrepreneurs mould, and how did they respond to, the great surge of environmentalism in the late 1960s?

Crenson's (1971) frequently cited study of the origins of clean air legislation in Gary and East Chicago, Indiana, looks at the first question. East Chicago, where no one employer dominated the town, got a clean air ordinance eighteen years before Gary, a company town so dominated by US Steel that it is even named after a former president of the corporation. Crenson concludes that US Steel was an important negative entrepreneur in that its baleful influence stopped the issue from ever reaching the political agenda. This conclusion has been very influential in the debate among political scientists about 'non-decisionmaking', but it is weakly supported by evidence. Crenson actually cites US Steel's official attitude of non-intervention in Gary's affairs as 'a critical obstacle to the development of the dirty air debate' (pp. 124–5). This seems on a par with accusing God of distorting the debate on His existence by refusing to intervene in it.

However, Crenson's book contains a much more interesting argument which neither he nor his followers have stressed sufficiently. When reform-minded politicians in both towns tried to raise the apparently glaring issue of the filthy air they were forced to breathe, they ran into bitter opposition from the 'machine' politicians who controlled both towns. Machine politicians are non-ideological entrepreneurs. They deliver private goods (jobs in the local administration, cash payments to party workers) in return for votes, and take their fees out of their share of the proceeds of municipal contracts. But clean air, as Crenson rightly says, is a 'benefit which does not lend itself to the machine politician's way of doing business' (p. 16), because it is a public good. If anybody kept clean air off the agenda, it was not US Steel, but the local politicians who did not want their trade in divisible benefits to be upset.

The man who brought clean air to East Chicago was a mystery to his fellow-citizens. They could not understand why he stayed on as city attorney and did not enter much more lucrative private practice (Crenson 1971, pp. 43–8). He was clearly an ideological entrepreneur, who was willing to sacrifice personal income in order to help get a public good. If it were not for people like him, there would be fewer public goods. Luckily, there are some altruists, and hence some charitable provision of public goods. In Gary the story had a slightly different twist. The first man to try to get clean air was seen off by the machine. The next was less of an ideological entrepreneur – he was described (Crenson 1971, p. 66) as 'a man in search of an issue' – but he did have a personal interest. He suffered from a respiratory disease. So he faced higher costs than the average citizen and a higher expected utility from clean air. It is not surprising that he became the successful entrepreneur.

Before 1970, entrepreneurs could turn clean air from a non-issue into an issue locally, but nobody had managed to do so on a national scale. The costs of motivating citizens would have been far too high, until they spontaneously developed an interest. The explosion of environmentalism in the late 1960s was not due originally to politicians, but once it had happened they had to adapt to it.

2.4.2 The 1970 Clean Air Act Amendments: Symbolic Benefits and Deferred Costs

It is a truism of American politics that when 'the public interest' and 'special interests' clash in Congress, the public interest loses out. According to this view, each Congressman depends on the votes and campaign funds of organised groups. Organised groups are groups which either have no free-rider problem of their own, or one which they can get over fairly easily. For instance, an industry may be dominated by large firms which stand to gain more from government contracts than it costs them to lobby for them. Or some citizen body will be dominated by the rich because they have more spare time and money to devote to campaigning than the poor. Congress is not necessarily corrupt, according to this view, but Congressmen have neither the time nor the opportunity to get beyond the interests to the public at large. 'You can reach [local leaders], but not the public generallly', as a Congressman told a researcher observing him at work in his district (quoted in Fenno 1978, p. 235).

There is much to be said for this view. But if it were always correct, there could never have been a Clean Air Act (nor a Sherman Antitrust Act nor a Pure Food and Drugs Act). These are clear-cut cases in which the public interest lay in getting a public good which benefited everybody, whereas the interests of virtually every organised group lay on the other side. As a citizen I have an interest in clean air; but as the owner of a power station I have an overriding interest in generating electricity as cheaply as possible. I am much more likely to join an association to promote the second interest than the first. So how did the Clean Air Amendments of 1970 (the first effective clean air legislation on a federal level) come to be passed?

Ingram (1978) argues that it was actually easier to pass a radical measure like the 1970 Act than the painstaking incremental legislation, with lengthy consultation with affected groups, which is more typical of areas where interest groups are active. The key lay in a combination of surprise and symbolism. Groups which would have had a vested interest in opposing the changes were taken by surprise because the required standards were much more radical, and covered more areas of activity, than anybody had anticipated. Some of the measures would hurt the public, in its capacity as polluter (e.g. as motorist) directly, but these were not due to be implemented until 1977. The public in 1970 took a generous view of the costs imposed upon itself in 1977. In the meantime, people felt involved, however symbolically, in the movement to protect the environment. Objectively the air was no cleaner the day after the Act was passed than the day before, but people felt better. If a politician can make people feel better at very low cost, he is bound to be interested. Here was an issue, unlike most of those where Congress can or must act, where there was no history of unsuccessful past attempts at reform, each marked by an interest group ready to block any future attempt at the same reform. If the motto of the successful conservative is 'Nothing should ever be done for the first time', perhaps the reformer ought to aim only to do things for the first time. After the first time, there are too many organisations with interests in seeing that there is no second time.

Not all congressmen who backed the 1970 Act were environmentalists. Most of them were pure profit-takers who saw that many votes could be gained and few lost from being in favour of the environment. To those few, such as Senator Edmund Muskie (Democrate Maine), who already cared about the environment, the spontaneous rise of the issue was a heaven-sent opportunity for ideological enterprise. (Maine is, in any case, an environment-consuming rather than a pollution-producing state.) Muskie said afterwards. 'The real reward was in being able to fulfil the mandate imposed on Congress by the founders – the opportunity to respond to an issue in the public interest and arrive at a result which was considerably more than an accommodation to the accumulated special interests' (quoted in Ingram 1978, p. 32). For the environmentalists themselves, legislation, which need only be organised once, showed a far better return to their activities than local dealings with individual polluters or cases of pollution. They made the same discovery as Keir Hardie ninety years earlier.

2.4.3 Coping with Reality

Symbolic politics is all very well, but the symbols sometimes have to be translated into reality. The Clean Air Act put the immediate costs of pollution control on to polluters, such as the operators of power stations. Of course they would transmit their increased costs to the consumer in higher electricity charges, but they would then be spread so thinly as to be almost painless. But once the Environmental Protection Agency (EPA) had to promulgate standards of emission reduction to be met by coal-fired power stations by a certain date, interest-group politics was back with a vengeance. A bizarre coalition of environmentalists and producers of dirty coal forced provisions mandating an inefficient and expensive form of control known as 'scrubbing' of effluent from new power station chimneys through Congress.

Muskie protested that 'the dominant thrust' of the scrubber campaign 'is not its relationship to clean air, but its relationship to the economics of the areas it is designed to protect. . . . I just see this as a first step . . . in regionalization around regional economic interests'(Ackerman and Hassler 1981, p. 46). In the best tradition of congressional logrolling, Senate Majority Leader Robert Byrd (Democrate West Virginia) allegedly told the Carter Administration in 1979 that he would not vote for the SALT II arms treaty unless the Administration promised to back power station emission controls lenient enough to allow high-sulphur coal from West Virginia to continue to be burnt (Haskell 1982, p. 100). Furthermore, the car emission controls, due to take effect in 1977, that seemed so symbolically attractive in 1970, became rapidly less and less so as 1977 approached, and people realised that they would have to pay for a better environment. The best the politicians could do was to promise to delay the implementation of the standards until 1982, and link them with a protectionist campaign against foreign cars. Congressmen have been unable to act as clean air entrepreneurs since 1970.

2.5 Entrepreneurs in a Party System: the Labour Manifestos of 1979 and 1983

Most of the theoretical writing on public choice is American. American scholars sometimes fail to recognise how abnormal their political system is. It is necessary, therefore, to extend the discussion of politicians as entrepreneurs by looking at a system which is more typical of the other democracies: a system where log-rolling goes on in the party office rather than on the assembly floor.

2.5.1 *Why Parties Make a Difference*

The two most unusual features of the American political system are the weakness of parties and the separation of the legislature and the executive. James Madison equated party with 'faction' and designed his Constitution to minimise the dangers of factionalism. The checks and balances of the Constitution are designed to ensure that no one individual, or faction, can control all the organs of government at once. There was to be no George III in the new republic; but there was to be no 'tyranny of the majority' either. Parties nevertheless grew up, and the duopoly of Democrats and Republicans dates back to the Civil War. At the end of the nineteenth century came another wave of party reform. The Progressives of that period blamed the ills of the cities and the corruption of national government on party, and particularly on party machines, so they sponsored a series of reforms (ballots to allow ticket-splitting, civil service reform, primary elections) to break the machines. They succeeded, but they broke up the parties in the process. In every democracy except the USA, a political party has two main functions: recruiting elites and formulating policies. In the USA they have only the first of these.

The Founding Fathers, determined to prevent the tyranny of the majority, also insisted that control of the legislature and the executive must be in different hands. The President of the US, unlike any other head of government, controls no divisions in Congress, and his power, in the old cliché, is the power to persuade. There can therefore be platforms, but no manifestos in American elections. A manifesto outlines what its authors will do in all the main policy areas. Presidential candidates cannot issue them, because they cannot guarantee that Congress will carry their legislative programme; and candidates for the Senate and the House of Representatives do not issue manifestos on national policy either, because they are running in (say) Wyoming, not in the USA, and their job is to represent the people of Wyoming, not the people of the USA.

In every other democracy, and Britain is reasonably typical, somebody must put together the programme on which each party fights each election. It need not be the party members. Mass parties began as organisations to mobilise support for parliamentary groups whose leaders decided their policy. The British Conservative Party still shows the marks of these origins. The job of Conservative activists was to get the vote out. It was not to make suggestions to Mr Disraeli, or the Marquess of Salisbury, or Mr Churchill, on how to run the country. This conception of the job has been challenged a number of times in the history of the party (see McLean 1982a, pp. 129–31) but it has never been overthrown. In contrast the Labour Party started as a pressure group outside Parliament, not a support organisation for MPs, so it has always been accepted that members of the party who are not MPs have a role in formulating the party's policy – although how they stand in relation to MPs has been fiercely debated ever since 1907 (McLean 1982a, pp. 131–3). But Clause 5 of the Labour Party Constitution states plainly that the party's election manifesto is to be drafted jointly by the National Executive Committee (NEC – representing the party outside Parliament) and the parliamentary leadership.

If the Labour Party were internally democratic, the NEC contribution to the manifesto would mirror the views of ordinary members. In fact it is a bogus democracy for two reasons. First, not every member may take part in policy-making, but only those who have been voted on to a constituency committee – who are obviously likely to be the most active members. Second, the affiliated trade unions have always had a large say in formulating Labour Party policy, and many do not consult their own members before doing so. At times in the history of the party, the second distortion has counterbalanced the first, but that has not been true in the period we are about to study.

Party activists are usually in the public goods business. They may have private motives as well – to become Prime Minister or to rub shoulders with the great. But their work is always aimed at one public good – the election of politicians of their party – and often at another – the policy of that party if elected. So why does anybody become a party activist? It is an altruistic act, but even altruists have to decide which of the many possible altruistic acts they are going to do in their scarce time. If there were no such people as party activists, politicians would still write election manifestos in which they would try to maximise their chances of election by offering the people what they wanted. A would-be activist who wants the same things as most people has no incentive to take part in manifesto-writing, as the politicians will get there without his help. On the other hand, a would-be activist who wants different things from most people does have an incentive to take part. There is then almost bound to be a struggle between the activist and the entrepreneur. It is a struggle which must enter any model of the real world of non-American policy-making.

2.5.2 The 1979 Manifesto

In 1979, Labour had held power rather precariously for five years. Elected with a minority of seats in February 1974, they scraped a bare majority in October of the same year; had to introduce tough deflationary and monetarist policies in November 1976 in return for a loan from the International Monetary Fund; and had to seek the consent of the Liberals to govern from March 1977 on, as they had lost their majority in by-election defeats. Throughout this time, left-wing activists had been disappointed at the government's failure to act on policies supported by the NEC and the Annual Conference of the party. Their problem was to get these policies into the next election manifesto; the problem for James Callaghan, the Labour Prime Minister, was to keep out those which were vote-losers. Surveys showed that several policies dear to the hearts of Labour activists were in this category, such as increasing trade union rights, nationalising more industries, and abolishing the House of Lords.

Callaghan won by successful prevarication. On behalf of the NEC, the party Research Department produced a draft in late 1978 calling for abolition of the House of Lords, compulsory 'planning agreements' with the hundred largest companies in the private sector, and the nationalisation of at least some banking and insurance companies. Callaghan did not summon the joint meetings of NEC and Cabinet representatives required by Clause 5 of the party constitution until the election was known to be close. This gave him a power of veto he would not otherwise have had. Parliament was dissolved after he had lost a confidence motion on Scottish devolution by one vote on 28 March, 1979, and the election was called for 3 May. The joint manifesto drafting committee met on 2 April, and Callaghan simply refused to agree to including any proposal he did not want. As a manifesto had to be produced quickly, it was an effective veto, backed by his threat to resign if the committee insisted on putting in the abolition of the House of Lords.

The manifesto stressed those Labour policies which the electorate wanted or could be expected to tolerate, and dropped known vote-losers. It promised price controls, reform of the Common Market's Common Agricultural Policy, job rights for the long-term unemployed, and a rather shadowy suggestion of discussions with trade unions on 'what the country could afford' in pay rises. As a policy entrepreneur, Callaghan had done a fairly successful piece of damage-limitation. But there were few positive proposals for achieving public goods (the anti-inflation pay talks suggestions were too vague to count for much) and the manifesto did not succeed in winning Callaghan the election. Perhaps nothing could have done.

(The sources for this subsection are Butler and Kavanagh 1980, pp. 144–53, and Bish 1979. The manifesto is printed in *The Times Guide to the House of Commons 1979*, London: Times Books 1979, pp. 295–309.)

2.5.3 *The 1983 Manifesto*

There were bitter recriminations about the drafting of the 1979 manifesto, and left-wing activists campaigned for full NEC control of the manifesto. This was one of three constitutional changes debated at the party's 1980 conference. The activists won on the other two issues (election of the leader by an electoral college of Labour MPs, trade unions, and individual members; and mandatory submission of Labour MPs to a reselection process by their constituency parties during each parliament), but lost on NEC control of the manifesto. Soon after, and not coincidentally, four prominent right-wing figures led a breakaway into the new Social Democratic Party (SDP), and Michael Foot was elected Labour leader. Foot was much closer to the activists, and much further from the electorate, than Callaghan. Unlike his predecessor, he was not interested in survey evidence on the popularity or otherwise of items in the Labour Party's programme. Not only did he not attempt to veto any NEC proposals for the 1983 election manifesto, he made no proposals for additions to it. Hence the manifesto which emerged was mostly the NEC's document, although various members of the Shadow Cabinet had added proposals in the areas of their departments. In addition, Denis Healey, the Deputy Leader, had insisted on inserting passages committing Labour to continuing in NATO and to including the British nuclear deterrent, Polaris, in any future international arms negotiations. This was widely felt to be incompatible with the commitment to unilateral nuclear disarmament found elsewhere in the manifesto.

The 1983 manifesto had a bad reception. A professor of English literature called it

appallingly written, and perfectly free from self-doubt . . . . Some pledges are repeated, almost verbatim, on different pages. Possibly the authors reckoned that readers who had nodded off the first time round might wake up for the replay . . . . At times the repetitiveness sets up a pleasant rocking motion which, you feel, might go on for ever: 'We intend to protect the rights of individual suspects, while providing the police with sufficient powers to do their job effectively whilst not infringing the civil rights of individual suspects.' While, of course, providing the police etc . . . . Socialists should demand, in anger, how this calamity came to be published. (Carey 1983)

A senior Labour frontbencher (Peter Shore according to Butler and Kavanagh 1984 p. 62; Gerald Kaufman according to Mitchell 1983 p. 64) called it 'the longest suicide note in history'. It is widely assumed to have contributed to Labour's disastrous defeat in the election, in which it got 28 per cent of the vote, its lowest share since 1918.

Although, alas, all too easy to make fun of, the 1983 Labour manifesto repays study, because it shows how hard it is simultaneously to 'draw . . . the party's competing factions together' and 'invite . . . voters to contemplate what a Labour government would actually do' (Kellner 1983). Some passages were clearly drafted for the first purpose: 'We will establish a significant public stake in electronics, pharmaceuticals, health equipment and building materials.' 'A national economic assessment . . . with the trade unions . . . will take a view on what changes in costs and prices would be compatible with our economic and social objectives.' In others, the first and second purposes violently clashed in successive sentences: 'We will propose that Britain's Polaris force be included in the nuclear disarmament negotiations in which Britain must take part. We will, after consultation, carry through in the lifetime of the next parliament our non-nuclear defence policy.' In others again, the conflicts between interest groups are all too plain: 'We will . . . eliminate lead in petrol by setting a date after which all new cars will be required to use only lead-free petrol. The interests of motorists will be safeguarded' (cited from *The Times Guide to the House of Commons June 1983*, London: Times Books 1983, pp. 304–33).

It all goes to show how hard a policy entrepreneur's job is in a party system. He must simultaneously try to give party activists a reason for continuing to work for the party, and put together a platform on which the party can win the election. The Labour manifesto of 1983 is at least a good example of how not to do it.

3

Choosing Between Governments:
The Voter as Consumer

3.1 Downs' Puzzle: Why Ever Vote?

This chapter will examine the analogy between the consumer in economic theory and the voter in public-choice theory. A vote is in some ways very like money. In both cases we can assume that citizens use them to maximise their satisfaction in some sense. This does not imply that all consumers are selfish, or that all voters are. I may buy bread to give to the poor; I may vote for the party that promises to give most aid to Ethiopia. In each case I get more satisfaction that way than from a more selfish use of my resources; that is what rationality implies. However, a lot of trouble has been caused by people confusing rationality with selfishness, and nowhere more than in the first topic we need to discuss: why vote at all?

One of the differences between the economic analysis of private choices and the public-choice analysis of voting lies in the need to ask the question at all. It is obviously rational to spend (or save) money; but it is not obviously rational to use one's vote, even though if not used it is lost for ever. It costs time and (sometimes) money to vote, and if the time and money would be better used in some other way, it would be irrational to vote. Downs (1957, chapters 3 and 14) wrote the classic account of the rationality of voting. In doing so he laid bare a puzzle which was not satisfactorily resolved for twenty-five years.

Downs assumes that everybody can compute his 'party differential'. This is his valuation of the difference to him between his favourite party winning and his next favourite. Some people will have large party differentials. It is not just – not even mainly – that they expect a government of one party to make them richer than a government of the other, but more that governments do a lot of things, like restricting experiments on animals or ensuring world peace, which people value highly even though they are not traded in the market and therefore do not have direct cash value. As we saw in chapter 1, laws are a form of public good that only governments can practicably provide, and it would be rational for people who value them highly to spend a lot of resources on providing a government to enact them.

So what is the problem? The problem is that there are millions of people in any large country, and each voter's party differential must be multiplied by the probability that he is the decisive voter, and then compared with the cost of voting, before the voter can decide whether or not it is rational to vote. Suppose that I live in Britain and my party differential is £5000. I have to calculate how likely it is that the next General Election will be decided by one vote. This would require both that the winning party gets in by a majority of one seat and that the parties in the seat where I live would tie but for my vote (or else that my vote would turn a one-vote deficit into a tie, which there would then be a one-in-two chance of my party winning in the tie-break). Neither of these events is terribly likely; both of them together are rather less likely. For the sake of argument I might surmise that there is one chance in 500 of a one-seat majority and one chance in 30 000 of a tie in my seat. The expected value of my party differential is now £5000/(500 × 30 000), or one-thirtieth of a penny. If I vote, I certainly spend more than that in shoeleather alone, even if the polling station is a hundred yards away. And I incur opportunity costs which are considerably higher: that is, I could have spent the five or ten minutes it takes to vote in innumerable other ways.

A number of ways out of the conclusion that it is irrational to vote have been proposed, some of them by Downs himself. It is said that it is rational to wish my party to get in with a majority of more than one seat, to protect it against by-election losses, and to wish my party succeed in in my seat, even if it does not win the election. There is the 'What if everybody thought like that?' argument. If everybody thought like that, then nobody would vote. But then it would be worth my while to vote. But if everybody thought like *that*, they would all vote after all, and it would not be worth my while to vote. And if everybody thought like THAT . . . Downs (1957, p. 267) calls this 'a maze of conjectural variation'. But it is not exactly Hampton Court. An easy way out is to assume that on average half of the population will flip on one side and half will flop on the other. So the expected value of my vote is not one-thirtieth of a penny, but one-fifteenth. This does not get us very far. Another line is to say that it is worth voting in order to save democracy from the collapse that would occur if nobody voted. But in saying this, Downs 'commits a common fallacy in social thought which most of the book turns on his avoiding, when he adds that our citizen "is willing to bear certain short-run costs he could avoid in order to do his share in providing long-run benefits" (page 270)' (Barry 1970, p. 20) It is the fallacy of assuming that what is in the interests of all is in the interests of each, forgetting that free-riding is individually rational. Downs' analysis is a marginal analysis; but for a moment he forgets the principles of marginalism.

A third line is to say that there are valuable spin-offs from voting – such things as meeting your friends on the way to or from the poll and being seen to do your duty. This one is empirically suspect. In any election where there is a choice of voting in person or by post, as often in unions and clubs, the overwhelming majority of voters vote by post. Note, though, that feeling warm because you have done your duty is subtly different from feeling warm because you have been seen to have done your duty. Many people agree with Jesus (see Matthew, chapter 6, 1–4) in regarding the first as morally superior to the second; and the first, unlike the second, can be satisfied by postal voting just as well as by voting in person.

None of the attempts to fit voting into a framework of rational *self*-interest is thus very convincing. (Perhaps the best is the half-serious claim that people will vote in order not to be pestered any longer by a succession of political canvassers asking them if they have voted yet.) It is possible to end the argument at this point by saying that it is just irrational to vote, and that Downs' attempt to show otherwise is a constructive failure. Constructive admittedly, because it shows how wrong-headed many arguments about civic duty are, and how it is rational to expect voting turnout to be lower when it is wet than dry, when voting is expensive (as in the USA) than when it is cheap (as in the UK), when the result is not expected to be close, and among the poor compared to the rich. (All of these expectations are borne out.) But a failure none the less. If Downs means it when he says (1957, p. 27) 'We assume that every individual, though rational, is also selfish. . . . whenever we speak of rational behavior, we always mean rational behavior directed primarily towards selfish ends', the cause is hopeless: nobody would ever vote, except in the improbable circumstances just discussed. I know two distinguished political theorists, both with strong (but different) political opinions, who practise what most of us in the profession merely preach, and never vote.

However, Downs is not consistent. Ten pages on from the passage just quoted, he says, 'There can be no simple identification of "acting for one's own greatest benefit" with selfishness in the narrow sense because self-denying charity is often a great source of benefit to oneself. Thus our model leaves room for altruism in spite of its basic reliance upon the self-interest axiom.' Most of his arguments actually work better on this second, more realistic, assumption than on the one quoted in the previous paragraph. People have views about, say, animal rights or the Panama Canal which are not self-interested in the narrow sense, but which obviously influence their political activities and make them feel that they are not wasting their time by voting. Voting is one of these little bits of altruism that makes the world go round. But that is not the end of the matter. We have to characterise altruism more carefully than we have done so far, because there are different kinds of altruism. And a rational altruist faces the same dilemmas and opportunity costs as a rational egoist. It may be worth while to go and vote for the party which says it will send aid to Ethiopia; but if I do that, I cannot at the same time be making jam for the 'Save Ethiopia' Bring and Buy Sale. Even as an altruist I may be rational to free ride on my fellow Ethiopia-savers, and assume that enough of them will go and vote for the Save Ethiopia Party to make it unnecessary for me to go as well.

This free-riding problem has often, but wrongly, been characterised as Prisoners' Dilemma (e.g. by McLean 1982a, p. 74). If I think there is no chance that my vote would make the difference between my favourite party winning and losing, then it is unconditionally irrational for me to vote; but if I think there is some chance that it would, then I am in not a Prisoners' Dilemma but a Chicken game with the other supporters of the same party (see chapter 7; also Taylor and Ward 1982). It is best if the others go and vote and I do not; next best that we all do; third best that I do and the others do not; worst if none of us does. The difference between Prisoners' Dilemma and Chicken is in the transposition of the third and fourth options. In Chicken games, such as the voting free-rider game, I would rather you contributed than contribute myself (as in

Prisoners' Dilemma); but if it comes to it I will contribute, on my own if necessary, rather than risk losing the good altogether. This is no less of a dilemma for altruists than for egoists. If I can free-ride, it is in my interest to do so; if I am an egoist, it frees me for more pleasure-seeking, and if I am an altruist it frees me for doing more good works.

Resolving the paradox 'why ever vote?' thus requires a careful description of altruistic contribution motives, such as that of Margolis (1982, esp. chapter 7). In his model there are two different sorts of altruism, which he labels 'goods altruism' and 'participation altruism'. In goods altruism my happiness (utility) is an increasing function of what other people have; in participation altruism it is a function of what I give. Most of us have some of both. We want the Ethiopian famine to end, and we want to feel that we have done our bit to end it. These are quite separate feelings. If you give money to a cause I support, then I am happy because the beneficiaries of the cause are better off, even though I did not give them the money. That is goods altruism. If I work in what turns out to be an unsuccessful election campaign, I do not feel all my work has been wasted afterwards – I feel the satisfaction of having taken part. That is participation altruism.

The three respectable arguments for the rationality of voting can be restated in Margolis's terms, two of them as goods altruism and the third as participation altruism. If my favoured party is going to produce public goods, I expect everybody to be better off by about the same amount as I am (my party differential). Even if the probability that I am the decisive voter is minuscule, the benefit is so huge – 50 million times £5000, say – that it is still worth voting from a goods-altruistic point of view, even if I could otherwise have been working for charity. Second, the 'Vote to save democracy' argument, which does not make sense in Downs' framework, does in Margolis's, again as goods altruism. Third, the feeling of having done my bit – to be distinguished, as already pointed out, from the feeling of being seen to have done my bit – is a typical piece of participation altruism which cannot be dismissed as irrational.

3.2 The Spatial Theory of Competition

The transition from microeconomics to public choice is smoother in the other part of Downs' analysis that has been widely discussed: the theory of spatial competition (Downs 1957, chapter 8). The basic theory is very simple. Imagine a street of 100 identically spaced houses on one side numbered from 1 at one end to 100 at the other. If you are going to set up a shop, and you think that just one rival entrepreneur may do the same, where should you put it? Obviously, at no. 50; because the best your rival can then do is go to no. 49 or 51. Then you will each get half the trade. If the number of houses is even, the first chooser cannot get to the exact midpoint, so there is no advantage from going first; if the number is odd, the first chooser has a slight advantage. If there are 101 houses, and I move first, I should go to 51. Then I am guaranteed 51/101sts of the trade to my rival's 50/101sts. But in either case the shops will be adjacent in the middle and the people at no. 1 and no. 100 (or 101) will have a long way to walk; but they will have to grin and bear it. For 'shops' read 'political parties' and you have a powerful general prediction of convergence on the views of the median voter.

Downs adds various refinements to make the model more realistic; and others can and should be added. I discussed these at length in my *Dealing in Votes* (McLean 1982a, pp. 20–4 and 76–88) and so will be much briefer here. First, the model needs to be modified to take account of party activists. As we noted in section 2.5, if policy-space is unidimensional party activists can be expected to be off the median position and trying to pull the politicians away from it. This follows from the fact that if they held median views, they could free ride upon the politicians who would get there anyhow in order to win the election. Second, the two-party model with parties convergent on the median depends critically on entry being difficult. This happens to be the case in both the UK and the USA, neither of which has proportional representation (PR). In the plurality electoral system which both countries share, it is next to impossible for a new party to challenge the existing ones for power unless it starts from a strong local base. If its supporters are evenly dispersed around the country, it could get 25 per cent of the votes in every electoral unit without winning a single parliamentary or congressional seat. Thus no new party has broken into US national politics since the Republican party was created in 1856. In the UK, none did between 1918 (the Labour Party) and 1981 (the SDP), and the success of the SDP/Liberal Alliance is by no means guaranteed even yet. It could still be squeezed out of existence as a national challenger for power by the Labour and Conservative parties returning to the Downsian median which they abandoned in the late

1970s. If they succeed, the SDP will have quixotically succeeded by its failure.

PR changes all these calculations. It lowers the electoral threshold because, under PR, parties no longer have to get around 35 per cent of the vote in any locality before they start to win seats. In the UK, lowering the electoral threshold would have two effects which pull in opposite directions. It would make it easier for extreme party activists to threaten to form breakaway parties if the vote-seeking leadership went too close to the Downsian median but, if the existing parties moved out in response to such threats, they would leave a gap which would be much more easily filled under PR than it has been under the plurality electoral system. The net effect of PR, assuming that party politics is unidimensional, would be to generate a number of parties arrayed along the street, each closer to its median activist than at present, but none large enough to govern without forming a coalition with its neighbours.

However, politics is not unidimensional. In few multi-party systems can the parties be arrayed from left to right on any single scale. Italy and the Scandinavian countries come closer than most; but even there the left-right dimension is crosscut by a religious/secular one (in Italy) or a rural/urban one (in Scandinavia). So it is unrealistic to talk about shops in a street after all. In two dimensions we could imagine the parties as being like showmen in a fairground, each looking for the best place to pitch his stand; in three dimensions (getting more desperate) like helicopter pilots jostling for the best view of the Boat Race; in more than three dimensions the physical imagination fails altogether, though the mathematical imagination does not. For the most part, Downs presents his model as a one-dimensional left-right one. This apparently leaves him wide open to criticism (see e.g. Stokes 1966; Butler and Stokes 1974, pp. 324–8) on the grounds that voters do not understand the left-right dimension. Although this has some truth in it, it is not as clear-cut as Stokes claimed; and in any case it underestimates the subtlety of Downs' work. As a student of Kenneth Arrow (see chapter 8) Downs realised before most people that his analysis would be undercut if politics really was multidimensional. So he introduced the one-dimensional model not because he thought it closer to reality but because it enabled him to evade the question whether there is such a thing a a median point in multidimensional space for parties to converge on. It has now been proved that, in general, there is not. This has serious consequences for both voters and politicians, as we shall now see.

3.3 The Insoluble Problem of *Full-Line Supply*

In subsection 1.3.2 we introduced Condorcet's paradox and gave Liverpool City Council's two-dimensional housing and open-space dilemma as an example. The councillors had to decide on two independent questions. Would they rather have housing or open space? And if they were to have housing, was it to be council or private housing? The outcome was a cycle: on a vote open space would beat council housing, on another council housing would beat private housing, and on a third private housing would beat open space. If the parties had been showmen trying to attract the median voter, they would have found that the fairground had no centre (or no 'core' to introduce the technical term used by social choice theorists). Norman Schofield and others have now proved (Schofield 1978, 1983) that most multidimensional voting games have no core. The non-mathematical reader will not be able to understand the proofs, but ought to find the implications easy to grasp. Suppose that there are five political issues in Ruritania. The first is the economy. Should demand be expanded (leading to high employment but high inflation) or suppressed (leading to low inflation but high unemployment)? Second, religion: should the government subsidise the Church, or tax it, or neither? Third, race: should policy favour black, brown, red or pink Ruritanians? Fourth, rural versus urban. Fifth, defence: unilateral disarmament, an arms race, or something in between? Each party which wants to form the government of Ruritania must take a position on each of these five issues. There are many possible positions on each one, but let us suppose that there are only three. There are then 243 (3^5) possible platforms. Schofield's theorems prove that there is almost certainly no platform which can win a majority of votes against each of the 242 others. This is an aspect of the problem of **full-line supply** (a term coined by Breton 1974). For a politician it is both a curse and a blessing; for the voter it is almost all bad news. To see how bad, compare and contrast for a moment the situations of voter and consumer.

At the moment I do most of the family shopping in one big store (Tesco's at Fiveways, Birmingham). It has most things we want, but anything it doesn't have can usually be got either in a city-centre department store, or in an Asian-owned shop on Dudley Road. Now suppose, first, that I was only permitted to shop at Tesco's; and, second, that my choice was restricted to one of four kinds of hampers put together by the store manager. There is only one consolation: the manager is democratically elected, and he can be voted out at the next election if people don't like what he puts in the hampers. As it happens, I love Marmite but I loathe eggs. All four of the hampers have too little Marmite and too many eggs for my taste. As my tastes are unusual, I cannot form a coalition of Marmite-loving egg-haters to get rid of the manager. Worse, even if I sacrifice some of my tastes to help build a coalition (no eggs and no Marmite), it may be beaten by some utterly different coalition, which takes the same position on eggs and Marmite but a different one on asparagus and cat food.

The analogy with the voter is not quite exact, but it is close enough to be painful. It is inherent in the human condition that most of us will never be able to get exactly what we want in the public arena unless public goods are supplied voluntarily (through altruism or anarchy) or by market exchange. Government is doomed to be a disappointment; the problem of full-line supply is insoluble from the voter's point of view. In the next two sections we shall look at how far voters got what they wanted in the two chosen policy areas.

3.4 Applying the Model in the USA

Public policy-making is a two-way process. Voters have views which they communicate to politicians, who try to give them what they want. Or else they try to make voters want what they have to give. Public-choice writers have sometimes been accused of making a naive (and smug) assumption of consumer sovereignty, which ignores one side of the interaction: the fact that politicians have 'state power' (incumbent ones do, anyhow) and can use it to shape voters' preferences (see e.g. Dunleavy and Ward 1981; Dunleavy and Husbands 1985, pp. 49–52). For the moment we treat voters' preferences as given ('exogenous' in economist-speak). However, in section 3.5 we shall look at a case where politicians and interest groups helped to mould voters' preferences.

A good deal is known about the preferences of environmental activists; less is known about the views of the mass American public on the environment. We need to establish two things: first, the *salience* of mass opinions, and second, their *direction*.

It is helpful to think of three levels of salience. At the top are issues which people consistently tell pollsters are among 'the most

important problems in this country today'. Without doubt, these
issues have a major impact on voting decisions and politicians will
always try to satisfy as many voters as they can on them. Lower
down come issues on which people have definite and relatively
stable opinions, but which are less likely to lead them to change their
votes. At the bottom lie a vast mass of issues on which voters have
no real opinion at all, even though they may tell pollsters that they
have one, either out of politeness or to avoid seeming ignorant (see
Converse 1964 for the classic discussion of this; also McLean
1982a, pp. 15–19).

In the USA, the environment is in the middle category. It has never
made the top three in Gallup's regular 'most important problem'
question (see Nie, et al. 1979, pp. 100–3 for evidence from the
1950s to the early 1970s; *Public Opinion*, Feb.–March 1980, p. 21
and April–May 1983, p. 25 for updates). But it is not a question to
which people give random answers either. People have fairly stable
and moderately salient views. In one 1982 survey the environment
ranked equally with a clutch of other medium-salience issues (taxes,
a balanced budget, the Middle East, the Equal Rights Amendment,
gun control and religion) each of which 2 per cent of a national
sample said would lead them to change their vote if their normal
party was unsympathetic. For comparison, nuclear war/nuclear
freeze, foreign policy, defence spending and social programmes each
scored 4 per cent, social security 13 per cent, abortion 15 per cent
and the economy 33 per cent (*Public Opinion* Dec.–Jan. 1983,
p. 21).

If the salience is medium, the direction is moderately
environmentalist. Of a number of criticisms of the Reagan
administration put to a series of samples from 1980 to 1983,
'spending too little on the environment' was the third most popular,
with 54 per cent agreeing with it (*Public Opinion* Oct.–Nov. 1983,
p. 38). In 1978 people thought that setting stricter controls for auto
emissions was worth the cost, and in 1977 opinion was exactly
evenly divided on whether to relax environmental standards on
behalf of the coal industry. There may be a very slight trend away
from environmentalism, in that a slight majority of those asked in
1981 leant towards the economy rather than the environment if
forced to choose, and the proportion of voters who think that Ralph
Nader has done an 'excellent' or 'pretty good' job on behalf of
consumers has declined from 54 per cent in 1976 to 39 per cent in
1982. There is a marked age difference in attitudes, with the cohort

born between 1944 and 1952 most strongly environmentalist, closely followed by the next younger five-year cohort and a steady downwards tendency in older age-groups (*Public Opinion* June–July 1980, pp. 38–9; April–May 1982, p. 28; Feb–March 1983, p. 40; Feb–March 1980, p. 38).

If the environment had been in the bottom category of salience, politicians and interest groups would be able to ignore public opinion altogether in forming policy. As it is, they are constrained, but not too seriously. The environment, like motherhood and apple pie, commands widespread approval, and it seems that the Reagan Administration may have suffered from its 'anti-environment' stance. But it is probably more a matter of presentation than substance. Two of the Administration's most disastrous appointees (James Watt and Anne Burford) were in the environmental field. The mass electorate probably reacts more to events such as Mrs Burford's resignation in 1982 or the jailing of one of her aides in 1985 after being convicted of perjury before Congress than to controversies on the issues.

3.5 Applying the Model in the UK

3.5.1 Are Modern British Politics Incompatible with Downs' Model?

In the last ten years, the main British parties seem to have moved sharply apart, although the basic Downsian model predicts convergence. However, both halves of that sentence have to be studied very carefully before rushing to the conclusion that the Downsian model is invalid.

Conservative and Labour rhetoric were certainly further apart from 1979 to 1985 than at any time since the 1920s. However, two qualifications are needed. Rhetoric is not the same as performance. On a number of issues (tax reform and subsidies to loss-making industries are examples) the policies of the Labour and Conservative governments have differed far less than their rhetoric. Neither, for instance, has dared to interfere with the tax privileges of house-owners with mortgages. And on matters where the Labour and Conservative parties have a common interest (for instance, in opposing electoral reform and resisting open government) the supposed adversaries are warm allies, (for a review of the evidence, see Rose 1984).

Another possibility is that the voters have moved apart as well. If that were the case, the 'move apart' of the parties would support, not undermine, the simple Downs hypothesis. So we must look carefully at the survey evidence on what voters think. There are two things to consider: what voters think are the salient issues, and what they think about them.

There are three issues which always make the top ten in answers to the regular survey question in Britain, 'What do you think are the most important issues facing the country today?' They are unemployment, inflation and industrial relations. Unemployment and inflation have an inverse relationship, at least in the short run; the more the government of the day concentrates on one of them, the more the other will rise in the salience list. This is not because people are bloody-minded, but because no modern government has discovered a way to ameliorate one without worsening the other. From March 1978 to September 1980, for instance, 'prices' declined steadily in salience from being mentioned by 72 per cent to being mentioned by 44 per cent of voters; 'unemployment' described a U-shaped curve from 71 down to 24 and back to 72 per cent. The salience of 'industrial relations' varies positively with the incidence of prominent disputes: it hit 73 per cent during a rash of strikes in February 1979 ('the winter of discontent'), but within two months was down to 24 per cent.[1]

Some other issues rise and fall dramatically in salience. This is due partly to changes in the outside world and partly to deliberate attempts to bring issues on to the agenda. As an example of the first, 'law and order' reached the top three briefly in July 1981 at the time of widespread urban riots. A probable example of the second is the surge in salience of race and immigration in late 1978 and early 1979 following a speech in which Mrs Thatcher complained that 'people can feel rather swamped' by coloured immigration. A certain example is the arrival from nowhere of defence and nuclear disarmament as a salient issue in 1982–3. From an incidence too low to be separately recorded, defence jumped to the second most salient issue in time for the 1983 General Election. The Labour leadership put defence on to the agenda, although the result was not what they wanted.[2]

The relationship between salience and effect on voting is complex. Obviously, issues which are not salient have little or no effect on voting, and therefore politicians, activists, and interest groups can negotiate policy more or less unconstrained by what the voters think. But it is not necessarily the most salient issues that have the most effect. Unemployment and inflation are what have been called 'valence' as opposed to 'position' issues. Unlike (say) selling council houses, they are not issues on which the parties are on opposite sides. All politicians say that they are against both unemployment and inflation, and the electors are left to judge them by how effectively each party can be expected to deal with them. For many voters the answer is 'Not very'; if this were not so, they would not be such enduring issues (see, e.g., Himmelweit et al. 1981, pp. 183–4). This helps to explain why the Conservatives won the 1983 General Election even though unemployment was overwhelmingly seen as the most important issue and was at heights unprecedented since the 1930s.

Much of the Labour activists' agenda – nationalising more industries, increasing trade union power, abolishing the House of Lords – comprised position issues. There is no evidence that voters were warming to the activists' view. If anything, the evidence points the other way. For instance, the proportion even of Labour sympathisers who favoured more nationalisation declined by 25 per cent between 1964 and 1979, and the proportion favouring more spending on social services declined by 28 per cent from 1964 to 1974 (Crewe 1981, p. 298; other evidence is in Crewe and Sarlvik 1983 chapters 8, 11; Dunleavy and Husbands 1985, chapter 7).

Thus it is clear that the voters have not moved but the parties have. So the simplest Downsian model is not confirmed. Note, however, that it is one of the very features of the simple model that has allowed the parties to diverge from it: the high electoral threshold. If it had been easier for new parties to enter the system, the parties would have had to respond more quickly than they have done to evidence that they have drifted away from the electorate. In mid-1986 the Conservative and Labour Parties were apparently converging on median electoral opinion in a deliberate attempt to squeeze the SDP/Liberal Alliance out of existence. The county council elections of 1985 were the first British elections ever in which the Alliance won seats in rough proportion to its share of the vote. That is a dangerous threshold for the Labour and Conservative Parties, and it was in their urgent (and joint) interest to push the Alliance back over it. No such threshold would exist if the barriers to entry were lower.

The main reason for the parties' divergence from the electorate is familiar: the tension between satisfying party activists and satisfying marginal party supporters. Empirical evidence for the gulf between these groups abounds (see McLean 1982a, pp. 124–9, 192). And, as we made clear in section 2.5, there is every reason to expect this to be a normal feature of political life. If my views are the same as most people's, it pays me to take a free ride on the process of convergence which will tend to bring the parties into line with my views; only if my views are not the same as most people's do I have an incentive to become a party activist (see McLean 1982a, chapter 6; Robertson 1976, especially pp. 31–3).

3.5.2 *The Voters, the Labour Manifestos, and Full-Line Supply*

Full-line supply is a problem for voters; for politicians it is both a problem and an opportunity. In 1979 and 1983 the Conservatives turned it to their advantage. With unpopular policies on unemployment – the central economic issue – the Conservatives nevertheless managed to win. In 1979 this was largely by persuading the electorate to think retrospectively rather than prospectively ('Labour Isn't Working' as the Conservative posters proclaimed). But in 1979 and to a much greater extent in 1983 the Conservatives chose to fight on what their own polls showed them was strong ground among the electorate: trade union reform, 'law and order', the sale of council houses – the last a policy actually suggested to them by their pollsters (Butler and Kavanagh 1980, p. 275; Butler and Kavanagh 1984, pp. 34, 135–40). In this way they hoped to mask the fact that they were vulnerable on unemployment. By presenting a hamper in which an unattractive packet of unemployment cure was balanced by highly attractive council-house vouchers and union reform packages, the Conservatives turned full-line supply to their advantage. Labour did not do so well.

Part of the problem is that Labour has always been more ambivalent about marketing than the Conservatives. This is partly a matter of style and partly a matter of values. Many Labour politicians, including Michael Foot, are deeply suspicious of the claims made by the pollsters, resentful of the brash American who has been the party's principal polling consultant since 1970, and hostile to the ethos of the advertising world from which opinion polling springs. Besides, it is not necessarily right to take voters' preferences as exogenous; many Labour politicians would agree that 'It is not the party's policy, but public opinion which needs to be changed' (J. Mortimer, General Secretary of the Labour Party, October 1983; quoted in Butler and Kavanagh 1984, p. 278). But in order to do that it is necessary at least to know what the voters' exogenous preferences and tastes are; and in 1983 Labour disastrously failed to do this. As its disgruntled pollster complained afterwards: '[R]esearch doesn't measure truth, it measures *perception*. For the public to perceive the Tories under Mrs Thatcher as the Party with the greatest concern for the majority of the public is nonsense; *yet that was the perception*. To ignore this is foolish. To fail to know it is foolish ignorance' (R. Worcester, quoted by Butler and Kavanagh 1984, pp. 140–1; emphasis in original).

By comparison, the 1979 manifesto had been a modestly successful exercise in full-line supply. Callaghan knew that Labour was vulnerable on most of the issues, although less so on Scottish devolution than everybody had assumed because the issue was not salient enough; his strength lay in his own personality, as he was seen as a better Prime Minister than Mrs Thatcher. So the manifesto came wrapped in a statesmanlike presentation of, and by, Mr Callaghan ('Together the people and the Labour Government, even without a parliamentary majority, have achieved much these past five years. . . . But nobody who cares about Britain can rest satisfied until far, far more has been accomplished'). It highlighted policy areas where the activists and the electorate were at one. Areas where they diverged were in the small print. The idea of nationalising a bank, for instance, had mysteriously evolved into a commitment to 'develop the Girobank and the National Savings Bank to their full potential . . . [to] ensure for the country a vigorous public banking sector'.

With the retirement of Mr Callaghan in 1980, the party faced a leadership election. It was still conducted by the old system, with only MPs voting, but the new system cast a long shadow in front of itself. MPs voted for party unity rather than electoral appeal, and on their second ballot they chose Michael Foot as the new leader. Table 3.1 shows the gap between their choice and the public's preference.

As we noted in subsection 2.5.3, Michael Foot was not interested in reconciling the demands of party activists and the preferences of voters when the 1983 manifesto was being drafted. This had several unfortunate consequences. First, policies were put in which were known to be desperately unpopular with the electorate (for instance, nationalising a clearing bank, fudged in 1979, was set forth starkly

Table 3.1   Labour leadership election 1980: MPs' first ballot votes
and public preferences (percentages)

	Voters	Lab. Voters	All electors
Healey	42	68	71
Foot	31	25	16
Silkin	15	6	9
Shore	12	1	4

Source: Mitchell (1983) p. 50.

as an option in 1983). Second, and more important, Labour gave the ineradicable impression of being disorganised and incompetent. It never became clear whether a Labour government would unilaterally scrap Britain's nuclear weapons or use them as bargaining counters in international negotiations. (Since foreign governments employ people who can read English, the two proposals were strictly incompatible.)

Thus the British electorate in 1983 faced an unappealing choice. Overwhelmingly the voters thought the most important issue was unemployment. But they did not trust any of the main parties to reduce it. The Conservatives had conspicuously failed in the previous four years; the SDP/Liberal Alliance was an unknown quantity; and Labour was perceived to be too incompetent. The next issue was defence, which Labour had put on to the agenda by bringing forward a new radical policy. But one part of that policy – unilateral disarmament – was overwhelmingly unpopular. The proportion of voters agreeing that 'Britain should give up its nuclear arms even if other countries do not give up theirs' fell from 28 per cent in October 1981 to 16 per cent in May 1983. Other aspects of the Labour defence proposals were popular – a plurality of voters favoured banning both American bases on British soil and cruise missiles (source: *NOP Political Social Economic Review* no. 42, 1983, pp. 15–16). But voters faced an acute problem of full-line supply. The effective choice was between a Labour package of unilateralism and no Americans and a Conservative package of Americans and no unilateralism. This was merely a microcosm of the overall problem before the voters. Labour was more popular than the Conservatives on unemployment but thought to be unable to get anything done about it. On most issues other than unemployment the Conservatives had more popular policies; but all the other issues were ranked far below unemployment and defence in salience. The 1983 election showed very clearly how much more restricted voter choice is than consumer choice. Labour politicians had made an unusually bad job of deciding what to put in the hampers and how to wrap it; but this merely highlighted a problem which was there all along, and is always there in every election.

4

Lobbying:
The Role of Interest Groups

4.1 How the Collective Action Problem Applies to Groups

An interest group is any organisation which tries to influence public policy. Unlike a political party or an official bureaucracy it is not directly involved in governing; but members and potential members of interest groups face similar public-goods problems to those faced by politicians and bureaucrats. They are more acute than the problems faced by potential voters because giving time or money to a lobby is a much larger action than voting. If Downs has shown that it is doubtful whether any rational person should vote, is it not all the more doubtful whether any rational person should take part in a lobby?

The work of Mancur Olson (Olson 1965, 1982) stands in the same relation to this chapter as that of Anthony Downs did to chapter 3. Olson posed the right questions and came up with some of the right answers; but neither his hypothesis nor his applications are entirely consistent. The first task of this chapter is to set out the hypothesis, with several variants; the second is to test it on our two running examples.

The basic argument is simple and, by now, familiar. Interest groups lobby for public goods. A government policy, unless it is wholly divisible, is a public good: it is there for everybody in the group to whom it applies, whether or not they have contributed to the cost of lobbying for it. Government policy cannot always be wholly divisible, even when the government and the lobby both want it to be. Consider a lobby for a tariff, for instance. Tariffs are normally bad for everybody except those in the industry they protect, for whom they are a good which is not wholly divisible. For instance, a government can give import protection to all firms in the textile industry. It cannot practicably give protection only to firms which are members of the Textile (Keep Out Foreigners) Industry Association. If the policy involves some indivisible element, potential members of every lobby are tempted to freeride. If some of them do freeride, the good is underprovided; if all of them freeride, the good is not provided at all.

Olson distinguishes between three categories of groups, which he calls 'privileged', 'intermediate', and 'latent'. These are roughly, but not exactly, the same as 'small', 'medium' and 'large' respectively. A privileged group contains at least one member who gains enough privately from the public good to be willing to supply it on his own if necessary. Privileged groups are usually small, but need not be. Late-night TV viewers in Las Vegas turned out to be a privileged group after Howard Hughes bought the TV station. Any industry which would benefit from a tariff is privileged if the gains to at least one member are higher than that member's share of the cost of organising the lobby. An intermediate group is one which is not privileged, but whose potential members are sufficiently few that each can be aware of the others' actions and inactions. Olson supposes that collective action will occur in some intermediate groups because the members will watch each others' behaviour, and by a process of threats, promises and conditional cooperation may come to provide the public good. Olson does not develop this idea, but it is obviously analogous to the 'evolution of cooperation' concept of writers like Robert Axelrod, which will be discussed in chapter 7.

Most groups, actual and potential, are neither privileged nor intermediate. Olson calls them 'latent'. A latent group need not exist at all. Everybody who is unemployed has a number of common interests. A rise in unemployment benefit would be a public good for every unemployed person. But the lobby of the unemployed, in both Britain and the USA, is not just latent; it is virtually non-existent. Olson advances various arguments to account for the fact that some latent groups exist. They may have been originally set up by the government (the American Farm Bureaus are an example). Their lobbying may be a by-product of actions which are more directly aimed at advancing their members' interests (Olson classes the political activities of trade unions under this heading, but his argument here seems confused). Or they may thrive on the selective benefits they offer their members. Selective benefits are excludable,

unlike public goods. An example is *Which?* magazine, which the
Consumers' Association – the principal British consumers' lobby –
sends only to its members. It does not sell it on the newsstands, nor
allow articles from it to be reprinted elsewhere. To get your personal
copy of *Which?* you have to join the Association, which thereby
acquires funds to use on public-goods lobbying.[1] Selective benefits
are the obverse of selective harms, which lobbies may also use: for
instance, a trade union which does various nasty things to
workpeople who are not in the union. If the price of free-riding is
being picketed or sent to Coventry, it may be no longer rational to
freeride on the wage rises the union negotiates.

At this point it is useful to interweave another three-way
classification of groups into Olson's. Groups may be described as
producer groups, consumer groups, or altruistic groups (see McLean
1982a, pp. 95–104). A producer group controls a factor of
production and is a strong bargainer because it can threaten to
withhold the factor it controls. A union can withdraw its labour, a
capitalist can shut his factory, a farmer can withdraw produce from
market. Consumer groups are typically weaker than producer
groups. Although no less self-interested, they have no sanctions –
control no factors of production – and therefore find it harder to
persuade governments to provide public goods for their members
and potential members. Altruistic groups may be even weaker
because they do not have the spur of self-interest. In terms of
Olson's classification, virtually all consumer and altruistic groups
are latent. (One or two may be intermediate: a group of people in a
smoke-filled room may achieve clean air by bargaining, for instance.
But apart from Howard Hughes's lucky Las Vegans it is hard to
think of a privileged consumer group.) Producer groups may come
into any of Olson's three categories. The fewer the producers in each
group, the more likely it is to be either privileged or intermediate. In
general, there are fewer capitalists than workers in any industry.
This would lead us to predict that their interests are more likely to
be protected in lobbying (Offe and Wiesenthal 1980).

Ever since the eighteenth century, some commentators have
always worried about lobbyists. From Rousseau to Madison to
Joseph Schumpeter, normative political theorists have complained
that groups distort democracy because politicians give the groups
what they want rather than try to find out what the people want.
Until Olson most modern political scientists were sceptical; following Bentley (1908 *passim*, especially pp. 226, 454–5) they argued

that if a group did not exist, that merely showed that nobody cared enough about the issue, and that the interplay of group pressures was not a distortion of democracy. Indeed to Bentley, the interplay of groups *was* democracy.

Olson's first book was a challenge to the complacency of this view; and in his second (Olson 1982) he takes a more radically critical view. In this book he concentrates on the sort of producer group discussed in the last paragraph (although he does not particularly distinguish between controllers of capital and control-lers of labour; for many purposes they are on the same side). Such groups are now labelled 'distributional coalitions' and are a Bad Thing. They grab an unfair share of resources, laying claim to things which are public goods to their members but public bads for everybody else (subsidies to loss-making industries and tariff protection are two common examples); and they lead to 'sclerosis' in old industrial societies. Only in places which are relatively free of them because of recent industrialisation or because old associations were swept away in war and replaced by new ones designed by occupying powers to maximise efficiency can there be fast growth. Thus Britain, France and most of the USA grow slowly; but Germany and Japan grow fast, thanks to their post-Second World War occupation by the British, the French, and the Americans.

4.2 An Evaluation of the Olson Model

The Olson model has great strengths. A lot of things which are said, both positively and normatively, about political institutions would not be said so readily if they were carefully scrutinised in the light of Olson. Like Downs, Olson works on the marginal principle. A rational potential lobby member does not ask 'Does this lobby pursue aims I support?' but 'Would my marginal contribution to this lobby increase its chances of success sufficiently to warrant my spending resources on it?' It is still commonly, but fallaciously, assumed in discussing all sorts of collective action that what is in the selfish interests of all is in the selfish interests of each. It is not only pluralists who make this mistake. Marxists do it too. Marx and Engels called the capitalist state 'a committee for managing the common affairs of the bourgeoisie' and argue that capitalism forces the bourgeoisie to follow its narrowly selfish class interest. But if each bourgeois followed his self-interest, he would free ride on the apparatus of the state, which could not therefore manage the common affairs of the bourgeoisie.

It is less clear whether Marx thought that the proletariat, too, followed its self-interest. If he did, then by the same argument there is no reason for any individual proletarian to be involved in the revolution. Possibly Marx is to be read as arguing that proletarians have, or may have once the possibility of revolution is pointed out to them, a more altruistic view than capitalists, so that they are prepared to work for the revolution out of class solidarity. But an appeal to altruism does not end the argument. For, as Olson points out, an altruist still has to measure the opportunity cost of any one altruistic act – say, taking part in the revolution – against that of all other possible altruistic acts like being kind to animals or looking after an elderly relative. Unless the value of the revolution, discounted by the minute probability that it is my participation which makes the difference between its success and its failure, exceeds the non-discounted value of an individual piece of altruism, I should still free ride. Unless, that is, the consequence of not participating is to be the first against the wall after the revolution. (A critique of Marxism on these lines from a scholar who regards himself as a Marxist is Elster 1985, pp. 349–71.)

Nevertheless, before we can test the model against our running examples, there are a number of critical points to make.

4.2.1 *How do Non-Privileged Groups get Going?*

Olson can explain why non-privileged groups do things other than lobby for public goods – issue magazines, do casework, and offer various other selective incentives – but he has no real explanation of how such groups get going in the first place. It cannot be that the selective incentives come first. If they did, the putative public-goods lobby would be disadvantaged compared to pure trading organisations which offered 'selective incentives' – namely, goods and services in exchange for money – without trying to carry a public-goods organisation on top. Olson's argument about selective incentives can only explain why lobbying groups also have to offer them, not how they come into existence.

Some groups, as he notes, are called into existence by governments. In other cases, new lobbies can piggyback on organisations that already existed for other purposes. Two American cases are the prohibition movement of the 1920s and Civil Rights in the 1960s.

Both used an existing network of churches – black churches in the case of Civil Rights – to supply the resources needed for a lobby. But in general Olson's work fails to provide an explanation of why any latent group comes into existence. We need to assume some sort of altruism, and some ideological entrepreneur.

4.2.2 Inconsistent Game-Theoretic Assumptions

Olson's treatment of 'privileged' and of 'intermediate' groups is not consistent. He assumes that there is no strategic interaction between members of a privileged group, but that there is, or at least may be, among members of an intermediate group. 'Strategic interaction' means that each actor bases his decision on some expectation about the decisions of the others, and that the outcome is a function of all the actors' interdependent decisions. The correct way to analyse this sort of thing is by using game theory. In writing about intermediate groups, Olson obviously had economists' theories of **oligopoly** in mind, in which players may act non-cooperatively and arrive at the **'Cournot equilibrium solution'** to the problem of how much to produce and what to charge, or they may, by behaving cooperatively, each secure larger gains. However, oligopolists are in a Prisoners' Dilemma with one another, and if there is a cartel to restrict prices and/or output, each player's **dominant strategy** is to undercut. There are cooperative solutions to this Prisoners' Dilemma if it is assumed that the players will often meet; in that case they can issue threats, make promises, and take decisions conditional on what the others did last time. These conditions do accurately describe the situation of (potential) members of a small lobby; they are discussed in chapter 7 below.

However, if they are applied to intermediate groups, they have to be applied to privileged groups as well. The smaller a group, the more likely there is to be strategic interaction among its members. Olson assumes that privileged groups will normally be smaller than intermediate ones, and his model must be modified to take account of the Chicken supergame in which privileged members of privileged groups find themselves. Recall that in Chicken my orderings are: best that the others contribute and I don't; next best that we all do; third best that I do and the others don't; worst that none of us does. When Chicken is played repeatedly (as, in this case, it is) it turns into a game of bluff and precommitment. If there is more than one player who would pay the full cost of the lobby if he had to, each of them has an incentive to precommit himself to not paying, and thus force the other(s) to pay. If there is only one, he still has an incentive to precommit in order to try to force the smaller actors to pay up. Olson seems to assume, without discussing the case fully, that he is bound to fail, and that therefore the small actors will free ride on the large – the 'exploitation of the great by the small' as Olson (1965, pp. 29, 35) calls it. A rigorous analysis of precommitment is needed before we can jump to this conclusion.

4.2.3 Problems with the 'By-Product' Argument

'The common characteristic which distinguishes all of the large economic groups with significant lobbying organisations is that these groups are also organised for some *other* purpose' (Olson 1965, p. 132; stress in original). Hence, he claims, their lobbying activities are by-products of their central purpose. But this claim is both empirically and logically suspect. Many of the most significant lobbying organisations in US national politics, for instance, are producer-group associations which exist for the explicit purpose of lobbying. The raison d'être of a typical trade association (like the Chemical Industry Association in the UK, or the National Association of Electrical Contractors in the USA) is to lobby on behalf of member firms. Sometimes, it is true, trade associations have other functions, such as arbitrating in disputes between member firms, but it is these functions which are by-products of an organisation set up to lobby, and not the other way round. Trade unions are in a different position from trade associations, but not in the position Olson assigns to them. Unions are mostly in the public-goods business in industrial relations as well as in politics. Therefore they face a free-rider problem from the outset (and Olson does not explain how any union could ever come into existence). But once they have conquered that problem, they are just as well equipped to lobby as to negotiate with employers. And lobbying may be much cheaper, as the example of Keir Hardie versus the Northumberland miners (section 2.2) was designed to show. Hence it seems wrong to call political lobbying by a trade union a 'by-product' of its industrial activities.

4.2.4 The Outcome of Lobbying as an Ultra-High-Value Public Good

The outcome of lobbying may be very lucrative indeed. We have already given examples from different fields: the miners' eight hour day and the Texan oilman's tax-break, for instance. In these cases, the law changed property rights without forcing the gainers to pay the losers (coalowners and American taxpayers, respectively). Laws are always doing this sort of thing, and therefore lobbies to change the law may be 'privileged' more often than Olson seems to allow for. Furthermore, this argument is not restricted to cash. As we argued in chapter 3, a voter's party differential has to be measured in utility income, not cash income. I may derive a stream of utility from the fact that from next year laboratory experiments on animals are banned. And if this is to affect the calculus of voting, it must also affect the calculus of lobbying. People say 'I would give anything to preserve Stonehenge/stop animal experiments/reduce the risk of nuclear war.' If that is not just a rhetorical exaggeration, we should not be surprised to find that they do in fact spend something on lobbies to achieve these ends.

4.2.5 *Taking Account of Altruism*

To formulate these ideas carefully, we need to bring in Margolis's model of altruism, as we did at the equivalent point in chapter 3. It may be altruistic to join a lobby to prevent nuclear war or to protect animals, but of course it is not irrational. None the less, a rational altruist has to weigh both altruistic actions against non-altruistic ones, and each altruistic act against each other. To do so he needs something like Margolis's model of goods altruism and participation altruism. Consider somebody thinking of joining the Sierra Club. The Sierra Club, with 178 000 members in 1977, is the largest environmental lobbying organisation in the USA. It costs $20.00 a year to join. A potential member has two questions to solve: first, should my last $20 go on an altruistic or a self-interested project? That will obviously depend on how much of the rest of my money has gone on each. Second, if it is to go on something altruistic, should it be a subscription to the Sierra Club or something else?

This choice has to be broken down into its goods-altruistic and its participation-altruistic components. I can compute the second directly; and if I can get a feeling of having done my bit from something as painless as sitting down and writing a small cheque, subscribing to the Sierra Club comes out well on participation altruism. On goods altruism, I reckon, (being an environmentalist) that the USA with the Sierra Club's aims achieved is worth thousands of dollars more to each and every one of the 250 million

Americans than the USA with the Sierra Club's aims unachieved. I therefore value the public goods involved in billions of dollars. The probability that my $20 will make all the difference is tiny, of course; but multiply ten billion dollars by a tiny fraction and you may still end up with a sizeable utility income. In section 4.4 we shall look at this sort of altruism in more detail.

4.3 Lobby Power Versus Vote Power

A more radical criticism of Olson's model is that he sometimes seems to forget about politics. This is especially notable in *The Rise and Decline of Nations*, in which politicians, bureaucrats, and voters hardly appear at all. But politicians care about votes as well as about interests. Indeed if we consider politicians as primarily vote-maximisers, as public-choice writers often do, then groups play a strictly secondary role. Politicians must still pay attention to them, for at least three reasons. First, groups may have vote power themselves. Very often, groups ask political candidates where they stand on the group's issue, and advise their members how to vote in the light of politicians' replies. As a candidate in local elections, I have been asked my views on abortion (by both sides), homosexual rights, and animal experiments, even though a British local authority has very few powers to change the way the world treats any of these. Second, politicians may need groups to help pay their expenses (see section 2.1 and McLean 1982a pp. 158–66). When politicians need support from suppliers of the factors of production, they also need to listen to their paymasters' views about policy, even if these views contradict those of the voters. It is of little use to have an election-winning policy if you cannot afford to put it before the electorate. Third, politicians often need the specialised knowledge and skill of groups to put their policies in the group's area into effect.

Nevertheless, lobby power and vote power often do pull in different directions, and politicians' choice of direction has to be influenced by both. We should not have any predetermined ideas about which pull is the stronger. That obviously varies from issue to issue. But the two extreme assumptions are clearly false. Vote power does not always override group power; if it did, the US Congress could not have passed either the tariff of 1824 or the Smoot-Hawley tariffs of 1930 (see Pincus 1975; Morison et al. 1969 pp. 424–6). But neither does group power always override vote power; if it did,

Congress could not have passed the Sherman Anti-trust Act of 1890 or the Clean Air Act Amendments of 1970. In the first two cases, Congress produced laws that were good for the producer groups but bad for everybody else; in the second pair, it produced laws that (at least in their intentions) were the opposite.

4.4 US Environmental Lobbies at Work: The NSPS Case

This section will discuss the efforts of the EPA to set New Source Performance Standards (NSPS). These are rules for emission control that all new factories emitting effluents, especially power stations, have to meet. Designed to reduce atmospheric pollution, the rules will in fact increase it; and yet they were mostly welcomed by environmental groups. In studying how this came about, we may learn something about how groups work and have some test of Olson's and rival hypotheses.

The story is so complex that an exasperated Federal judge, at the end of a hundred-page ruling on the principal case under it, said:

> We have read the record with as hard a look as mortal judges can probably give its thousands of pages . . . . Cases like this highlight the enormous responsibilities Congress has entrusted to the courts in proceedings of such length, complexity, and disorder. Conflicting interests play fiercely for enormous stakes, advocates are prolific and agile, obfuscation runs high, common sense correspondingly low, the public intent is often obscured.[2]

I shall try none the less to summarise the main events (for fuller summaries see Ackerman and Hassler 1981; Haskell 1982; McLean 1984).

The EPA had to propose clean-up standards under the Clean Air Act Amendments of 1970. For existing plants, the rules demanded that the total *ambient level* of sulphur dioxide pollution in the local atmosphere must not exceed a certain threshold, but for new plants the rules demanded a *reduction* in emissions from what they would otherwise have been. Controlling levels is a rational policy, but stipulating reductions is not, because if the local atmosphere is already at a level which is tolerated elsewhere there is no point in demanding a reduction; and if the local atmosphere is below par, it is in principle more sensible to determine a level and leave it to the polluters to decide how to meet it. The consequence of seeking reductions (later changed, to tighten the net, to 'technological reductions') of effluent from new plants was to increase their cost, and hence to make plant-owners keep less efficient, and dirtier, plants in use for longer than they otherwise would. The most recent summary of the achievements of the NSPS programme is that by 2000 it will cost $3 billion a year more than a policy based on ambient pollution levels, and will also leave the air dirtier, because of old, dirty, power stations being kept on stream instead of new ones made too expensive by the NSPS requirements (estimates from the Congressional Budget Office, cited by Palmer and Sawhill 1984, p. 145; cf. also Justice Stevens in *Chevron USA Inc.* v. *NRDC*, US Supreme Court 1984, 21 ERC 1049–62).

This outcome resulted from an odd coalition of environmentalists and coal producers against power station operators (privately- and publicly-owned utility companies). To the environmentalists, emission control was a tangible gain and technological emission control by 'scrubbers' in power station chimneys was more tangible than a change in utilities' behaviour brought about by pricing or ambient-pollution-level rules. To the producers of dirty coal, scrubbing was a lifeline which enabled them to continue marketing coal that otherwise could not have been sold because utilities would have railed in low-sulphur coal from other parts of the country. Let us look in a little more detail at the lobbies and their Olson problems.

4.4.1 The Environmentalists

Two main environmental organisations fought the NSPS battle – the Sierra Club and the Natural Resources Defense Council (NRDC). Sierra Club members are disproportionately drawn from the ranks of the better-off (Mitchell 1979; Hardin 1982 especially pp. 69–135). This fits Crenson's evidence that protecting the environment appeals more to the young, affluent and/or well-educated than to the opposites of each of these. Hardin also suggests that clean air may be a 'superior good': 'that is to say that the well-off; demand proportionately more . . . than do the less well-off' and maybe in addition a complementary good to private goods such as fast cars (you are more likely to be able to get to a National Park and enjoy its clean air if you have a fast car than if you have not) (Hardin 1982, pp. 69, 88). Members were contributing some $7.2 million a year to the Sierra Club in the late 1970s, of which about $1.9 million went directly on lobbying and most of the rest on goods for members. The Club also got lobbying money from charitable foundations – its Legal Defense Fund would not exist 'without the generosity of the Ford Foundation', according to the executive director of the fund (quoted by Hardin 1982, p. 117).

The NRDC relied less on members and more on the foundations – in 1984, for instance, one of its staff estimated that only 15 per cent of its income came from members.[3] This was deliberate policy. It was set up primarily as a litigating body, not as a campaigning-cum-social body like the Sierra Club, and its activities largely depended on what foundations were willing to pay for. There has never been a careful study of this, but there are strong indications that fashion plays a large part. The environment swung sharply into fashion in the early 1970s, and although it has swung out again to some extent, foundation money still comes in fast enough to maintain the NRDC's programme of litigation.

These two organisations faced a severe public-goods problem; how did they overcome it? Hardin estimates (in Mitchell 1979 p. 123) that the US spent $15 billion on pollution abatement in 1977, but that the total campaign income of the main environmental organisations was only $10 million. If this is read to mean that every $1 of campaign donation brought in $1500 of pollution control, it makes campaign contributions a very good bargain indeed. But this can be looked at in two ways. A would-be contributor still knows that quite a lot of pollution control will come about without his efforts and he has the usual incentive to free ride on others' efforts. This is not an all-or-nothing case; presumably, the more lobby income the Sierra Club gets, the more lobbying it can do, and the prospects of legislation favouring the Club grow incrementally. However, the contributor's dilemma has a flavour of Chicken: the more others contribute, the less I should, and the less they contribute, the more I should. This dilemma is not exactly captured by Olson's model, nor by any of the proposed amendments to it (Moe 1980; Hardin 1982; Taylor and Ward 1982). It can be read two ways. Confronted by a half-full cup, some people are surprised that it is not full and others are surprised that it is not empty. In proportion to the number of American citizens who say they are concerned about the environment (see section 3.4), the number who contribute to campaigns seems pitifully low and heavily weighted towards the rich. But in relation to Olson's original prediction about latent groups, the number of environmental activists seems high. They contribute for a mixture of reasons – Hardin, drawing on another empirical survey, suggests that sheer confusion and mis-taken logic are not insignificant[4] – but their contributions are enough to ensure that producer-group lobbies do not have the field to themselves.

A group like the NRDC evades free-riding in another way. By relying on foundation funding, it depends on bodies whose purpose is to be charitable, or in another word altruistic. The question 'Why should a charity be altruistic?' is nonsensical, of course, whereas the question 'Why should an individual be altruistic?' is not. But charities have to have some yardstick to judge the cost-effectiveness of their contributions. What that is, and how they decide to allocate money to the environment (or any other particular cause) are matters on which empirical research has scarcely begun, and therefore I can say nothing useful about them.

4.4.2 *The Industrialists*

Two producer groups were involved in the NSPS case – the power station operators and the coal companies. Both were internally divided. Utilities which planned new power stations were very much affected by NSPS; those which did not were not. Coal producers whose coal was naturally low in sulphur, mostly located in Western states, were not interested in scrubbers. Those whose coal was high in sulphur, located in mid-Western and Eastern states, very much wanted scrubbers, which alone would permit their coal to continue to be burned.

The utilities mostly belonged to a relatively large and rather amorphous trade association called, by 1977, the Edison Electrical Institute (EEI). It and its predecessors employed a staff of counsel and Washington lobbyists, but the industry was caught unprepared by the innovative Clean Air Act Amendments of 1970 (see Ingram 1978) and still more by the Amendments of 1977, which imposed more stringent controls on new sources than before. It suffered for classic Olsonian reasons. Members undercontributed, especially in staff, by sending inexpert delegates to its meetings; it operated by a *de facto* unanimity rule, and therefore members particularly threatened by legislation could push the Institute into an unrealistic position of outright opposition and unwillingness to negotiate with other interests. Large utilities who were particularly vulnerable to NSPS but saw the need to negotiate and litigate therefore set up an *ad hoc* body called the Utility Air Regulatory Group (UARG) in

1977. UARG was a privileged group. Each member had a large enough interest in the outcome of regulation to be willing to take a share of the burden of organising UARG irrespective of the contributions of others. It was also protected against Chicken precommitment strategies, because only the members affected by any particular proposal send staff to the UARG committee meetings discussing that proposal. Hence any member who threatened his colleagues with a precommitment to free-riding would simply not have his concerns dealt with. Not surprisingly, it was the privileged UARG, not the intermediate EEI, which sponsored the utilities' litigation over NSPS.[5]

The coal industry was also divided. The National Coal Association represented both low- and high-sulphur producers, and therefore its contribution to the lobby was restricted to producing a tendentious map with regional boundaries drawn in such a way as to make the coal industry appear to suffer far more from NSPS than it actually did (Ackerman and Hassler 1981, p. 99). The United Mine Workers Union, almost all of whose members are in the East, 'had no difficulty coming out publicly for universal scrubbing' (Ackerman and Hassler 1981, p. 31). Other lobbying for coal was apparently conducted by individual producers and directed at Congressmen, who easily perceived an electoral threat if they did not advance their constituents' interests. The climax of this lobby was the reported threat by Sen. Robert Byrd of West Virginia to refuse to support President Carter's SALT treaty unless NSPS was adapted to make it more favourable to coal producers (*Washington Post*, 5 May 1979, p. A-1). Thus it appears that the coal lobby beat the Olson problem in three ways: individual producers in the East were privileged; the union (the UMWU) could not exist at all if it had not solved its basic collective action problem, and therefore found lobbying for high benefits for its members very cheap; and the coal industry was able to use vote power as well as lobby power.

4.4.3 Accounting for the Outcome

We have not yet explained why the NSPS story ended so unsatisfactorily for everybody except the coal producers and the lawyers. I suggest three reasons. First, the consumer interest was not represented at all. The ultimate sufferers from NSPS are the American public, who will get both dirtier air and more expensive electricity than they need have done. But no consumer lobby ever took part in the bargaining over NSPS. This is as Olson predicts. Consumers are an extreme example of a latent group. The expected marginal utility to an individual of taking part in a consumer group lobby on a matter of national policy is infinitesimal. The power companies and regulatory analysts in the Carter Adminintration fought a surrogate battle on behalf of consumers, but the first were seen as self-interested (which they were) and the second had no impact on Congress. Second, the environmentalists misperceived their interests. They appear to have argued throughout that forced scrubbing was better than no forced scrubbing, and that more scrubbing was better than less. Nowhere do they seem to have acknowledged that the effect of tough rules for new plants would be to keep dirty old plants going for longer and hence increase pollution compared with that which laxer controls on new plants would produce. Third, they suffered from a voting paradox because lobbying went in two stages. In 1977 the issue was forced scrubbing versus no forced scrubbing. The environmentalists and the coal industry combined to enforce scrubbing on the utilities. In 1979 the issue was the level of scrubbing; and 'the utilities welcomed their errant friends from the coal industry back into a dirty coal–dirty air alliance to resist the low ceiling' (Ackerman and Hassler 1981, pp. 98–9). Hence the final outcome was forced scrubbing but at a lenient level.

A little diagram shows the environmentalist dilemma. Let x stand for 'no forced scrubbing' y for 'lenient scrubbing' and z for 'stringent scrubbing'. In descending order from best to worst, the groups' preferences were:

Environmental	Utilities	Coal
z	x	y
y	y	z
x	z	x

The first vote isolated option x. The choice seemed straightforward; the two groups for whom it was the worst combined to beat the group for whom it was the best. This left the choice between y and z. But in the 'run-off', z was bound to lose to the new coalition which preferred y. In securing at least their second-best by the first vote, the environmentalists were doomed to lose their best on the second. (The classic analysis of this sort of dilemma is Farquharson 1969; see also chapter 8.)

4.4.4 *Olson Versus Bentley: the Case Study as a Test of Hypotheses on Lobby Power*

The NSPS story shows that Bentley's group theory is inadequate. Not all the groups which had an interest expressed one; the consumer interest could never practicably have been expressed at all; and the strength of group pressures bore no relationship to the number of citizens each group represented. These defects are fatal not only to Bentley's model but to all later pluralist models that do not take account of the collective action problem.

However, Olson's formulation is not sophisticated enough either. It needs to be refined to produce a more accurate prediction of the numbers likely to join (for instance) an environmental lobby than 'none' or 'too few'. It also needs to take account of the interaction between lobby power and vote power. One reason why the Eastern coal industry came out on top is that it alone mobilised votes in Congress. The utilities, which had no votes in Congress, did much better in the courts (especially in the two cases cited, *Sierra Club* v. *Costle* and *Chevron USA Inc.* v. *NRDC*); but from 1977 to the present there has been a cycle in which the utilities lose in Congress, win a favourable interpretation of Congress's legislation in the courts, and then lose again when Congress rewrites the legislation.

4.5 Lobbies and the Labour Party Manifesto

The Labour Party relies on the trade unions for about 80 per cent of its finance. This fits the prediction that most campaign finance comes from suppliers of the factors of production. But the channels in the UK differ from those in the USA. Suppliers of capital give money almost exclusively to the Conservative Party, and of labour almost exclusively to the Labour Party. He who pays the piper calls the tune: not all of it, but the parts that most people whistle in the street. Both in 1979 and in 1983 the Labour manifestos closely reflected the interests of suppliers of labour, or at any rate what the leaders of trade unions believed these interests to be. Much agonised bargaining lay behind the phrase 'national economic assessment' which appeared both times: the nearest the party dared go to suggesting an incomes policy, and the most the union leaders would accept. Other pledges were less painful, for instance import controls 'using tariffs and quotas, if these prove necessary' (1983). There were pledges for specific industries which reflected the relative strength of different producer groups. Both documents promised to encourage coal production and discourage nuclear energy; the 1983 one specifically pledged to nationalise firms in a number of sectors of the economy, a demand supported by the trade unions in each of them except banking.

However, consumer groups helped to shape the manifestos as well. In 1979 the party promised to make heavy lorries carry their full share of road costs and to refuse to increase the maximum allowed vehicle weight.[6] The most successful consumer groups were those demanding women's rights and nuclear disarmament. Both got substantial coverage in 1983. The section headed 'A Better Deal for Women' included 23 specific pledges, from 'End VAT on sanitary protection' to 'Appoint a cabinet minister to promote equality between the sexes'. The travails over nuclear disarmament have already been discussed in chapter 2. The fact that the issue was so prominent in the manifesto, and indeed in the entire election campaign, is a tribute to the Campaign for Nuclear Disarmament (CND), whose membership rose from 3000 in the early 1970s to 40 000 in 1982, and which claims a further 200 000 supporters 'in local peace groups . . . . Only one political party – the Conservative – is larger' (Byrne and Lovenduski 1984, pp. 226–7). Apart from the lorry-weight pledge (which may have resulted from producer-group lobbying by railwaymen) there was little of note about the environment. Environmental groups had less agenda-setting success than either the nuclear or women's groups or their American counterparts.

The main ground gained by strictly altruistic groups was in animal rights. Both manifestos promised to restrict animal experiments and to ban hare coursing and stag hunting (fox hunting was added in 1983). Both added rather hastily that their proposals would not affect angling or shooting. The distinction seems to relate more to the social class of humans who kill animals in different ways than to the forms of animal suffering.

Public-choice analysis can account for some, but not all, of this pattern of lobbying. It correctly predicts that much of it comes from suppliers of the factors of production, but does not say which suppliers or which factors. To fill in the gaps we need to know some history. The Labour Party has always been financed by suppliers of labour (not land or capital) because it was created that way. It came into existence to redress damage to the legal position of trade unions which had been done in the courts and could only be undone in Parliament. A struggling coalition of socialists founded in 1893 would have got nowhere if it had not been joined by trade unions in 1900 to form the Labour Representation Committee. That title tells more clearly than the title Labour Party (which replaced it in 1906) who financed the body and why. But not all suppliers of labour have an equally effective voice in the Labour Party. It favours coalminers against nuclear industry workers, and railwaymen against drivers of heavy lorries. The reason is again largely historical. Coal and railways were there in 1900; nuclear power and heavy lorries were not. It takes time for a lobby to get organised. This is one of the main themes of Olson (1982): as lobbies have to surmount their internal collective goods problem, it may be some decades after the formation of the interest before there is an interest group to represent it.

Yet even this modification of Olson's theory does not help to explain the rise of the feminist, anti-nuclear and animal rights movements. A partial explanation for both of the first two lies in the concept of the ultra-high-value public good. A law which improves the lot of every woman, or a policy which secures world peace for everybody, may be attractive enough for goods altruists to think it worth while devoting some resources to it. But this does not explain why some latent groups come into existence and others do not. What about the majority of British people who opposed unilateral disarmament? They are presumably as much (or almost as much) in favour of world peace as their opponents, but have not formed a lobby for it. To explain this disparity we would have to look at social psychology to explain why some sorts of groups, and some sorts of ideologies, seem to have the potential to generate mass movements while others do not.

Of course, party manifestos are not the only objects of lobbying in Britain. But the parties and bureaucrats set great store by manifestos: if a proposal is in the manifesto of the party that wins an election, it feels that it has the right to carry it out, and others have a duty not to hinder it. So we come back to the problem of full-line supply. Ordinary voters, even ordinary Labour voters, have no influence over what goes into the manifesto. It is a product of pressure-group lobbying, but which lobbies are present and which are successful is a matter of chance and history. Nuclear power workers and heavy lorry drivers have the same, very restricted, choices as everybody else. They cannot choose the policies they want from a selection of different parties but must buy one of the three or four bundles they are offered. Policy-making may be less chaotic than in the USA, but that does not guarantee that it is any more democratic.

5

Bureaucracy

5.1 The Sociological Perspective

Every society of any size needs bureaucracy. Not all social interactions can be managed by altruism, anarchy, or the market. Of course, some societies have much more prominent bureaucracies than others. But the main point of this chapter is to try to establish what features are common to bureaucracy in all sorts of different societies.

The word 'bureaucracy' was apparently invented in France in 1764 (Albrow 1970, p. 16) and the sociological study of the concept goes back almost as far. From the beginning writers on bureaucracy have mixed up description and evaluation. Most of them thought of bureaucracy as a bad thing. The word has pejorative overtones in ordinary usage today, and that is nothing new. A German dictionary of 1813, for instance, defined it as 'the authority or power which various government departments and their branches arrogate to themselves over their fellow citizens' (quoted in Albrow 1970, p. 17). The best-known sociological writer on bureaucracy, Max Weber (1864–1920), took the opposite view – 'The decisive reason for the advance of bureaucratic organization has always been its purely technical superiority over any other form of organization' (Gerth and Mills 1948, p. 214). But Weber mixes evaluation with description as much as everybody else. This chapter will aim as far as possible at a description which is not loaded on either side.

Weber saw human history as a long march from the magical to the rational. Though mankind was sometimes sidetracked and sometimes even backtracked, the normal direction was forward to rationality. For Weber, as for another universal systematiser of a century earlier, G.W.F. Hegel, 'rationality' often seems remarkably similar to what goes on in contemporary Prussia. According to Weber, there are three sorts of authority, which he calls traditional, charismatic, and 'rational' (the quotation marks are Weber's). Some rules, or people, are obeyed because they always have been. This is traditional authority, as exercised by a hereditary priest or by the English common law. Some people are obeyed because of their exceptional personalities which command direct obedience from their followers – a Christ, a Mohammed, or a Napoleon. This is charismatic authority. But there are often no charismatic people around, and traditional authority cannot cope with complex administration, so the general trend in modern societies is towards 'rational-bureaucratic' authority. Weber sees six characteristic features of bureaucracy. First, the task of government is divided up into 'fixed and official jurisdictional areas'; second, there is a hierarchical pyramid of authority within the office; third, 'the management of the modern office is based upon written documents ("the files")'; fourth and fifth, officers are specially trained and work full-time at their jobs; sixth, the office itself is run according to fixed rules (Gerth and Mills 1948, pp. 196–8).

All modern discussions of bureaucracy derive from Weber, and everybody more or less accepts his characterisation of bureaucracy. In passing, he notes points that have become central in modern discussion, as when he remarks (p. 233) 'Every bureaucracy seeks to increase the superiority of the professionally informed by keeping their knowledge and intentions secret.' He also draws attention to an important but controversial distinction when he claims (p. 235), 'Errors in official statistics do not have direct economic consequences for the guilty official, but errors in the calculation of a capitalist enterprise are paid for by losses, perhaps even its existence.'

There are, however, one or two oddities in Weber's account that have not been generally followed, and are often not noticed. One of his themes was that bureaucracy was more rational, that is more technically efficient, than democracy. Like many other scholars of his time, he was fascinated by the 'boss system' of urban politics in the USA. This led him into making a curious distinction between bureaucratic and democratic politics. In many urban machines, administrative jobs were handed out to supporters of the machine. Weber's attitude to this practice was ambivalent. On the one hand, if the head of the administration was elected rather than a career bureaucrat, this led to inefficient administration and was, presumably, 'irrational'. On the other hand, service in the party machine itself was a form of bureaucratic career which might lead to 'rational' administration even though there was no entrance examination to service in the party machine. 'The French, English, and American bureaucracies have for a long time foregone [sic] such examinations entirely or to a large extent, for training and service in party organizations have made up for them' (Gerth and Mills 1948, p. 240).

Weber tried to be a universal scholar. His method is one of grand inductive generalisation and he drew examples as freely from ancient China as from contemporary England. He knew a great deal about a large number of places at many different times. Unfortunately he knew rather little about contemporary Britain or the USA, as the passage just quoted begins to warn us. There is worse to come. Weber vastly exaggerated the importance of urban 'machines' in staffing the bureaucracy of both countries; in the USA in his day it was relatively small and in the UK it was non-existent. His reference (p. 225) to 'the caucus democracy of Gladstone–Chamberlain' suggests a man with a very shaky grip on British politics, whose knowledge probably derived from the inaccurate account given by Ostrogorski (1902) and not from first-hand acquaintance. The British Civil Service was created in its modern form by the Northcote-Trevelyan Report of 1854 and conforms so exactly to Weber's 'ideal type' that it is sometimes mistakenly assumed that he had it in mind in making his famous scheme of classification. However, it is apparently just a lucky coincidence; it seems that Weber knew nothing at all about the British Civil Service.

Modern sociologists mostly follow Weber, except that they are less inclined to assume that bureaucracy is for the best in the best of all possible worlds. One influential view is called 'functionalist'. On this view, patterns of behaviour are to be explained by the function they serve; it is assumed that everything has *some* function.[1] The bureau has the official function of carrying out the policy of the government as cost-effectively as possible. But individual bureaucrats have all sorts of other aims which do not point entirely in the same direction. Some may want a quiet life; their actions can be interpreted as functional towards that aim. Therefore if a clerk in the reception area of a local social security office behaves coldly and uninterestedly to the clients who come in, it may be because he will suffer less emotional and physical stress that way than by being

involved on clients' behalf and actively trying to remind them of
their rights. Others may want to maximise the budget of the bureau;
for them the opposite sort of behaviour would be functional, and
they might propose that teams of bureau staff be formed to go round
the neighbourhood to find out if any clients are failing to claim
benefits they are entitled to.

One study showed how far life at the bottom of French
bureaucracy deviated from Weber's ideal type. Routine staff 'do not
participate in any way in the goals of the organization'. They 'are
trying to evade face-to-face relationships and situations of personal
dependency whose authoritarian tone they cannot bear. . . .. They are
accustomed to rules and routinism'. Staff joined in 'delinquent
communities' like school gangs, as 'a protective device against
external authority' (Crozier 1964, pp. 50, 54, 220). Crozier
concluded (p. 222) that 'The French bureaucratic system of
organization is the perfect solution to the basic dilemma of
Frenchmen about authority. They cannot bear the omnipotent
authority which they feel is indispensable if any kind of cooperative
activity is to succeed.'

5.2 The Economic Perspective

Beginning with Weber, then, sociologists have defined and described
bureaucracy in a way which stresses that the informal goals of those
involved are not necessarily the same as the official goals of the
organisation. The joky contribution of C. Northcote Parkinson
(Parkinson's Law: 'Work expands so as to fill the time available for
its completion', Parkinson 1958, p. 4) gave wide currency to their
ideas. But the whole thing rests, at best, on anecdotal evidence. To
make progress the theory needs to be stated in a more rigorous way,
so that it contains some testable propositions; the propositions then
need to be tested. In the last twenty years a small number of
economists have made considerable progress on the first front.
Much less has been done, unfortunately, in the more humdrum
business of testing.

To understand the economists' analysis of bureaucracy, we need a
short diversion to consider how classical microeconomics works.
Any good that is traded in the market has a 'supply curve' and a
'demand curve'. Both are measured in a space in which price is
measured along one axis and quantity along the other (see figure

5.1). At any price from zero upwards we can find out how much of
the good manufacturers would be prepared to supply. Each
combination of price and quantity represents one point in the space
defined by the axes and the supply curve is the line which links all
the points. For instance, point (5,10) is on the supply curve. This
means that if the price is £5, 10 items will be supplied. Normally, the
supply curve slopes upwards from left to right across the diagram:
the higher the price, the more of the good people are prepared to
put on the market. Similarly, for any price from zero upwards we
can find out how much of the good consumers would buy. The
demand curve links all these combinations of price and quantity.
The point (5,40) is on the demand curve; this means that if the price
is £5, there will be a demand for 40 items. Normally the demand
curve slopes downwards: the higher the price, the fewer consumers
are prepared to buy. If the curves slope in the way stated, they are
bound to cross somewhere providing that the demand curve started
above the supply curve. (That is, if the good is free, more people
want it than are prepared to supply it. If this is not the case, there
will be no market for the good. There is no market for smallpox
viruses, although a number of laboratories are capable of growing
them.)

The point where the curves cross is called the **equilibrium** point.
In equilibrium, a particular quantity of the good is made and sold at

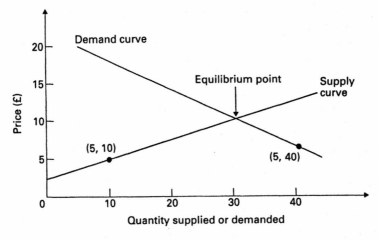

Figure 5.1 *Supply and demand curves*

a particular price which exactly 'clears the market'. Manufacturers have no unsold stock on their hands and every buyer who wants one of the goods can have it. In a perfectly competitive market, whenever the price and/or the quantity move away from equilibrium, the resultant unsold stocks or unsatisfied demand will send signals which automatically adjust supply and/or demand so that the market clears at a new equilibrium. (Economists differ very widely on the key question of whether most markets in practice do clear, but they all accept the above model.)

The public-choice analysts of bureaucracy have tried to treat the supply of and demand for government goods and services in the same way as classical microeconomics treats the demand and supply of traded goods and services. Although almost all attention has been focused on supply, the first important contribution was on the demand side. The immediate demand for bureau products comes from the government. In a democracy, the government is answerable to the electorate who have a rough sort of control. If the government asks the bureaux to produce much too much or much too little, it risks being turned out at the next election. Most public-choice writers have assumed that the government is prepared to pay for more bureau services than the electorate would choose if they could buy them themselves. But Downs (1960) titled his paper, 'Why the Government Budget is Too Small in a Democracy'. It was too small, he argued, because governments would underprovide public goods. If the benefits of a navy are indivisible (and also *invisible* unless the country is successfully invaded) the government will get less kudos from the electorate than it will get by providing divisible goods to special interests. There might be a too-small navy berthed in a too-big base in the district of an influential politician.

Since then, most public-choice writers (including Downs 1967) have paid remarkably little attention to the demand curve. The most comprehensive, and mathematically elegant, model of the supply of bureau goods and services is that of Niskanen (1971). It is worth quoting his key (and controversial) assumption.

Among the several arguments that may enter the bureaucrat's utility function are the following: salary, perquisites ∴.., public reputation, power, patronage, output of the bureau, ease of making changes, and ease of managing the bureau. All of these variables except the last two, I contend, are a positive **monotonic** function of the total *budget* of the bureau during the bureaucrat's tenure in office. (Niskanen 1971, p. 38; stress on 'budget' in original)

This is a move away from the traditional assumptions of microeconomics, a move paralleled by writers on the firm. The traditional assumption was that the firm seeks to maximise its profits, that is, the difference between its total revenue and its total costs. Maximising output (for a bureau, read: maximising budget) means going on producing goods until the last marginal item you produce adds nothing at all to your total revenue. (Readers who know some calculus and/or microeconomics should turn to the appendix to this chapter for a more formal presentation of the Niskanen model.) A justification for assuming that bureaucrats maximise budget, not profit, is that they cannot normally appropriate any 'profits'. A monopoly capitalist would make very fat profits for himself. Bureaucrats are usually monopoly suppliers of their goods; but in democracies they must usually rest content with fixed salaries which do not reflect the 'profits' made by their bureau.

Both economists and ordinary citizens usually deplore 'monopoly power' but they do so for subtly different reasons. We often think of a monopolist as somebody who can hold us to ransom by supplying as little as he wants of his product and/or charging us as much as he feels like. But even monopoly power is not boundless. Monopolists face a downward-sloping demand curve in the same way as everybody else. British Telecom is not free to charge what it likes for phone calls because if it charges too much people will just stop using their phones. The most powerful sort of monopolist is a 'discriminating monopolist'. With divisible, traded goods, some people are often prepared to pay more for them than others. A producer, including a monopoly producer, can appropriate some of the 'consumer surplus' for the good if he can charge a top price to the person who is prepared to pay the most, sell the second unit of the good to the person who is prepared to pay the next highest price, and so on until the last unit is sold at a price where marginal revenue just equals marginal cost (for a profit maximiser) or where marginal revenue is zero (for an output maximiser).

It is hard to play this trick with tangible goods, because some people will buy them at a low price and resell them at a higher price, thus undercutting the would-be price discriminator. But with services that cannot easily, or at all, be transferred from one purchaser to another there is ample scope for price discrimination. Good examples are transport, electricity, and health care. That is why rail fares are expensive for commuters, on Fridays and on early-morning long-distance trains but cheaper at other times and extremely cheap for pensioners who otherwise would not travel at all.

All three of these goods are sometimes produced by governments and delivered by bureaucrats. According to Niskanen (chapter 10, especially p. 97), a bureau delivering untransferable goods will discriminate by price and supply more of the good than a market provider. The National Health Service (NHS) is such a bureaucracy (if I get an operation I cannot transfer it to you); but Niskanen's model is not a recognisable picture of the NHS, which delivers less health care per head, but at a lower unit cost, than the private medical system of the USA, and which does not price-discriminate. A health service delivers the private good of cures (with public overtones in the case of infectious disease) and the mixed public-private good of disease prevention, and has to decide how to switch its budget between them. The Niskanen model is silent on this important topic.

An important supply factor to which Niskanen draws attention is the opportunity some bureaux have to be *monopsonists* of factors of production. 'Monopsonist' means 'sole buyer' as 'monopolist' means 'sole seller'. If you are the only buyer of land, labour or capital, you will be able to pay less for it than if there were other buyers, especially if you have compulsory legal powers to acquire it. Quite often governments give bureaux powers to acquire one or other factor compulsorily, especially in time of wars or rumours of wars. Somehow the compulsory acquisition of capital (other than through taxation) does not seem to happen as often as that of other factors. Niskanen worked in the US Department of Defense under Kennedy. He notes sarcastically that there is a perceptible 'difference in attitudes toward military programs between young men and defense contractors' (p. 52). It might be tempting to ascribe some of the low price of NHS services in Britain to the position of the Health Service as monopsonist of medical labour. On the face of it, there seems no other way of accounting for the astonishingly low wages it pays to doctors and nurses.[2] But there are alternative buyers of doctors' and nurses' labour in the private medical sector. There must be a powerful element of altruism in the behaviour of medical staff who offer their services to the NHS for considerably less than they could get elsewhere.

Niskanen distinguishes between a 'budget-constrained region' and a 'demand-constrained region'. The bureaucrat's problem is to maximise his budget subject to the constraint that the budget must be at least as great as the total cost of providing the output. This sets an absolute limit to output at the point where an extra unit of output provides the bureau with no extra income at all. This is the demand-constrained region. But the budget constraint bites if providing another unit of output would cost more than it brings in. This is the budget-constrained region. The conditions under which, given Niskanen's assumptions, the bureau is in each of these regions are given in the appendix to this chapter, as is a proof of the proposition that, still given these assumptions, a budget-maximising bureau will produce exactly twice the amount of output which would be produced in market conditions of perfect competition for the same good.

Niskanen does not have much to say about how the demand function for bureau services is determined – that is to say, how the government decides how much it is willing to spend on bureau services. But he does devote a chapter to the claim that local government will be more responsive to its electorate than central government. In the public-choice literature, this is called the 'Tiebout hypothesis' (see Tiebout 1956) and is based on the idea that, if moving were costless, people would move to the area which gave them the mix of local services they wanted. Following this, Niskanen claims that local bureaucracy will be less liable to expand beyond what the people would be willing to pay for market provision than will central bureaucracy.

5.3 A Critique of the Economists' Model

The public-choice model is an improvement on its predecessors in that it is clear what is being claimed, and the claim is in principle amenable to empirical testing. It goes beyond anecdotal claims that bureaux are 'wasteful'. Indeed it does not necessarily claim that bureaucrats waste resources in the ordinary sense, but merely that bureaux produce more, leaving fewer resources available for producing other goods, than would be the case under perfect competition. In economists' language, Niskanen claims that bureaucracy is 'allocatively inefficient' but not that it is 'X-inefficient'. The forbidding term 'X-inefficiency' merely means 'waste' as you or I understand it.

Nevertheless, there are serious problems with the Niskanen

model. They start with the budget-maximisation hypothesis. As Niskanen admits in introducing it, we know that many 'arguments' enter a real-life bureaucrat's 'utility function'. In non-economists' language, many different things make bureaucrats happy at work. Even by Niskanen's own admission, not all of them can be bundled up into a desire to maximise the bureau's budget. He admits that 'ease of making changes' and 'ease of managing the bureau' do not increase with the bureau's budget but blithely continues to regard the budget as the **maximand**. He offers an anecdotal justification: 'Consider ... the consequences of contrary behavior ... the probable consequences for a subordinate manager who proves without question that the same output could be produced at, say, one-half the present expenditures' (Niskanen 1971, fn. to p. 38)

There are certainly real-life stories in which the consequences have been unhappy for the cost-cutter. Leslie Chapman cut the costs of maintaining public property in the part of the UK for which he was responsible. Chapman's superiors palmed off an investigating committee of the House of Commons with a cock-and-bull tale that he had not made any real savings, and that the apparent savings were merely due to the Army moving out of his region. The Comptroller and Auditor-General, who is in theory a servant of the legislature who looks into bogus claims coming from the executive, singularly failed to pursue this one, a job which was left to Chapman himself, who had by this time left the Civil Service, (see Chapman 1979, chapters 8 and 22 and appendices 1,2, 8 and 9). However, one story does not clinch an argument. Many bureaucrats fervently deny that they are trying to maximise their budget. Sometimes assiduous cutting, or willingness to cut, can be an avenue for promotion. For instance the Thatcher Administration in the UK in 1979 set up what were known as 'Rayner reviews' after the chairman of Marks & Spencer, who was put in overall charge. The Rayner exercise was based on a (?mis-)reading of Niskanen; the government expected to find substantial X-inefficiency. High-flying young civil servants at the head of these teams led elaborate exercises to see where costs could be cut in the departments they were investigating. The personal rewards could be high. One particularly successful member of such a team was personally invited by Mrs Thatcher to present a review to the Cabinet, and was awarded an OBE and accelerated promotion to the grade of Assistant Secretary. His name was Clive Ponting, and he later fell out spectacularly with Mrs Thatcher's Administration (see Ponting 1985, pp. 9–11).

Of course, bureaucrats who firmly deny that their aim is to maximise their bureau's budget may be fooling themselves, or trying to fool others. We review such empirical evidence as there is in the next section. On the demand side, Niskanen's only substantial claim, that local bureaucracy will produce a smaller excess quantity of output than national, is based on the Tiebout 'theory of pure local expenditure'. It is hard to see why this theory is taken as seriously as it is in some quarters, because its assumptions are hopelessly unrelated to the real world of local politics in the USA or anywhere else. The Tiebout theory assumes that there is free movement of capital and labour from one local authority area to another. But of course there is not. People who are rich enough to move out from the high-tax city to the low-tax suburbs will do so, while still using the city's roads and sewers every day without paying for them. Factory owners in the city are stuck with their location for a long time, and the urban poor are stuck forever. These facts account for the fiscal crisis in US cities in the 1960s and 1970s, when a number of major cities, including New York, Boston, and Cleveland, teetered on the edge of bankruptcy. There is thus no reason to have much faith in a model which relies on the Tiebout hypothesis for one of its predictions (see e.g. van Mierlo 1985, pp. 62–3).

A much better argument for assuming that bureau services are overprovided depends on bureaux' *monopoly of information*. Weber noticed this, as we have seen. The people in charge of the files know better than anybody else how many land-use planning applications were made last year and how many staff processed them. If they tell the government that they need more staff because more applications are coming in or the existing staff are overworked, there is no independent way for the government to check the claim. It may be genuine; it may be bogus; but it is hard to see how such claims can be checked without erecting another bureaucracy alongside the first one with the job of checking the claims made by the first bureaucracy.

In both Britain and the USA there are some checks of this sort – in the USA they are provided by the General Accounting Office (GAO) and in the UK by the Comptroller and Auditor-General's department (see McLean 1982a, pp. 149–51), which has recently been joined by the Audit Commission for Local Authorities. But the checks are weak. An effective checking system would require a branch of the government – perhaps a legislature – which had an interest in controlling executive expenditure, served by a bureau which, even if it wanted to maximise its own budget, was willing and able to make recommendations for cutting the budget of every other bureau.

In the USA the first condition is met to some extent, but no single bureau could ever monitor the entire range of expenditure by all others, so that the GAO rarely gets beyond exposing specific instances of extravagance – lavatory seats for which the Department of Defense paid $400 each for example. In the UK even less checking is done; this is partly the fault of a legislature, the House of Commons, most of whose members seem more interested in the tribal rituals of Prime Minister's Questions than in the reports of the Public Accounts Committee, and partly the fault of the Comptroller and Auditor-General for failing to ensure that his department does its job (if the Chapman affair is anything to go by). The new Audit Commission has a different constitutional status. It is not a legislative check on the executive, but a national executive check, set up by central government to report on the performance of local executives – that is local authorities. It may be a more effective check on extravagance than the Comptroller-General, but it has already proved willing to say things its sponsor did not want to hear. In April 1985 it reported that waste in local authorities' capital spending was the fault of central government for trying to meet mutually inconsistent objectives through an irrational system of capital controls (Audit Commission 1985); and in June 1985 its Director was reported as saying that the bureaucratically-run waste disposal service in Sheffield was more cost-effective than its privately-run equivalent in Southend.[3]

At best these agencies can check on X-efficiency but hardly at all on allocative efficiency. Their first task is to check on fraud; if they have the resources, they can sometimes go on to check on waste; they virtually never have the resources, or the inclination, or the power to ask 'Is this bureau supplying too little, too much, or the right amount of the goods it produces?' or 'Should this good be allocated by bureaucracy or the market or anarchy?'

The budget-maximisation hypothesis has another important and subversive implication which neither Niskanen nor his campaigning colleagues appear to notice. Advocates of laissez-faire have always said that the market is more efficient than bureaucracy. Weber agreed with them, as he commented that bureaucrats were not under the market discipline of failure (although he does not seem to have reconciled this observation with his main theme about the superior rationality of bureaucracy). An inefficient firm under perfect competition, the argument goes, will not survive; therefore the search for profit maximisation will ensure that only those firms which produce with a minimum of bureaucratic waste will survive.

At first sight the Niskanen hypothesis appears to back this view, but in fact it does not. The laissez-faire view relies on a classical model in which the firm seeks to maximise its profits, and everybody within the firm is seen as simply a part of the profit-maximising machine. This model, Niskanen rightly perceives, cannot be applied to bureaucracy. It is not realistic to suppose that everybody in the bureau has the same aim as the official aim of the bureau, still less to suppose that profit-maximising is either the official or an unofficial aim. But the classical model cannot realistically be applied to the firm either, and never is any longer outside the pages of elementary textbooks and laissez-faire tracts. It has fallen to two distinct but related objections from the real world. One is based on the concepts of 'bounded rationality' and 'satisficing'. The classical model assumed that all economic actors had perfect and costless information about each other's behaviour. This is obviously unrealistic. We don't go to all the butchers in town to find out who has the cheapest meat. (Apart from anything else, it would cost more to go round them than we would save.) We fix in our minds a combination of price and quality which is 'good enough' and we search until we find it, or until we decide that there would be no point in further searching.

This procedure is called 'satisficing' and it is a much more realistic description of human behaviour than the traditional concept of 'maximising'. Some scholars have argued that it applies particularly to administrative behaviour in both market and bureaucratic bodies: 'Administrative theory is ... the theory of intended and bounded rationality of the behavior of human beings who satisfice because they do not have the wit to maximise' (H.A. Simon, quoted in Jackson 1982, p. 86). For Simon, 'administrative theory' is just as much a theory about General Motors as about the US government. No large organisation, private or public, has the information necessary to maximise its profits, and so its officers settle for satisficing, sometimes known as 'the science of muddling through'. General Motors does not succumb through loss of profits, as the classical theory predicts, because over at Ford and Chrysler they have identical problems. At most the threat of bankruptcy could only filter out a firm which was markedly more wasteful than all the others in its industry.

The second related objection to the laissez-faire classical view of the firm insists that 'the firm' cannot be treated as an individual. Individuals have motives; firms do not. The motives of a shop-floor employee of General Motors are not the same as those of its executive vice-presidents, which are not the same as those of its engineers, nor its sales managers, and so on. What is needed is a 'Behavioral Theory of the Firm' (the title of Cyert and March's (1963) influential book). Up to now, the behavioural theory of the firm has proved better at pointing out the fallacies in the classical view than at presenting an agreed alternative.

The main fallacy is one we shall examine at length in chapter 7: the fallacy of assuming that what is in the interests of all is in the interests of each. Many people would deny that managers and workers within a firm have the same interests at all. But even if, for the sake of argument, we assume that it is in the interests of everybody who is paid by the firm that it should maximise profits, it does not follow that each should do his bit towards maximising profits. Suppose I am a worker who has the choice of working fast and shoddily (and getting home early) or slowly and carefully (and getting home late). I know that if everybody works fast and shoddily the firm's profits will be reduced. But that is no argument for working slowly and carefully. For if everybody else works fast and shoddily my slow careful work will not save the firm; and if everybody else works slowly and carefully my fast shoddy work will not ruin it. Hence there are really no grounds for assuming that the aims of each member of 'the firm' are the same as the aims of 'the firm' in microcosm (for more on this, see Jackson 1982, p. 55). On the constructive side various hypotheses as to the actual maximand of firms have been put forward – sales (parallel to the budget-maximising hypothesis for bureaux) and managerial perquisites have been suggested, for instance – but there is no agreement on which is the most realistic model, (for details see any intermediate microeconomics text, e.g. Koutsoyiannis 1979, chapter x).

Thus there is no more, and no less, reason to suppose that the aims of a bureau are identical to its members' aims than to suppose that the aims of a firm are identical to its members' aims. 'It is not from the benevolence of the bureaucrat that we expect our research grant or our welfare check, but out of his regard to his own, not the public interest.' Thus Gordon Tullock, a distinguished public-choice theorist and scourge of bureaucrats, has reworked a famous saying of Adam Smith's (quoted by Jackson 1982, p. 121); but it is equally true that a worker, sales manager, engineer, vice-president, or any other member of a 'firm' has regard to his own, not the firm's interest. Hence the public-choice theory of bureaucracy fails to support the laissez-faire prediction that bureaucratic service delivery is less efficient than market delivery.

5.4 Some Empirical Findings on Bureaucracy

Nevertheless, this is the only prediction about bureaucracy which has been extensively tested. The tests are not very reliable, partly because they have been conducted by people who were looking for one particular conclusion. Borcherding's (1977) contributors, and Frey (1983, especially pp. 102–20) argue that in general bureaucratic provision is more expensive. But this amounts to no more than saying that they have found more cases where it is more expensive than where it is cheaper. Writers of this school place quite inordinate emphasis on one study which showed that of two roughly comparable airlines in Australia, the state-owned one was more expensive than the private one. However, the publicly provided electricity in Los Angeles is cheaper than the privately provided electricity in San Diego (Spann 1977) and the public rubbish collection in Sheffield is cheaper than the private service in Southend (see above, section 5.3). This argument promises to get absolutely nowhere for the foreseeable future.

There is little progress even in establishing the basic proposition that bureaucracy always and everywhere is growing, whether measured by staff numbers or by budget. There are serious problems of measurement of both. As to staff, there are always large categories which might or might not be classified as bureaucrats, and which can be arbitrarily added to or taken away from the payroll by changes in government policy. Two notorious hard cases are employees of government-owned trading organisations and officers performing functions that are transferred between national and subnational government. In the UK, for instance, employees of British Rail have never been officially classed as 'civil servants'; employees of the Post Office were from 1660 to 1969, but are no longer; employees at the publicly owned naval dockyards still are. Again, the Thatcher government reduced the number of civil servants at the stroke of a pen in 1984 by transferring the administration of housing benefit from central to local government;

but that proves nothing about the growth or decline of bureaucracy. You can construct tables more or less at will to show that the trend in numbers of national-level bureaucrats in the UK is up or down (see e.g. Hood and Dunsire 1981, pp. 8–11); but it seems clear that the number of bureaucrats employed by local government is rising in clear contradiction of the Tiebout hypothesis (for more on the problems of defining 'the public sector', see Breton 1974, pp. 18–20; Lane 1985, pp. 6–17).

The argument about trends in public expenditure is usually conducted at far too simplistic a level. Politicians are as guilty as anybody else, because they deliberately or accidentally use inconsistent definitions of what is to count as government spending. The British government, for instance, in defiance of all accounting conventions, lumps capital and current spending by public authorities together, although the implications of a cut (or growth) in one are utterly different to those of a cut (or growth) in the other. There is also an important, and far too rarely observed, distinction between public spending including and excluding transfers. Transfers are payments by government which are not in return for any good or service. Examples are state pensions and interest payments on the National Debt. If transfer payments are included, the Thatcher administration in Britain is the highest-spending in history, both absolutely and relative to GNP. This is because unemployment has soared since 1979, and unemployment benefit – which is a transfer payment – has soared with it. But whatever else the figures show, they are not evidence for the proposition that the Department of Health and Social Security is a Niskanen-type budget maximiser.

The proper basis for measuring trends in public expenditure is probably to exclude both transfers and public-sector capital spending. Very little work seems to have been done on this basis, but some US data reported in Borcherding (1977) is worth reproducing (see table 5.1). These figures confirm most people's impression that the government budget has been rising through the twentieth century, but note the remarkable blip between 1929 and 1939. The New Deal, which began in 1932 and is normally thought of as a vast expansion of government activity, actually saw a reduction in the government share of GNP. Much of the New Deal expenditure took the form of transfers, which are strictly irrelevant to the debate about the growth of bureaucracy.

The only direct test of any of Niskanen's hypotheses seems to be a neat little paper by McGuire (1981). The detailed argument of the

Table 5.1 Estimated share of GNP taken by federal and subfederal government spending, excluding transfers, USA 1903–1969

Year	% of GNP
1903	5.8
1929	17.5
1939	13.5
1949	18.0
1959	22.0
1969	25.1

Source: Borcherding 1977, p. 25.

paper depends on some standard microeconomic theory which there is no room to expound here, but the basic idea can be set out. If the prediction that supply of services is at twice the equilibrium level (see the appendix to this chapter) is correct, the demand for services will always appear elastic. That means that a given percentage cut in costs will lead to a greater percentage increase in demand. McGuire examined a large number of local programmes in the USA funded partly by Federal grants and partly by local taxation. The cost to the local taxpayer of local services is cut whenever a Federal matching grant is raised. On the Niskanen hypothesis the output would go up by a larger proportion than the cost came down, but McGuire found that this was not the case for his data, and neither did the demand for government employees appear to be elastic. Hence the hypothesis was not confirmed.

The process by which bureaux ask for money and sponsors grant a proportion of what they have asked for has been more thoroughly researched (Wildavsky 1964; Davis et al. 1974; Heclo and Wildavsky 1974). There is a collective action problem analogous to that faced by the fast shoddy worker in the last section. The head of each bureau knows that every bureau tends to apply for more than it expects to get; he also knows that the sponsor knows that, and will probably cut each bureau's request by roughly the same percentage. Fewer tears would be shed if every bureau applied for exactly what it thought it needed; but no bureau chief has any incentive to do that. Hence the basic procedure is *incrementalist*: after all the blood has been shed, each bureau gets what it got last year plus a percentage addition which is roughly the same for each bureau.

Shocks from the outside world such as the Russians beating the Americans into space and the war in Vietnam have some effect on US agency budgets, but not as much as one might expect; changes in political control of Congress or the Presidency have a slightly more noticeable across-the-board effect (Davis, et al. 1974, especially pp. 432, 438–9). From time to time, governments try to reform the budgetary process and move from incrementalism to so-called 'zero-based budgeting' – that is, a system where each agency has to justify every single request from scratch every year and cannot assume it will get last year's budget plus a little bit. It never works. There is far too much information to cope with, and most of it is in the hands of the bureaux rather than the sponsor. Nevertheless, the public-choice school is wrong to forget about the demand side of its equation. Voter pressure leads politicians to compete with each other in their claims to be the most efficient cutters of the bureaucracy. Like Olson, Niskanen has forgotten that interest-group power may be balanced by vote power.

5.5 Bureaucrats at the Polls

The empirical work done so far on the public-choice hypotheses about bureaucrats is thus scrappy and inconclusive. There is one smaller and more self-contained issue, though, on which more progress has been made. It seems reasonable to assume that bureaucrats, like other people, usually prefer more to less of good things like pay or jobs. This is a much less stringent assumption than profit- or output-maximising. But it may still lead to interesting predictions. One which seems to be valid is that public employees are significantly likelier to vote than the rest of the electorate. This was first noticed a long time ago (Tingsten 1937; Dupeux 1952). Over a wide range of European elections, from the French *département* of Loir-et-Cher in 1871 to the Swedish general election of 1924 and the Zurich city elections of 1933, the turnout of public employees was higher than that of the rest of the electorate (although the data have never been subjected to modern statistical analysis or significance testing).

It has been rediscovered not only by the public-choice writers but also by scholars in a quite different intellectual tradition who are examining the impact of 'structural cleavages' on voting. It has long been known that class, however defined, is a poor predictor of voting behaviour in most democracies, and getting worse. But although class is in decline as a predictor, economic influences on voting patently are not. One promising new way to categorise them is by 'consumption' and 'production' cleavages (see Dunleavy 1980). People may consume either primarily collectively provided goods (council housing and public transport, for instance) or primarily individually provided goods (private houses and private cars). On the production side, people who work in the public sector have clearly distinct economic interests compared to those who do not; and these interests crosscut traditional class divisions. In the UK in 1983, for instance, public-sector employees in all social classes were more likely to be trade union members than anybody else; and public-sector employees, both manual and non-manual, were more anti-Conservative than private-sector employees, as table 5.2 shows.

Table 5.2   UK: reported vote by production sector and social class, 1983

		Lab. %	Con. %	SDP/Lib. %	N
Manual	Public	48.5	23.3	28.3	99
	Private	42.6	30.5	26.8	190
Non-manual	Private	12.2	59.7	28.1	221

Source: Dunleavy and Husbands 1985; recalculated from table 6.10, p. 132.

By 1983 it was well-known that the Conservative Party was in favour of cutting down both the numbers and the pay of public employees; so the differences shown by table 5.2 are in the direction expected. At the same time, the legal position of public employees who wished to run for public office was being called into question. The Civil Service has always had rules which allow lower grades to run for office under party colours anywhere, intermediate grades in local but not national elections, and upper grades not at all. Local authority employees are not allowed to run for office on the authority which employs them, but are for another authority. Thus for instance teachers and social workers, who are employed by county councils, are eligible to run for district councils; and housing managers, who work for district councils, are eligible to run for county councils. The Conservative Government was reportedly alarmed at this phenomenon, which was becoming increasingly common in the 1980s. Few of the individuals in question are Conservatives. The Government appointed an enquiry in 1985 into 'the conduct of local authority business'. It has not reported at the time of writing, but it was widely expected to recommend that the practice of 'cross-membership' should be outlawed. The Association of District Councils, on which the Conservatives have the largest number of seats, recommended it to do so, and it is no secret that the Government wishes to (see, e.g., Association of District Councils 1985). It seems that both public-sector employees and the Conservative Party are pursuing their rational self-interest.

Appendix: The Basic Niskanen Model of Bureaucracy

The bureau faces linear demand and supply curves where

$$P = a - bQ$$
$$C = c + dQ$$

(P = unit price; C = unit cost; Q = quantity demanded/supplied; a, b, c, and d are parameters; b and d $>$ 0.)

Budget (B) = total revenue = $PQ = aQ - bQ^2$

Marginal revenue = $\dfrac{dB}{dQ} = a - 2bQ$

Total cost (TC) = $CQ = cQ + dQ^2$

Marginal cost = $c + 2dQ$

A budget-maximising bureau maximises B subject to the constraint that B must be at least as great as TC. Hence (first-order condition) it sets dB/dQ to 0 i.e. $a - 2bQ = 0$. Second-order condition for a maximum is fulfilled as $d^2B/dQ^2 = -2b < 0$ (b $>$ 0).

Thus $Q = \dfrac{a}{2b}$ if constraint does not bite $\qquad(1)$

The constraint bites if B = TC, that is:

$$aQ - bQ^2 = cQ + dQ^2 \text{ or } Q = \frac{a-c}{b+d} \qquad(2)$$

From (1) and (2), if $\dfrac{a}{2b} = \dfrac{a-c}{b+d}$ then $a = \dfrac{2bc}{b-d}$ $\qquad(3)$

Hence bureau produces $Q = (a - c)(b + d)$ if $a < 2bc(b - d)$(the budget-constrained region), and $Q = a/2b$ if $a \geq 2bc(b - d)$(the demand-constrained region).

By contrast, a profit-maximising entrepreneur would maximise profit Π.

$$\Pi = B - TC$$

To maximise Π, set $d\Pi/dQ = 0$ (first-order condition), that is:

$$\frac{dB}{dQ} - \frac{d(TC)}{dQ} = 0$$

that is: $\qquad a - 2bQ = c + 2dQ$

That is: $\qquad Q = \dfrac{a-c}{2(b+d)} \qquad(4)$

Second-order condition for a maximum is fulfilled as:

$$\frac{d^2\Pi}{dQ^2} = 2(b + d) < 0 \text{ (b and d}> 0)$$

Comparing (2) and (4) shows that a bureau in the budget-constrained region produces exactly twice the equilibrium output under perfect competition.

If a bureau is a discriminating monopsonist, its costs go down in relation to the basic model; if it is a price-discriminating monopolist, its revenue (= budget) goes up in relation to the basic model.

If a bureau in the budget-constrained region faces a choice of production methods, it can be shown by the Lagrange technique that it will mix methods in such a way that the marginal cost of production by each method is the same.

Problems with this model include:

1 There is no reason to suppose that supply and demand curves are linear; the assumption is made in order to make the algebra tractable.
2 There is no empirical method for estimating the parameters a, b, c, and d.

For fuller expositions, see Niskanen (1971), *passim*, especially pp. 25–8; Jackson (1982), pp. 125–35.

6

Winning Elections and Winning Power:
The Theory of Political Coalitions

6.1 How to Win Elections: A Summary

In chapters 2 and 3 we looked at the manoeuvres of politicians trying to win elections in Downsian issue space. If policy space is one-dimensional, a Downsian politician should go as close to the position of the median voter in that dimension as he can without mortally offending the activists in his party. If policy space is multidimensional, and if there is an analogous median position, it will pay politicians to go to it in the same way (See Enelow and Hinich 1984). However, unless opinion is distributed in an implausibly symmetrical way – so that every voter who stands on one side on each issue is balanced by another who stands on the opposite side on every single issue – there is no such unique median. The set of winning platforms will be cyclical. That is, within the set there will be no platform that cannot be beaten by another. An elementary example is the Liverpool City Council housing versus open space dilemma introduced in subsection 1.3.2. Governing a country is (slightly) more complicated than governing Liverpool, the number of policy dimensions and possible positions on each dimension is higher, and the likelihood of such cycles accordingly greater.

If democracy means 'the people's choice', this is thoroughly bad news for voters and for democratic theorists. It implies that there is no such thing as 'the best' policy for governing the country; and, for those who maintain that democracy gives voice to the will of the people, it poses the awkward question 'what if there is no such thing?' (a question to which we shall turn in chapter 9). For politicians, it is a mixture of good news and bad news. The bad news is that there is no platform which cannot be beaten by another. The good news is for persistent losers and (perhaps) for politicians faced by contradictory demands from their supporters and from the need to win an election. Persistent losers may be able to find an issue on which they can break up the persistently winning coalition and form a new set of coalitions. Politicians faced by contradictory sets of demands may be able to satisfy different groups by putting together a platform which beats the previous best, especially if the new elements involve issues which are not salient to most of the electorate. Both of these manoeuvres involve making and changing political coalitions.

All politics involves coalitions. This follows from the fact that there are many voters, each with political preferences, but there are only a few political parties and only one government. But coalition-building takes quite different forms in countries with few, large, parties, from those it takes in countries with more, smaller, parties. In the first case, coalition building mostly goes on within parties; in the second case, mostly between them. Britain and the USA are in the first category. The USA always, and the UK often, has only two parties challenging for power on a national scale. In the US, the Republican–Democratic duopoly of power goes back to 1860. In terms of parliamentary seats, and therefore of power, the UK has had a two-party system from 1867 to 1910 (with an interlude in 1885–6) and from 1931 to 1970. Neither country has a proportional electoral system; therefore in both the thresholds that any new party has to surmount are very high. So people who are dissatisfied with the range of options on offer must usually try to change it by changing the policies of an existing party. There will be complex and shifting coalitions within each party.

Most European democracies, on the other hand, are multi-party systems. Because they have proportional electoral systems, the entry threshold is lower than in Britain or the USA. So on average, there are more parties and each party is smaller and more homogeneous. So there is less coalition-building within parties, but more between them. In particular, no party is likely to win a majority of seats outright at most European elections. Therefore, after every election there will be a bargaining session in which politicians try to form a government coalition, trading jobs and ideologies with one another.

This is where the theory of political coalitions comes in. It is much more fully developed for the multi-party case than for the two-party case, and most of this chapter will be devoted to that. I shall try to show that, in spite of what I have just said about the UK, it has more to tell us about British politics than is usually assumed. There is no formal theory of political coalitions in two-party systems. But there are some interesting suggestions, most of which have been made by William Riker (see Riker 1962, chapter 7; Riker 1982, chapters 8 and 9; Riker 1984).

The first is a point about size. Downs said that politicians aim to win as many votes as they can; Riker says that they aim to win just enough votes to get into power. Too many votes may be almost as bad as too few, because more votes mean more campaign promises and obligations to more people. If the size of the cake to be distributed is fixed (a key assumption for Riker) then the fewer people who get a share the better. However, the contradiction between Riker and Downs may be more apparent than real. For mass elections there may be not much difference between their predictions because of the impact of uncertainty. If I am (say) a Labour Party strategist halfway between elections I am tempted to think, 'Let's forget about trying to get back the votes of the skilled white working class in Southern England. We can win the next election with a coalition of Scots, Welsh, Irish, northerners, the unemployed, blacks, and gays.' But I am also tempted to think 'I don't *know* that that coalition is big enough; if not enough of its members turn out we may lose. Therefore we should appeal to the skilled working class in the South as well, especially if we can do so without losing anybody else from the coalition.'

The clash between Downs' and Riker's principles is more obvious in coalitions among small groups, such as MPs. In the 1983 General Election campaign, Francis Pym, a former Conservative Chief Whip, said that he was apprehensive about the probability that the Conservatives would win by a very large majority ('Landslides on the whole don't produce successful governments'); Mrs Thatcher rebutted him ('That is the natural caution of the Chief Whip') (quoted from Butler and Kavanagh 1984 p. 89). Pym took a Rikerian view and Thatcher a Downsian one; in the event there was a landslide in seats for the Conservatives and Pym was immediately sacked as a Minister. However, in April 1986 the Conservative Government was defeated by a backbench revolt on its Sunday Trading Bill, which was one of the main pieces of legislation announced in the 1985 Queen's Speech (the annual statement of the government's programme). No twentieth-century government with a secure majority had ever previously lost a bill in this way.

Riker's second point relates to cycles and persistent losers. The losers have an interest in trying to bring new issues on to the political agenda, and to keep on trying until they find one that breaks up the existing winning coalition. He illustrates this with a discussion of the emergence of slavery as an issue in national politics from 1820 to the Civil War (Riker 1982, chapter 9). From the foundation of the new republic, slavery was a delicate issue and the Constitution contained a number of fudges that were needed before all 13 states could be persuaded to sign it. It was tacitly agreed that the states which had slaves should be allowed to keep them, but those which had not would not be expected to allow slavery. This left unsettled the question of whether slavery would be permitted as 'territories' (the parts of the continent which did not yet have enough white settlers to qualify as states) entered the Union. The Missouri Compromise of 1820 said that southern territories would be allowed to become slave states so long as northern territories, which would be non-slave states, were admitted to the Union at the same rate. The issue went back to sleep but woke again with a series of controversial decisions in the 1840s and 1850s (the Kansas-Nebraska affair, the Dred Scott judgment on a runaway slave, and the judicial revocation of the Missouri Compromise) which led up to the Civil War.

There are various traditional interpretations of the backgound to the American Civil War. Some historians see it as a triumph of a moral principle over the evil of slavery, others as a conflict between agrarian (Southern) and industrial (Northern) economic interests. Riker takes a distinctive view. For him, the appearance of slavery on the agenda was the work of the persistent losers in the coalition politics of the period from 1816 (when the Federalist party collapsed) to 1856 (when the Republican party emerged). The central division in American politics, he claims, was indeed between agrarian and commercial interests, but not inherently betwen North and South, because there were many wholly rural districts in the North. The agrarian coalition was put together by Thomas Jefferson (President from 1801 to 1809) and Andrew Jackson (President from 1829 to 1837). From 1828 it was gathered together under the title of the Democratic Party, and it won nearly every election. It was a coalition between Southern farmers, who had slaves, and Middle Atlantic and Western farmers, who had none. This left urban and North-Eastern Americans as a persistent minority. They tried various issues in the hope that they would split up the Democratic coalition: for instance a campaign against Freemasons and another against immigrants. Neither of these worked.

The one which did work was a campaign against slavery, which held out the hope of splitting the Southern and the non-Southern elements in the Jackson coalition. So a number of northern politicians took up the slavery issue for reasons which their opponents saw as pure expediency, and dangerous expediency at that:

The slavery question is assuming a fearful and most important aspect. The movement . . . if persevered in, will be attended with terrible consequences to the country, and cannot fail to destroy the Democratic party, if it does not ultimately destroy the Union itself. Slavery was one of the questions adjusted in the compromises of the Constitution. It has, and could have no legitimate connection with the war with Mexico . . . . Of course, Federalists [i.e. the northerners who were raising the slavery issue] are delighted to see such a question agitated by Northern Democrats because it divides and distracts the Democratic party and increases their prospects of coming to power. Such an agitation is not only unwise but wicked. (President James K. Polk, diary entry, January 1847, quoted by Riker (1982) p. 224)

Polk turned out to be quite right. Raising the issue of slavery did break up the Jacksonian coalition and it did destroy the Union. Few politicians in the 1840s can have anticipated how horrendous the consequences of agenda-manipulation would be, and there is no point in condemning it with the wisdom of hindsight. If Riker is right, it is only to be expected from those who persistently lose out in two-party politics.

6.2 Coalition Theory: An Introduction

It is time to turn to the more formal side of political coalition theory. In the previous section we stated that Britain 'often' had two-party parliamentary politics, but this has by no means always been true. Table 6.1 classes twentieth-century General Elections by the winning party's margin in seats. Thus only thirteen out of the twenty-three elections this century have given the leading party a clear majority of the seats. (Incidentally, only in 1900, 1931, and 1935 did any party gain as much as 50 per cent of the vote. If the UK had a system of proportional representation, and if voters cast their first preferences in the same way as they mark their crosses at

Table 6.1 British General Elections since 1900: proportion of seats won by largest party

Over 52% of seats	50–52%	Under 50%
1900	1950	Jan. 1910
1906	1951	Dec. 1910
1922	1964	1918
1924	Oct. 1974	1923
1931		1929
1935		Feb. 1974
1945		
1955		
1959		
1966		
1970		
1979		
1983		

Source: Butler and Sloman (1980) p. 206, except for official versus independent Irish Nationalist numbers, which are from Halevy (1961) pp. 533–4.

present, there would hardly ever be a government which was not an overt coalition. But the British electoral system almost always magnifies the lead of the party with most votes into a much greater lead in terms of seats.) Those who think of the UK as normally a two-party country tend to forget, for instance, the Irish Party, which won most of the seats in Ireland from 1874 to 1910 inclusive. (The whole of Ireland was part of the UK from 1800 to 1922.) For the rest of this chapter, formal coalition theory will be explained and tested with reference to three of the elections of this period. Their results in terms of seats are in table 6.2.

6.2.1 The Shapley-Shubik Power Index

It is obvious from table 6.2 that the Liberals were able to form a government unaided in 1906, without formal promises to any of the other parties. This they did, and neither the Irish nor the Labour parties (nor, of course, the Conservatives) could do anything to influence government policy. But no party unaided had a majority in 1910. However, their power was not a simple function of the

Table 6.2. The General Elections of 1906 and 1910

| | 1906 | | Jan. 1910 | | Dec. 1910 | |
	Seats	*%*	*Seats*	*%*	*Seats*	*%*
Conservative	157	23.4	273	40.7	272	40.6
Liberal	400	59.7	275	41.0	272	40.6
Labour	30	4.5	40	6.0	42	6.3
Irish	83	12.4	71	10.6	76	11.3
Ind. Irish	–	–	11	1.6	8	1.2

Source: Butler and Sloman (1980) p. 206, except for official versus independent Irish Nationalist numbers, which are from Halevy (1961) pp. 533–4.

number of seats each controlled – a number called their 'weight' or 'size'. (Henceforth, I shall use 'size'.) A quick glance at the percentage figures shows that the official Irish party had a potential power out of proportion to its size. It could ally, or refuse to ally, with either of the big parties and help that party to victory. The Labour and independent Irish parties, on the other hand, had no power – of this sort – at all. There was no coalition that they could turn from a losing to a winning coalition by joining, or from a winning to a losing coalition by leaving.

More formally, define a 'winning coalition' as any coalition which commands enough votes to win. Then the set of all those voters not in the winning coalition must be a losing coalition. Any coalition which is neither winning nor losing is called a 'blocking coalition', although there are none in this example. In every n-person game there are 2^n possible coalitions, including the grand coalition of all members and its opposite, or 'complement', the coalition with no members at all. If there are no blocking coalitions, then 2^{n-1} are winning and the same number losing [1]. In the British Parliamentary game, your coalition wins if you have 50 per cent of the votes plus one: that guarantees you victory in a Commons vote. In the 1906 game there were eight possible winning coalitions and in the 1910 games there were sixteen. The game is assumed to be constant-sum. You either win or you lose, and if you win the prize (government) is of a constant size. This prize can be represented by any number, so we might as well choose 1. Next we define a 'pivot'. A pivot is a player whose departure from a winning coalition turns it into a losing one. If the Liberals, the official Irish and the independent Irish had formed a coalition in 1910 and first the independent and then the official Irish had left it again, the official Irish would be the pivotal party.

The power index of each player (here each party), first proposed by Shapley and Shubik (1954), is the proportion of winning coalitions to which the player is pivotal to all winning coalitions. To calculate the power indices, it is necessary to examine every possible route by which a coalition could break down from the grand coalition to the empty coalition. As the members drop out one by one, there always comes a point at which the coalition turns from winning to losing. For 5 players, there are $5 \times 4 \times 3 \times 2 \times 1 = 120$ (called 5! and read '5 factorial') different ways in which they can be laid out in a line. We could set out a small part of the 120-line table for January 1910 as follows:

Lib.	Con. /	Lab.	Irish	Ind. Irish
Lib.	Lab.	Irish /	Ind. Irish	Con.
Lib.	Irish /	Ind. Irish	Con.	Lab.
Irish	Ind. Irish	Lab.	Lib. /	Con.

In each line of this extract from the table, the symbol / is printed after the party which is pivotal – here the Conservatives once, the official Irish Party twice, and the Liberals once. The reader should check with table 6.2 to see that in each case it is the withdrawal of that party which brings the coalition down below 50 per cent of the votes in the Commons. In fact, for both 1910 elections, the Independent Irish party and the Labour Party are never pivotal, and each of the other three parties is pivotal one-third of the time. Table 6.3 shows the array of Shapley–Shubik indices for the three elections.

This illustration is just to give a more formal shape to the intuition that the Irish Party is unusually strong for its size when it holds the balance of power, but utterly powerless when it does not. Like other economists' analyses of politics, it brings out the importance of the *marginal* principle. It is not just the absolute size of a party that matters, but its marginal contribution to a coalition. The marginal contribution of the Irish Party to a Lib./Irish coalition is 100 per cent: if it withdrew, the coalition would no longer exist. In theory, then, the Irish Party should have an equal share with the Liberal

Table 6.3   Power indices, 1906 and 1910

	1906	1910 (Jan.)	1910 (Dec.)
Con.	0	1/3	1/3
Lib.	1	1/3	1/3
Lab.	0	0	0
Irish	0	1/3	1/3
Ind. Irish		0	0

Party in such a coalition, and each Irish MP should have far more power than each Liberal MP (because there are far fewer of them). The Irish ought to be in a position to demand half the seats in a coalition cabinet, should they want them.

This model captures some, though not all, of the reality of British parliamentary politics at the time. Throughout 1910, for instance, the Conservatives accused the Liberals of being in the pockets of the Irish Party, while the Liberals were forced against their will to promise Home Rule for Ireland. But the power index does not tell the whole story. It does not tell why there was a Liberal–Irish, rather than a Conservative–Irish or Conservative–Liberal pact; and it does not explain why there should have been any concessions at all to either the Labour Party or the independent Irish, although there actually were some. We must start to tell a more complicated story.

6.2.2 The Minimal Winning Coalition and the Size Principle

The idea of the minimal winning coalition comes from the fundamental treatise on zero-sum game theory by von Neumann and Morgenstern (1947). A zero-sum game is one where the winnings of the winners exactly cancel out the losses of the losers. A constant-sum game, like the coalition games we are discussing, is analytically the same as a zero-sum game. These games differ fundamentally from the variable-sum games like Chicken and Prisoners' Dilemma that we have come across so far in this book. In Chicken and Prisoners' Dilemma, there are some outcomes in which the total payoff to all the players put together is higher than in others; therefore players have a certain degree of common interest in going for those outcomes. In a zero-sum game, they have no common interest at all. And if the prize is fixed, then the fewer players who have to share it, the more there is for each winner. Hence von Neumann and Morgenstern predicted that winning coalitions would be minimal (Liberal plus Irish, not Liberal plus Irish plus Labour, for instance). The spoils of office are not to be shared around more players than necessary. But note that minimal winning coalition theory says nothing, strictly speaking, about the size of players. Liberal plus Conservative is just as much a minimal winning coalition as Liberal plus Irish. In either case, the desertion of one player would turn the coalition into a losing one.

Riker (1962) attempted to make the model more realistic by introducing his 'size principle'. The terminology of his account was confusing, as he switched between 'minimal' and 'minimum' to describe what he had in mind, and did not always make the distinction between his principle and von Neumann's clear, but I shall follow de Swaan (1973) and Taylor and Laver (1973) in describing Riker's as the 'minimum size principle'. The minimum size coalition is the minimal winning coalition of the smallest size, that is controlling the smallest total number of votes. Thus Lib./Irish, Lib./Con. and Con./Irish are all minimal winning for January 1910, but only Con./Irish is minimum size. The idea, again, is the sharing of spoils. The number of government offices is fixed; better to spread them out among 51.3 per cent of MPs than among 51.6 and far better than among 81.7.

6.2.3 *The Minimal Connected Winning Coalition*

A number of theorists complained that all this utterly ignored ideology. Arithmetically, a Con./Irish coalition had a minute advantage over a Lib./Irish coalition in January 1910, but the Liberals and the Irish were far closer than the Irish and the Conservatives (the 'Conservative and Unionist Party', whose opposition to Home Rule for Ireland was expressed in its very title). The best-known of the coalition theories which take ideology into account is Axelrod's (1970). He predicts that a 'minimal winning connected' coalition will form: that is, from the set of minimal winning coalitions all those which leapfrog over parties on some ideological spectrum are ruled out. If (and it is a big if) the British parties in 1910 could be arranged along a line like that shown in figure 6.1 then a Lib./Con. coalition is ruled out because it is not connected (the Irish lie in between) and a Con./Irish coalition is ruled out because the independent Irish are in the way. The example is perhaps unconvincing, but there is obviously something in the idea.

Figure 6.1 *The British parties in 1910: a hypothetical ordering in a single dimension*

6.3 Testing the Theories: Britain in 1910

From now on we shall label the 'minimal winning coalition' hypothesis MW; the 'minimum size coalition' SW, and the 'minimum connected winning coalition' MCW. MW predicts that one out of Lib./Con., Lib./Irish, and Con./Irish would form; SW predicts Con./Irish in January and either Con./Irish or Lib./Irish in December; MCW predicts Lib./Irish. What actually happened? (This section will inevitably refer to a number of long-dead politicians. Table 6.4 lists the principal actors by party.)

Table 6.4   Coalition-building 1906–1910: principal actors

Conservative	Liberal	Labour	Irish	Ind. Irish
A. Balfour	H.H. Asquith	A. Henderson	T.P. O'Connor	T. Healy
Marquis of Lansdowne	H. Campbell-Bannerman	R. MacDonald	J. Redmond	W. O'Brien
F.E. Smith	W. Churchill			
	H. Gladstone			
	D. Lloyd George			

One vital factor brought out by none of the coalition theories is that there are two overlapping games going on all the time in parliamentary bargaining. There is coalition-building on the basis of the (known) result of the last election; and bargaining in anticipation of the (unknown) result of the next one. Immediately after an election the first swamps the second, which gradually increases in relative importance until just before the next election. Politicians have a rough idea of the strength of other parties, but in the British electoral system they are unlikely to have any idea how many seats either their own or other parties will win next time because the relationship between votes and seats is so erratic. In 1906 the Liberals won 406 of the 670 seats. One might expect, therefore, that they had had no need to indulge in pre-election bargaining. But that would be quite wrong. In 1900 they had been crushed, winning only 184 seats (though with only 4.4 per cent less of the popular vote than in 1906). So it is no refutation of Riker's size principle to discover that the Liberals negotiated with both the Labour and the Irish parties before the 1906 election. After the election, they turned out not to need either, but they had no grounds for knowing that beforehand. In 1903 they negotiated the famous 'Gladstone–MacDonald Pact' with Labour, in which each party gave the other a free run in a number of seats. This enabled Labour to win its 30 seats in 1906. Without the pact, not only would Labour have been restricted to about five seats at most, but the Liberals would have won far fewer because a split 'Progressive' vote would have enabled the Conservatives to win.

At the same time the Irish were more of a known quantity to the Liberals. The number of seats Labour could win was utterly unpredictable within wide limits; the Irish would predictably win between eighty and eighty-four seats in Ireland, and one (Liverpool Scotland) in England. But pre-election bargaining with them still mattered because they controlled, or at any rate were universally believed to control, large numbers of votes among Irish voters living in Great Britain. The Irish Party leaders had used these voters as a weapon since 1885, in which election they had been advised to 'vote Tory', and evidently did. Hence in November 1905 Campbell-Bannerman made a pact with Redmond and O'Connor. The Liberals promised that if they won they would pass 'some serious measure which would be consistent with and lead up to' Irish Home Rule, although not Home Rule itself; in return the Irish promised the votes of their 'friends' in Great Britain to the Liberals (quoted from Murray 1980, p. 54). There are no records of pacts or discussions between the Conservatives and any of the other three parties in the approach to the 1906 election.

After that election, the Liberals treated their allies as coalition

theory predicts: they ignored them. Labour got the Trade Disputes
Act of 1906, which was based on radical Labour proposals instead
of more conservative Liberal ones; this may have been because
Campbell-Bannerman did not understand what was at stake when
he dropped his own party's bill in favour of the Labour one (see e.g.
McLean 1975, pp. 118–19). Labour got no further concessions
during the 1906–10 parliament, and there was no direct bargaining
as the next election approached. The Liberals were content with the
position they had brought about with the Gladstone–MacDonald
Pact. Labour was still to have a free run in a small number of seats,
but if it tried to break out, the Liberals would threaten to retaliate.
Many Liberals saw the Labour Party as the (very) junior partner in
the Progressive alliance. Lloyd George wrote to the Clerk of the
House of Commons in November 1909: 'The greatest danger to the
Liberals will arise from a split between Liberalism and Labour'
(quoted in Murray 1980, pp. 206–7) and proposed extensive
legislation in the interests of labour – old-age pensions, employment
exchanges, national insurance. But the Liberals distinguished
sharply between the interests of labour, which they wished to
promote, and the interests of the Labour Party, which they wished
to kill off. Unlike the Trade Disputes Act, none of the Liberal
proposals emanated from the Labour Party. The Labour Party
wanted legislation in all these areas, but it was not consulted on
Lloyd George's proposals, which were clearly designed to capture
and keep working-class votes for the Liberals.

The Irish Party honoured its 1905 promise to the Liberals (see e.g.
McLean 1983, p. 192), but the Liberals did not honour theirs. Only
two very minor pieces of Irish legislation were passed between 1906
and 1909. In April 1909 O'Connor told the Liberal Chief Whip that
unless the Liberals offered them something, 'We shall be able no
longer to resist the trend for our people to vote for the Tory' (quoted
in Blewett 1972, p. 59). They got nothing immediately, because the
Liberals were fully occupied with the crisis over Lloyd George's
Budget of that year, which the Lords were threatening to reject
because of the allegedly crippling land taxation it contained. The
Irish were in a dilemma: they welcomed any moves against the
House of Lords, but deplored the spirit duties and licensing charges
proposed in the Budget itself. They were reported as 'frantically'
demanding concessions on the duties from Lloyd George so as not to
have to vote against the Budget in the Commons (Blewett 1972,
p. 196). In November, the Lords rejected the Budget by 350 votes to

75. This action, unprecedented since the seventeenth century, forced a General Election. It also put reform of the House of Lords on the agenda. The previous Home Rule Bill, passed by the Commons in 1893, had been thrown out in the Lords by a huge majority. Any reform of the Lords brought about by their repeat performance on the 1909 Budget would thus have momentous consequences for Home Rule.

Therefore the Irish demands on the Liberals were stiffer than in 1905–6. Redmond asked Asquith for a pledge to introduce Home Rule, without which 'we will most unquestionably have to ask our friends to vote against' the Liberals. Asquith took the request to the Cabinet, which decided that he would make a carefully worded pledge of support (Blewett 1972, pp. 91–3; Murray 1980, p. 238). It satisfied Redmond, who advised Irish voters in Britain to vote for the most effective anti-Unionist candidate. In practice, this invariably meant the Liberal. Redmond had deprecated 'hopeless and wrecking' Labour candidatures in his message to the Irish in Britain, and his supporters took this to mean virtually all Labour candidatures (Blewett 1972, p. 351; McLean 1983, pp. 192–4).

The Labour Party could make no bargains with anyone. When Arthur Henderson announced on behalf of the party that it supported the Budget, there was nobody left in the Commons to hear him (Murray 1980, p. 234). Labour had a grievance of its own – the Osborne Judgment of 1909, which had outlawed contributions from trade unions to party funds – but it seems to have been swept aside in the January 1910 campaign. No other party offered to support Labour calls for a reversal of Osborne.

As in 1906, there seem to have been no negotiations involving the Conservatives. Redmond used them as a threat in his negotiations with the Liberals but does not seem to have met them. One of the grounds on which O'Brien split from Redmond was Redmond's alleged dependence on the Liberals. But O'Brien does not seem to have negotiated with anybody either.

After the election result was announced, it was up to the Liberals to make the first move. (The convention at the time was that a retiring Government remained in office unless and until defeated when the House of Commons first met.) The Conservatives were unable to form an anti-Budget, pro-Lords coalition. The only partners who could count were the Redmond faction. They were anti-Budget, but they were also anti-Lords, because they saw that if the Lords' powers were curtailed, it would at last be possible to get

Irish Home Rule on the statute book. The O'Brien faction was too small to be of use to the Conservatives, and the Labour Party was both too small and ideologically indistinguishable from the Liberals.

So, once again, the bargaining that mattered was between Redmond and the Liberals. Redmond faced a tactical problem. He had the Liberals at his mercy; would he aim for a certain victory over licensing duties in the Budget, or would he play a riskier game for far higher stakes, and demand a cast-iron commitment to curbing the Lords' veto on Home Rule? He decided on the latter, and stated his terms: 'no veto, no Budget'. The Liberals must introduce a bill for removing the Lords' veto before reintroducing the Budget; if they did not, Redmond's supporters would vote against the Budget en bloc. He indicated that he was not interested in concessions on whiskey duties or licenses. This was a calculated risk not only in the post-election January game, but in the pre-election December game, because it left Redmond wide open to attack from O'Brien, his only competitor for votes in Ireland. If O'Brien could paint Redmond as callously uninterested in the problems of the Irish drinker and the Irish licensee, Redmond might suffer heavily in the coming election.

None the less, Redmond stuck to his demands, and won. In February the Government went part of the way towards meeting the Lords-before-Budget timetable. Churchill told the King: 'If Mr Redmond's words have carried weight, it is not because he held the power of altering the balance of voting strength in the House of Commons but because the counsels which he urged were in full harmony with the views of by far the greater part of the Ministerial majority' (quoted in Murray 1980, p. 269). This was poppycock, and Edward VII would have had to be very gullible to believe it. Lloyd George now tried to stop the concessions going any further by negotiating, or appearing to negotiate, with O'Brien on Budget concessions (Murray 1980, p. 275). This seems to have been designed explicitly to put pressure on Redmond, not to get the support of O'Brien's eleven men. This tactic did force Redmond to discuss concessions, but luckily for him no agreement was reached before the Government gave way completely to him on the Lords' veto timetable. On 13 April 1910 the Cabinet agreed to seek guarantees from the King that he would create enough peers to force House of Lords reform through the House of Lords. Asquith told a colleague that Redmond had admitted to having been 'completely outmanoeuvred' (quoted in Murray 1980, p. 285; cf also Jenkins

1968, pp. 131–4). But the boot was on the other foot. It was the 275 Liberals who had been held to ransom by the 71-strong Irish Party against the will of the Conservatives and the O'Brien faction and with no input from the Labour Party at all.

However, before the Government could negotiate the guarantees with King Edward VII, he died suddenly. This led to a dramatic change of course: Asquith told the new king (George V) that he 'would endeavour to come to some understanding with the Opposition to prevent a General Election and [that] he would not pay attention to what Redmond said' (quoted in Jenkins 1968, p. 147). The Liberals proposed a constitutional conference involving only themselves and the Conservatives, who accepted. The conference lasted from June to November 1910 (it was suspended during the summer sporting season because the Conservatives refused to meet in the country houses of any of the Liberal delegates). It discussed at length a remarkable memorandum from Lloyd George proposing a Liberal–Conservative coalition. This document listed an extensive common programme which Lloyd George believed the parties could agree on. On Ireland, he said 'The advantages of a non-party treatment of this vexed problem are obvious. Parties might deal with it without being subject to the embarrassing dictation of extreme partisans, whether from Nationalists or Orangemen' (quoted in Jenkins 1968, p. 163). This came from the man who had just been denouncing the Conservatives and the peers with such force that 'Limehouse' (the scene of a Lloyd George speech) had become a term for political abuse, and was addressed to the party which was supposed to be dying in the last ditch in defence of the House of Lords and the union of Britain and Ireland. But it was treated with remarkable seriousness. Negotiations got as far as the proposed share-out of offices (Asquith to remain Prime Minister but go to the Lords, Balfour to become leader of the Commons, government jobs to be split equally between the two parties), but in the end Balfour rejected the plan when his chief whip warned him the backbenchers would not stand for it.

The Conference broke down in November and another election was inevitable. The Labour Party pressed both big parties for a pledge to reverse the Osborne judgment. They got a flat refusal from Balfour and a very qualified agreement from Asquith (Blewett 1972, pp, 154, 162–3). The overall result of the December election was virtually the same as in January (though many seats changed hands in ways which cancelled each other out). Therefore the Liberals were bound to advance the programme of their effective coalition partners, the Redmond faction (O'Brien's challenge having faded). The House of Lords veto was reduced to three years by the Parliament Act 1911. The Irish Home Rule Bill was accordingly brought forward twice, defeated twice by the Lords, and finally became law without the Lords' consent in 1914. By this time a world war had got in the way and by the time that was over Redmond and his party had been destroyed. But nobody foresaw that in 1911. The partial reversal of Osborne came much lower on the Government agenda and eventually appeared as the Trade Union Act, 1913.

How far can coalition theory help in interpreting this narrative? The Lib./Irish coalition which emerged from both of the 1910 elections is as predicted by MCW and (for December) by SW. All three coalition theories would predict that Labour and the O'Brien faction would be 'dummy' players, with no influence at all. That is not quite true, but it is truer than the belief of most historians (even one of the prime sources for this account – see Murray 1980, p. 10) that the Liberals were in some sense dependent on Labour. Apart from the Trade Disputes Act and the belated reversal of Osborne, I can find no concessions to the Labour Party in the record. Of course, there were substantial concessions to labour, but that is a different matter. The Liberals were trying to smother the Labour Party by taking over its votes, whereas they were in no position to do that to the Irish.

Coalition theory can also cope with the proposed Lib./Con. coalition of 1910, which traditional historians apparently find very mysterious.[2] The coalition is consistent with MW, although not with SW. It is consistent with MCW if one believes that there was an ideological dimension on which the Liberal and Conservative parties were adjacent. In the light of Limehouse and the constitutional crisis, this may seem odd. But Lloyd George was looking for a centrist solution to the Irish question, on which the extremes were the Irish Party and the Orangemen (Protestant opponents of Home Rule from Ulster, who were a small part of the Conservative Party) and on which the Labour Party could be ignored. In the immediate aftermath of 1910 his hopes looked wildly optimistic, as the Conservative Party took over (or was taken over by) the Orange interest in its most strident version and lent its support to armed rebellion in Ulster in 1914.[3] But after the First World War Lloyd

George proved that the coalition he had proposed in 1910 was feasible after all. In his own coalition government comprising part of the Liberal Party and all the Conservatives, he managed to settle the Irish Question for fifty years by partitioning off two-thirds of Ulster as 'Northern Ireland' within the UK, and setting up the rest of Ireland as an independent 'Free State' by the Treaty of 1921 (for the details of how he pulled it off, see Jones 1971; Longford 1967).

6.4 A Summary of Empirical Tests of Coalition Theory

In the previous section, we used coalition theory to illuminate a chapter of British political history. By showing it in a new light, the theory justified its existence. But one story does not constitute a test of a theory, and in any case the story is consistent with a number of different versions of the theory. However, several scholars have tested the versions by seeing which best predicts the actual pattern of coalition formation in the multi–party democracies of Europe since 1918 (de Swaan 1973; Taylor and Laver 1973; de Swaan and Mokken 1980). The tests are rather inconclusive, because it is not clear what is to count as a 'connection' in testing MCW and its variants. De Swaan ranks all parties in all European multi-party systems along a left-right dimension and tests MCW by that. Taylor and Laver quite rightly object to this procedure. It begs the question in a fundamental way, as should be obvious from the example in the previous section. It might be acceptable to range Labour, the Liberals and the Conservatives from left to right in that order, but where are we to put the Irish (either faction)? They just do not belong in the left-right dimension, and the Nationalist-Unionist dimension, which was much more important in the politics of the time, cannot be forced into a left-right one without grave distortion. However, Taylor and Laver have no acceptable substitute for the left-right dimension as their 'subjective estimates' (p. 216) beg the question in a different way.

Two things, none the less, stand out from the empirical analyses. First, only 87 out of the 132 coalitions in Taylor and Laver's set were nominally winning at all. The rest were of less than minimum winning size. This is partly a matter of definition. In some countries, including the UK, the political culture seems to favour a minority government rather than a formal coalition. The Liberal governments of 1910 are examples (and so are the Labour governments of 1924,

1929–31, 1974 and 1977–9). In these cases, one party took all the government offices. But it was still just as much involved in bargaining as if it had shared out government offices. The Irish party did not want government office. It wanted Home Rule, and got it.

Second, Riker's 'size principle', SW, does rather poorly as a predictor. The tests agree that MCW, in some version or another, is a far superior predictor. In other words it is much more important that you and your coalition partners should add up to a coherent ideology than that they should add up to the barest majority of seats. But there are severe problems in measuring 'connectivity'. If you try to measure it by some preordained dimension, you run into the objections set out in the last paragraph but one; if you measure it by parties' actual votes in parliament, you are trapped in a circular argument because parties' votes are a function of the alliances they have formed. Therefore you cannot use the votes to predict the alliances.

Overall, then, coalition theory is in a slightly unsure position. It can illustrate political history. But will it ever become a predictive science? Public choice theorists are divided. On one side, Enelow and Hinich (1984) believe that meaningful spatial measures can be devised whereby each voter can assess his distance from each party, and each party from each other, in multidimensional Euclidean space. If that is true, then the concept of MCW can be given a precise meaning. On the other side, Riker (1982, 1984) argues that politics is typically in disequilibrium, or in other words that there is a cycle of options, none of which can beat all the others. If that is true, then all coalitions will be 'connected' by definition, and MCW will be trivially true, but will not help explain upheavals like the American realignment of 1816–56 (?or the Unionist flirtation with Orange militancy from 1912 to 1914). I think Riker is closer to the mark than Enelow and Hinich, but the argument still has a long way to go.

Part II

Theory

7

How People (and Animals) Cooperate

7.1 Positive and Normative Public Choice

Up to now, this has not been a book about 'ought's. The previous chapters have tried to describe and understand the behaviour of voters, politicians, bureaucrats, and so on, not to say what ought to happen. We now move closer to some of the classic questions of political theory: questions such as 'Why should I obey people in authority?' or 'What is democracy, and is it a good thing?' Closer to everyday politics, but still 'ought' questions, are ones such as 'Should blood supply be governed by altruism or the market?' or 'Should the UK unilaterally disarm?' I have opinions on all these questions but I am not going to say what they are because my opinions are worth no more than the next person's. It is not the job of a book like this to provide answers to these questions, but it will try to suggest approaches – to set questions like these in a clear framework in which the good arguments on each side can be separated from the bad ones.

The general arrangement of the rest of the book is as follows. In this chapter we look more abstractly than hitherto at collective action problems and free-rider dilemmas. We shall find that the public-choice approach casts new light on questions of political obligation which have been disputed since Hobbes, and it also shows an unexpected convergence on arguments in evolutionary biology. In chapter 8 we pick up the problem of aggregating preferences from where we left it in section 1.3 and lead up to the fullest statement of the problem in Kenneth Arrow's famous General Possibility (or Impossibility) Theorem. In chapter 9 we examine what all this means for democratic political theory.

7.2 A Classification of Collective Action Problems

Collective action problems may be divided into three classes according, roughly, to how severe the problem is. These classes are Assurance games, Chicken games and Prisoners' Dilemma games. (From now on these will often be abbreviated to AGs, CGs and PDGs.) They may also be divided into games involving just two players, games involving more than two players which take the form of encounters between the players two at a time, and games involving more than two players which do not take this form. The last two are called, respectively, *compound* and *non-compound* n-person games (terminology invented by Hamburger 1973). The game people play in a street market is an example of a compound game. There are many customers and many stallholders, and at each stall where any trading is going on one customer is dealing with one stallholder. Each player has an opportunity to cheat or to be honest. We could look at the whole market as the sum, or compound, of all these two-person games. Consider by contrast the game of whether or not to vote that was the subject of section 3.1. There is no way in which this game can be broken down into two-person subgames. We are all in it at once and together; the decision of each of us interacts with the decisions of all the others.

There is yet a third important dimension: whether the game is to be played once only, or is one in a sequence of repeated plays of the same game by the same players. The latter is called a *supergame*. If I meet somebody I have never met before and never expect to meet again – say a stranded motorist whom I can, if I choose, help by changing his flat tyre – the game we play is a one-off affair. But if I am the government of the USSR conducting arms control negotiations with the government of the USA I know that I have to live with my fellow-player all the time, unless we blow each other up. Our game is a supergame, and what is rational in a one-off game is not necessarily rational in a supergame (and vice versa).

It is not easy to keep control of all these dimensions at once, and I do not find three-way tables very helpful. Here is a route map instead. I shall start with two-person one-shot games, considering the three types (AG, CG, and PDG)[1] in turn. Next I discuss two-person supergames, then compound n-person supergames, and lastly non-compound n-person games and supergames.

7.3.1 *Assurance Games*

Consider the telephone reconnection problem of chapter 1. We are in the middle of a conversation and we get cut off. What do we do? Obviously, we cannot communicate. Each of us has two options: dial and wait. If we both dial, we will both get the engaged tone. If we both wait, we shall wait, and wait, and wait (and probably both end up by dialling at once). The solution which is best for both of us is that one should dial and the other should wait. There is a slight advantage to waiting: the person who waits does not have to pay the bill.

This is a non-zero-sum game. The strategy pairs 'Dial/wait' and 'Wait/dial' are obviously better overall than 'Dial/dial' or 'Wait/wait'. For each player there are three distinct outcomes (Dial/dial and Wait/wait have the same effect, so they can be lumped together). The worst is silence. The best is reconnection without paying for it. Reconnection at one's own expense is intermediate. We could represent this ordering by numbers – any numbers will do so long as they are in the right order, but 0, 1 and 2 seem to be a sensible choice. These numbers represent *only* an ordering. They say nothing about the distance between each pair of outcomes. We shall use cardinal rankings later in this chapter, but not yet. Figure 7.1 represents this game in what is called 'normal form'.

In the normal-form representation of a two-person game, there is a row chooser who (obviously) chooses one of the rows, and a column chooser who chooses one of the columns. In each cell there are two numbers separated by a comma. The number before the comma is what the row chooser gets, and the number after the

	You	
	Redial	Don't redial
Redial	0, 0	1, 2
Don't redial	2, 1	0, 0

Figure 7.1 *A two-person AG*

comma is what the column chooser gets. So for example if I don't redial and you do, I get 2 (representing my best outcome) and you get 1 (representing your second-best).

Many social dilemmas have either the same form as figure 7.1 or the even simpler figure 7.2. Figure 7.2 is an AG in which there is no element of competition between the players; in other words a pure coordination problem. The 'Drive on the right/left' game of chapter 1 is an example. If I am approaching you on an empty road, and if there is no established rule of the road, it does not matter in the slightest whether we veer right or left, so long as we both do the same thing. A game like figure 7.1, in which there is an element of competition as well as of cooperation between the players, is labelled 'Battle of the Sexes' by game theorists, accompanied by this rather sexist story: He wants to go to a boxing match, but She wants to go to the opera. But they would rather do things together than separately. The only difference between Battle of the Sexes and the telephone connection game is that in Battle of the Sexes each wants to do the same as the other, whereas in the telephone game each wants to do the opposite to the other. But this difference is irrelevant for our purposes. Both are AGs with an element of competition as well as one of coordination.

How do one-off AGs ever get solved? Schelling (1960) conducted some well-known experiments on pure coordination games by asking groups of students to solve various familiar problems. You have to meet somebody in New York City, and you have failed to specify where and when? Make it the information booth at Grand Central Station at 12 noon. There is an infinity of possible places and 1440 possible times if only exact minutes are allowed; but over half the subjects chose Grand Central Station and nearly all of them

		You drive on the Right	You drive on the Left
I drive on the	Right	1, 1	0, 0
	Left	0, 0	1, 1

Figure 7.2 *A pure coordination AG*

chose 12 noon. Colman (1982, pp. 35–7) repeated Schelling's experiments with British students. The most popular rendezvous in London was Piccadilly Circus and overwhelmingly the most popular time was again 12 noon.

The rendezvous game is a figure 7.2 (pure coordination) game if each possible rendezvous is equally convenient to each player. If different rendezvous suit the different players best, then it is a figure 7.1 (impure coordination) game and Schelling's 'prominent' solutions are less certain to work. Grand Central was 'prominent' because all his subjects were in New Haven and all the trains from New Haven run into Grand Central. But suppose I (from Oxford) and you (from Leeds) have to meet in Manchester. My train arrives at Piccadilly station; yours at Victoria. I might be rather selfish and assume that you will come to Piccadilly, or I might be altruistic and go to Victoria to save you the bother of crossing the city. Of course, if you too are rather altruistic, our taxis will cross in the middle of Manchester; we will then be no better off than if we had both been rather selfish. To solve this coordination game, I have to work out what you are thinking about what I am thinking about what you are thinking . . . and so do you. If there is no obvious 'prominent' solution, this sort of game is quite hard to solve for a one-off encounter. If it is a supergame it is much easier. In section 7.3 we shall look at social conventions considered as Assurance supergames.

7.3.2 Chicken Games

The road from Jerusalem to Jericho is notoriously dangerous. It is plagued with muggers who operate in broad daylight. There are two good and busy men, a priest and a Levite. The priest lives in Jerusalem and works in Jericho; the Levite lives in Jericho and works in Jerusalem. One day they are approaching each other along a straight stretch of the road when they notice a fellow-traveller who has been mugged lying on the road in between them. The priest and the Levite both think that somebody should help the injured traveller. In fact, each of them reasons, 'It is best that this man I see approaching should help the injured man; next best that we both should; third best that I should help on my own; worst that nobody should.' Their preferences are as shown in figure 7.3. The priest and the Levite are both quite sophisticated men, and each realises that if he gives out a signal to indicate that much as he would love to help,

| | Levite | |
	Help	Pass by on the other side
Priest Help	2, 2	1, 3
Pass by on the other side	3, 1	0, 0

Figure 7.3 *A two-person CG*

he is terribly sorry but he has to get urgently to work where somebody in severe distress is waiting for him, then the other may be forced to stop and help the injured traveller. Unfortunately, the signals go out at the same time. Both men look at their watches in a preoccupied sort of way, and hurry past on opposite sides of the road, leaving the injured traveller to his fate.

The story is contrived, of course; but it stands for a very common situation. We all see people in distress in the street from time to time but we do not always stop to help. When we do not, we often have a guilty conscience and offer various rationalisations. In an experiment conducted on the New York subway (of all places!) it was found that when a man pretended to collapse, 59 out of 65 times when he was 'sober' fellow-travellers came to his aid, and even 19 times out of 38 when he was 'drunk'. The excuses offered when nobody came to help were such as 'It's for men to help him' (from a woman), 'I wish I could help him – I'm not strong enough', 'I never saw this kind of thing before – I don't know where to look', and 'You feel so bad that you don't know what to do' (quoted in Heath 1976, p. 142).

Perhaps there is an explanation here for the tragic and puzzling cases where somebody dies in full view of numerous onlookers – such as Kitty Genovese, whose screams woke thirty-eight neighbours as she was attacked by a maniac (quoted in Heath 1976, p. 90) or the six-year-old boy who drowned in the Serpentine in London on a summer's day in 1985 in the midst of hundreds of other bathers. It is much easier to assume that somebody else will help when there are many others than when there are few. However, this takes us away prematurely from the two-person one-shot game.

The game in figure 7.3 is Chicken. We have met Chicken before and it is now time to define it formally as any game where the orderings of the players are those given in figure 7.3. Remember, again, that the numbers are only orderings. The best option is shown as 3 and the worst as 0. If the players rank the options in the order shown, they are playing Chicken, whatever the exact values they attach to the **payoffs** in each cell.

Chicken gets its name from the 'dare' game played by James Dean in *Rebel without a Cause*. Two drivers head for each other on a collision course. The first to swerve is 'chicken'. Obviously, my best option is that you should swerve. If we both swerve at once, we both lose some face, but I do not lose as much as if I alone swerved. And, of course, if neither of us swerves, that is worst for us both. In October 1962 John F. Kennedy and Nikita Khrushchev were on just such a collision course as Khrushchev refused to turn away Russian ships heading for Cuba with a load of missiles and Kennedy threatened to attack the Russians if they came any further. Everybody who lived through the Cuba Missile Crisis remembers the agonising feeling of foreboding that neither would swerve and a world holocaust might ensue. In the end it was Khrushchev who swerved and the world's most desperate game of Chicken ended cooperatively (see Allison 1971).

7.3.3 Prisoners' Dilemma Games

The most notorious coordination game is Prisoners' Dilemma. Suppose that the administrations of the USSR and the USA have just signed a test-ban treaty. They have made promises to each other; but as Hobbes observed a long time ago, 'Covenants, without the Sword, are but Words, and of no strength to secure a man at all.' There is no effective international authority to wield a sword against the superpowers if they break their promises. Each superpower has the technical ability to conduct tests underground or in very remote places with a fairly high probability that such cheating will not be detected. If I am the government of either superpower, do I keep the agreement I have just made, or do I cheat? Obviously, it is better that both of us should keep the agreement than that we should both break it. If that were not so, we would not have signed the agreement. But my best option of all is to cheat while the other party keeps the agreement (so that I can perfect my weapons of destruction while his become obsolete) and my worst is the opposite: to obey while the other cheats. This gives us the classic matrix of figure 7.4. If I am the row chooser (here the USSR) I do not know whether the other will obey or cheat. But I do know that if he obeys, I shall get 3 from cheating and 2 from obeying; so I should cheat. And if he cheats, I shall get 1 from cheating and 0 from obeying; so I should cheat. It is thus a cast-iron certainty that it is in my interest to cheat, no matter how likely I think it is that the other player will. The argument is exactly symmetrical for the column chooser.

If the PDG really is a one-off two-person game then it is unquestionably in the interests of both parties to cheat, and there is no other equilibrium solution. But most PDGs in real life are more complicated games. The superpowers are not really playing a one-off game; if they do not blow each other up they have to carry on coexisting. The same is true of most other social PDGs. The PDG ordering (best that I cheat and you obey; second that we both obey; third that we both cheat; worst that you cheat and I obey) is very common. It can be seen in dilemmas about whaling, incomes policies, arms control, and the provision of public goods. But the games in question are not one-off two-person PDGs. They are usually between parties who will interact again in future (hence supergames) and usually involve more than two parties, although they sometimes can be split into two-party encounters (compound n-person PDGs). So we have to analyse more complicated cases.

	USA Obey test ban	Cheat
USSR Obey test ban	2, 2	0, 3
USSR Cheat	3, 0	1, 1

Figure 7.4 *Obey or cheat; a two-person PDG*

7.4 The Two-Person Supergame

A supergame is an indefinite series of one-off games.[2] Some things which are puzzling and paradoxical about the games just analysed cease to be so when they are considered as supergames; but some new puzzles arise.

Take first the pure coordination Assurance supergame ('Drive on the Left' or 'Rendezvous', for instance). During 1985, my wife met me about twice a week at New Street Station in Birmingham. It is hard to park a car there, and even if we fixed a time for her to pick me up, she could not always keep it because she was circling around looking for a parking space. To begin with, we were constantly looking for each other in the wrong places. I would be at the barrier while she was waiting at the taxi set-down point; then I would go to the phones to see if she had been detained at work while she came to the barrier; then I would go to the taxi point while she phoned to see if I had been detained at work.... After a bit we evolved a supergame equilibrium. I always went to the taxi point and waited, however long it took. We were never disappointed after that.

Thus when the parties can communicate and meet frequently, the coordination Assurance supergame becomes trivially easy. Even when they cannot, the notion of a 'convention', which is a more general form of Schelling's prominent solutions, is a sort of supergame equilibrium. There need be no rhyme nor reason to the convention. In some societies it is bad manners to leave your knife and fork on the plate at the end of a course. In other societies it is bad manners not to. But once the convention, whatever it is, is established and understood, it helps people choose.

The AG which is not a game of pure coordination also has supergame equilibria. An obvious one in Battle of the Sexes is that we go to His and Her entertainments on alternate nights out. An equally obvious one in the telephone game is that the person who initiated the calls is the one who redials. In none of these arrangements is government necessary. Anarchy is all that is needed.

Chicken supergames are tougher. In the long run, it must pay both parties to reach a cooperative equilibrium. If the Priest and the Levite are constantly encountering victims of muggings, they will come to some arrangement. It might be an arrangement to help the victim together every time they meet one, or to take turns. But there is a problem of *precommitment*. Suppose one player in the original

CG throws the steering wheel away so that he could not make the car swerve even if he wanted to. Providing the other player knows this, the first player is bound to win the game. The second player knows that the first has already chosen the uncooperative strategy ('Pass by on the other side' in figure 7.3). There is no longer any doubt about what the second should do. He will get his worst option by acting uncooperatively and his second-worst by acting cooperatively, therefore he must cooperate. The second player may try to even the score by precommitting himself to non-cooperation in the next round. There need be nothing disastrous about such a sequence; but if in any round the players both precommit themselves at once they would both end up with their worst option.

A farsighted Chicken player might announce a supergame strategy: 'I shall precommit myself to non-cooperation in each and every ordinary game'. This might force his opponent into cooperation. But an equally intelligent opponent might make the same announcement. This simply reproduces the original CG at a higher level. For each player the best option is 'I precommit, you don't'. Second best is 'Nobody precommits'. Third best is 'You precommit, I don't'. Worst is 'Both precommit'. We have got an infinite regress. The game of choosing a Chicken supergame strategy is itself a game of Chicken. Hence Chicken supergames may be harder to solve cooperatively than they look. Brams (1983, chapter 4) argues that an omniscient God would lose at Chicken. God, unlike you or me, *knows* whether his opponent really has thrown the wheel away or is just bluffing. It is dangerous to precommit against me, because I might mistakenly think you were bluffing, drive straight on, and crash. But it is safe to precommit against God. God knows you are not bluffing, and therefore will have to swerve to protect himself. Therefore God cannot be both omniscient and omnipotent. This argument is unlikely to appeal to theologians, but it is a good mental exercise to try to pinpoint just what is wrong with it.

The Prisoners' Dilemma supergame, unlike the other two, has been extensively studied. It has long been obvious that if two people play PDG over and over again, they will each gain more in the long run from cooperating each time they meet than either of them can hope to gain from defecting once followed by punishment in every subsequent game. Therefore if the players do not know when the last game is going to take place, they can say to each other, 'I shall cooperate in the first game, and thereafter I shall do in every game what you did in the game before.' This is called Tit-for-Tat (henceforth TFT).

When is it best to play TFT, and when should one always defect (henceforth ALL D)? If one values future payoffs as highly as immediate ones, then it is always best to play TFT, because there must be some point in the future at which the value of getting the second-best outcome time after time outweighs the value of getting the best once and then the third-best time after time. But often people discount the future. A bird in the hand is worth two in the bush. There are two quite distinct reasons for devaluing future benefits: one is that they are uncertain and the other is that they are in the future. Both can be combined in the assumption that everybody has a *discount parameter* which we shall label w. The discount parameter is the valuation of any payoff at time t + 1 as a proportion of its value at time t. So if I think a payoff next time is worth 80 per cent as much as the same payoff this time, my w is 0.8. Another way of saying the same thing is that my discount *rate* (1 – w) is 20 per cent or 0.2; w must lie between 0 and 1 both inclusive for everybody.

To get any further, we have to move from ordinal to cardinal measurement. That is to say, we need to know by how much each outcome is better than the next worse. We can then work out the *temptation ratios* for any two-person Prisoners' supergame from the payoffs given for the ordinary game. The payoffs in the ordinary game are conventionally labelled as shown in figure 7.5. If (and only if) $T > R > P > S$ and $2R > T + S$, the supergame is PDG. The letters stand for Temptation, Reward, Punishment, and the Sucker's payoff respectively.

		You: Cooperate	You: Defect
I	Cooperate	R, R	S, T
	Defect	T, S	P, P

Figure 7.5 *PDG: the conventional labels for the payoffs*

The temptation ratios (T – R)/(T – P) and (T – R)/(R – S) define the minimum value of w at which it is worth while for a player to play TFT. A formal derivation of them is in the appendix to this chapter. To understand what is going on, consider a supergame in which the ordinary game payoffs are those shown in figure 7.6. In this matrix, (T – R)/(T – P) is 1/2, and (T – R)/(R – S) is 2/3. So the discount parameter w must be at least 2/3 for both players for TFT to be best for them. If either of them values w at less than 2/3, he should defect on the first game.

		You	
		Cooperate	Defect
I	Cooperate	3, 3 R, R	0, 5 S, T
	Defect	5, 0 T, S	1, 1 P, P

Figure 7.6 *The payoff matrix for each ordinary game of Axelrod's PDG tournament*

7.4 Axelrod's Tournament and the Evolution of Cooperation

Temptation ratios for the two-person Prisoners' Dilemma supergame were first worked out by Michael Taylor (1976). But the fullest use of them has been made by Robert Axelrod (1984) in a book which ingeniously combines experimental and pure theoretical research. His work started with a two-stage computer tournament reported in 1980 (Axelrod 1980a,b). In the first round, he invited fourteen colleagues to submit a programme each to play the PDG shown in figure 7.6. Each programme was played 200 times over against each of the others and against itself. The simplest programme (submitted by Anatol Rapoport) was TFT, and it won the tournament. Axelrod then circulated the results and invited entries for another round. This time 62 competitors entered, and TFT, again submitted by Rapoport, won again. This was a pleasant surprise to those who are in favour of cooperation. Everybody who entered the second round knew that TFT had won the first. So entrants might have reasoned, 'A lot of people will submit TFT, or something like it, because they know it succeeded last time. Therefore I shall submit a nasty programme which rats on TFT.' If this had happened, the nasty programmes would certainly have defeated TFT, but everybody would have done worse than in the first round. Actually, more of the entrants drew the moral 'TFT does well; therefore to do well I should play TFT or something like it' than drew the moral 'TFT does well; therefore I will do even better than those whose reasoning stops there by exploiting it.' Both arguments are perfectly sound; but the first road leads to a cooperative society, and the second to a cheating society.

The argument has started to move away from the two-person case to the compound n-person case. The computer tournaments were models of societies each of whose members interacts with each other. Axelrod next defined a *collectively stable strategy* (CSS). A CSS is a strategy which renders a society safe from invasion. Individuals have strategies, societies do not; but individuals' strategies can determine whether society is stable or not. If every individual in a society plays the same strategy, and if individuals playing each other do at least as well as invaders do against members of the host population, the society can repel the invaders; no individual has an incentive to switch strategies; and the strategy is collectively stable.

There may be more than one CSS. Always Defect (ALL D) is always a CSS. If everybody always defects in every interaction with any other, the only alternative is a strategy that cooperates at least sometimes. When it cooperates, it gets less than ALL D. So if everyone else plays ALL D, no individual ever has a reason to play anything else. But TFT is sometimes a CSS. If everybody's discount parameter w is high enough, everybody will do better in the long run by playing TFT rather than ALL D. In such a society, there are at least two equilibria: one in which everybody plays TFT, and one in which everybody plays ALL D. The first is better for everybody than the second, so it should be easy for everybody to agree to the first.

This problem of 'which supergame strategy should I choose?' is itself an AG. If everybody else chooses ALL D, I should choose ALL D, and if everybody else chooses TFT, I should choose TFT. There is an interesting contrast with the Chicken supergame strategy discussed above. That was itself a CG, so there was no breaking out of the dilemma but merely an infinite regress. However, the game of deciding whether or not to play TFT in an Axelrod tournament is not itself a PDG. It is thus possible to answer Yes to the age-old question posed by Hobbes, 'Could perfectly self-interested people in a state of nature cooperate in order to get out of it?' (For a fuller version of this argument see McLean 1982b. However, Smyth 1972 and Ward 1982 both claim that there *is* an infinite regress of PDGs.)

When he ran his tournament, Axelrod believed that it was impossible to prove that TFT or any other strategy was 'the best' if everybody had a high discount parameter. But the success of TFT in the tournament prompted him to find a general deductive argument in its favour. This argument is in two parts. First, it is shown that if TFT is collectively stable against ALL D and against Negative (or Nasty) TFT ('Defect on the first game, and thereafter do what your opponent did in the previous game') then it is stable against any strategy whatever. Then the conditions for TFT to be collectively stable against ALL D and NTFT are derived. Axelrod presents them as if they were the same for the compound n-person case as for the two-person case, in other words that TFT is collectively stable if for every individual w is at least as great as the greater of $(T - R)/(T - P)$ and $(T - R)/(R - S)$. However, this is not quite correct.

To see why we need to look closely at the concept of 'collective stability'. A society is immune from invasion if its members on average do at least as well in all their social interactions as invaders do. There are three values to consider: what the invader gets, what the invaded individual gets, and what everybody else gets. Axelrod ignores the second category. But every time a cheat (an ALL D player) interacts with a new TFT player that player gets the Sucker's payoff, S. Of course he will never cooperate with the invader again but his suffering brings down the average payoff to each member of the society. If there are n (strictly n + 1) members of society, of whom k are invaders, the temptation ratios should be

$$\frac{n(T - R) + k(R - S)}{n(T - P) + k(P - S)}$$

and

$$\frac{n(T - R) + k(R - S)}{n(R - S) + k(T - R)}$$

The revised temptation ratios are derived in the second part of the appendix to this chapter, which goes through the argument in more detail. They make the prospects for cooperation somewhat less rosy than they are in Axelrod's formula. For any finite value of n the revised ratios are above the originals, but they come down towards them as n tends to infinity. Recalling that the higher the temptation ratios are, the less likely cooperation is to pay, this means that the larger a population, the better it is able to withstand invasion. In chapter 9 we shall compare this finding with some that point the other way in n-person games.

7.6 The Market for Lemons

The previous section may have been a little hard to follow because it was necessarily abstract. Here is an (almost) real-life Axelrod game to put it in context.

You are a trader in a street market, selling second-hand cars. It is a rather primitive market, in which there is no money, only barter. You will sell a car to anybody who produces one car's worth of goods in exchange. I come along to your pitch with a box full of home computers, which I have made, and I offer you three computers for a car. In principle we both think a car is worth three computers, but there is a problem. I am a computer technician, not a vehicle mechanic, and you are the reverse. I can see that every car on your pitch is shiny and clean, and it sounds smooth when I drive it round the block. You can see that each of my computers works when you first try it. But I do not know which of your cars will break down as soon as I get home and find the gearbox full of sawdust. You do not know which computer will expire the day after you buy it. However, some of your cars are 'lemons' and some are good buys – you know which are which, just as I know which computers are 'lemons' and which are not.

Each of us has two choices: offer good goods, or offer 'lemons'. The interaction of the choices leads to four outcomes, as shown in figure 7.7.

Obviously, this game is a PDG. It is best for me to offer 'lemons' in return for a good car; next best if both sets of goods are of high quality; third best if both are of poor quality; worst if I offer good goods in return for a lemon.

Introducing money makes the story more realistic and only a little

You

Offer a good car   Offer a 'lemon'

	Offer a good car	Offer a 'lemon'
Offer good computers	2, 2	0, 3
Offer 'lemons'	3, 0	1,1

Figure 7.7 *The 'market for lemons' as a two-person PDG*

more complicated. Everybody in the labour market is sometimes a buyer and sometimes a seller of goods and/or services. The generalisation of the dilemma just set out is 'Best buy good goods and sell shoddy ones; next best buy and sell good goods; third best buy and sell shoddy ones; worst buy shoddy goods and sell good ones'. If everybody interacts with everybody else, the market is a compound n-person PDG.

Akerlof (1970), in his seminal paper on the market for 'lemons', draws a typical economist's conclusion. The market PDG is a bad thing not because people cheat each other, but because trade which would otherwise happen does not. Cheating is just a redistribution of proceeds, and welfare economists invariably refuse to comment on issues of distribution but restrict themselves to considering obstacles to maximising the proceeds. In this case the obstacle is a familiar one to every honest person who has ever had an old car to sell. The best way to sell it is to another private individual, with no traders taking their cut. I know that my car is a good one; but how can I persuade potential buyers? It doesn't matter how fervently my advert in the local paper says that the car is a 'good runner'; too few would-be buyers are willing to take the risk of a private purchase, and they go to a big garage instead. So the price and quantity of cars sold privately are both depressed from the level they would attain in a perfectly functioning market. (Incidentally, if a buyer does come armed with a cheque-book, I had better assume that all his cheques are lemons.)

Why do used-car buyers go to big garages in preference to private sellers or street-corner pitches, even though big garages charge more for used cars? Obviously, because buyers know that if the car turns out to be a lemon, the garage will still be there next week to handle their complaints. Besides, the garage has a reputation to protect, and will not want to risk fiddling the records (turning the odometer back, for instance) if there is any substantial chance of being found out. This is just an Axelrod Prisoners' Dilemma supergame. There are some transactions where the parties normally meet only once and never see each other again. Private used-car deals are an example; house purchases are another. It is notorious that more cheating and attempted cheating goes on in this sort of transaction than in the sort where the parties are liable to meet again. Dealings with any established trader are in the second category; so are international trade deals, and dealings between (say) a village store or a corner shop and their customers. This could be put into Axelrod's terminology simply by observing that in the house or private car sale the value of w for each party is 0 or very low. The value of w partly reflects the probability of a further encounter between the parties; if that is low so is w. In the international trade and corner shop cases, the value of w is correspondingly higher, as the parties know that they are likely to meet again in future rounds of the supergame.

7.7 How Animals Cooperate

Our next illustration is not about human beings at all, but a safari in the animal kingdom may be worth while. For decades biologists have been puzzled by 'cooperative' animal behaviour. Animals sometimes pull their punches: for instance, a dog victorious in a fight does not kill the loser even though it easily could. Other animals seem to go further and sacrifice themselves for the good of the group: for instance, honey bees that sting intruders to protect the hive, but then die from the consequent damage to their own organs. Many popular accounts, even some written by biologists, praised such 'behaviour for the good of the species' and suggested that selfish man should learn from unselfish animals. But the concept of 'self-sacrifice for the good of the group' was inconsistent with any coherent account of evolution. Evolution proceeds by differential breeding. Qualities that make an animal better at reproducing itself than others of the same species will (obviously) tend to spread as such animals have more offspring than others. Animals which make a habit of sacrificing themselves for the good of the species are unlikely to have many offspring to which this excellent habit can be transmitted.

However, 'self-sacrificing' animals exist; how can their existence be accounted for? One possibility is that genes help their copies in other individuals. All the suicidal worker bees in a hive are infertile daughters of the same queen. The 'selfish gene' may be operating at the level of kin selection (Hamilton 1972; Dawkins 1978, pp. 184–94). Kin selection may explain many other cases of animal 'altruism', but cannot explain observed cases of cooperation among individuals which are not closely related. Trivers (1971) proposed an alternative explanation which he called 'reciprocal altruism'. He observed a symbiosis between large fish of one species and small ones of others, which pick parasites off the large fishes' bodies, teeth, and gills. Why do the large fish not wait until the little ones are inside and then eat them? Probably because in the long run they do better from being frequently cleaned than from once having a good meal but then being cleaned less often because there are fewer cleaner-fish around. (I am not suggesting that fish think logically. But fish which are genetically programmed to behave in this 'cooperative' way will breed more offspring than any programmed to behave in an alternative 'cheating' way.) In general, animals can be said to be reciprocal altruists if they follow a TFT behaviour pattern – 'You scratch my back (which is dirty and which I cannot reach) and I'll scratch yours.'

This pattern is exactly the one modelled by the Axelrod Prisoners' Dilemma supergames, and his model has been taken up by biologists more enthusiastically than by social scientists, (see Axelrod and Hamilton 1981; Hofstadter 1983). Biologists had evolved the concept of an evolutionarily stable strategy (ESS) which is virtually the same as a CSS (Maynard Smith 1974; Williams and McLean 1985). ESS reasoning can explain the existence of animals which behave 'altruistically' even towards non-relatives, in a way no earlier formulation could. Recall that it is individuals, not groups, which have strategies. However, a strategy may be stable for a group without being optimal for an isolated individual on a single occasion. TFT, which is another name for reciprocal altruism, may be such a strategy. If everybody in a group plays TFT, and if the values of w are high enough, the group is invulnerable to invasion by cheats. As its members generally do better (and are able to have more offspring) than any individual in neighbouring groups which have settled at the ALL D ESS, reciprocally-altruistic groups may be able to expand by colonising places where cheating groups have killed themselves off. (This highly compressed account owes a great deal to Dawkins 1978 and 1981, Mackie 1978, and Maynard Smith 1982, to which you should turn if you are intrigued or puzzled.)

Vampire bats are apparently reciprocal altruists. An experimental study (Wilkinson 1984) showed that

unrelated but closely associated bats are capable of sufficient recognition to reciprocally exchange blood.... Blood was donated preferentially to individuals in dire need from the same population.... Starved bats which received blood later reciprocated the donation significantly more often than expected had exchanges occurred randomly.... [But] the only bat with low association ... was not fed even when in need.

We have thus arrived back unexpectedly at the discussion of blood and altruism raised in chapter 1. Are human beings like vampire bats? Is human altruism TFT writ large, is it complex nepotism, or is it something else? I shall not even try to answer these questions until chapter 9, but I hope this section has illustrated some of the uses of Axelrod's model of the compound Prisoners' Dilemma supergame.

7.8 N-Person Supergames and the Free-Rider Problem

We first met the free-rider problem right at the beginning of this book. By definition, a public good is one from which it is hard or impossible to exclude anybody, whether or not he has contributed towards paying for it. Therefore it is to be expected that most public goods will be underprovided or not provided at all. We have looked at a host of examples. Three typical ones are clean air, a government of the party I favour, and an effective association to lobby for the interests I wish to see promoted. Free-rider games are non-compound. It would not be practicable to bring about clean air in the USA by a series of agreements between each pair of US citizens. (There are about 30 000,000 000,000 000 such pairs.) Therefore the analytical techniques of the last two sections do not apply.

Usually, if all the other possible contributors are lumped into one person called Everybody Else, each individual orders the outcomes in the PDG way: best that Everybody Else contributes and I don't; next best that we all do; third best that nobody does; worst that I do and Everybody Else does not. However, Everybody Else is not one

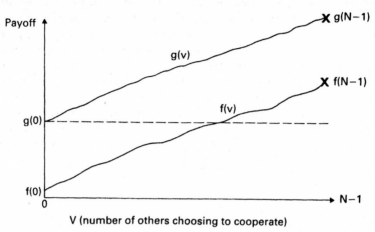

Figure 7.8 *Diagram of a free-rider's dilemma*

N = *number of players*
f(v) = *the payoff to me of cooperating when v others cooperate*
g(v) = *the payoff to me of defecting when v others cooperate*
g(v) > *f(v)* *for all values of v*
f(N − 1) > *g(0)*
g(v) *and* *f(v)* *are positive monotonic functions of v*

Sources: Diagram – Schelling (1973), *passim*; notation – Taylor (1976), pp. 43–4.

person. The situation in which everybody else contributes is different to that in which about half the others contribute, which is different again from that in which only one or two others contribute. In some contributors' dilemmas my best strategy is to free ride *irrespective* of the number of others who are contributing; but in others that is not the case.

Another dimension is binary versus non-binary. A decision is binary if there are only two choices. The voting game of section 3.1 involves binary choices – each player has only the options Vote or Abstain. But 'contributing-to-lobby' games are non-binary. Each potential contributor has an infinite range of options from contributing nothing to contributing all his wealth. Only binary choices have had any rigorous analysis. A useful starting-point is the diagram invented by Thomas Schelling (1973) and reproduced in figure 7.8. This shows the options open to any one player in a binary free-rider game. Each player, including him, has just two options, Cooperate and Defect. His payoff is on the vertical axis. The line marked g(v) represents what he gets if he defects, and the line marked f(v) represents what he gets if he cooperates. The horizontal axis measures the number of other players who cooperate. Assuming that there are N players, the number of others who cooperate can be anything between 0 and N − 1, and the axis is labelled accordingly. The expressions g(v) and f(v) are a form of algebraic shorthand called 'functional notation'. If we call payoff P and mark it with a superscript C or D to indicate cooperation and defection, we can write

$$P^D = g(v)$$

and

$$P^C = f(v)$$

In words, this reads 'The payoff from defecting is a function of (i.e. depends on) the number of others cooperating, and the payoff from cooperating is another function of the same thing.' A classic free-rider dilemma has three features of note, each of which can be expressed algebraically. The individual is always better off by defecting than by cooperating (g(v) > f(v) for all values of v). But if everybody cooperates each individual is better off than if everybody defects (f(N − 1) > g(0)). And the more people cooperate, the higher everybody's payoff (f(v) and g(v) are monotonically increasing: that is, their graphs both slope continuously upwards to the right).

If these three conditions are met, we can justly say that we have a pure n-person PDG (henceforth nPDG). The catalytic-converter case of section 1.2.5 is an example. No matter how many other Californian motorists have converters, I am better off without one than with, because the cost of it always exceeds the value of the extra air quality which *my own* converter would bring me. Second, the world in which everybody has a converter is better for one and all than the world in which nobody has. Third, the more people have converters, the cleaner the air is irrespective of whether I have one myself or not. These facts correspond to the three algebraic requirements of the last paragraph. We have here what philosophers call the 'Sorites paradox'. Every individual brings one stone to the top of the mountain. One stone does not make a cairn, nor do a small finite number of stones. We cannot pin down the point at which one extra stone added to a pile which is not a cairn turns it into a cairn. And yet that point must exist, because after many people have climbed the mountain with one stone each there is a cairn at the top. Each person has made an imperceptibly tiny contribution but they add up to a perceptible, and useful, thing.

However, many free-rider dilemmas do not take this form. Often the good to be provided is 'lumpy'. Up to a certain number of contributions, none or very little of it is provided. But there is some critical number of contributors who are just enough to provide the good. If the number, excluding me, is just below the magic number, then it is better for me to cooperate than to defect. The first condition for an nPDG — $g(v) > f(v)$ for all values of v — is not met.

An election is an extremely lumpy good. If our candidate gets one vote less than a majority, we get nothing. If he gets a majority of one, we get everything. So the voting free-rider game cannot be an nPDG. Suppose (to simplify) that I know for certain that the other side will get exactly 30 000 votes. I want my candidate to win, of course. But I am tempted to free-ride on the other $N - 1$ supporters of my party ($N > 30 001$). Here Cooperate means Vote and Defect means Don't bother. If $v < 29 999$, our candidate will not get in even with my help, and if $v > 30 000$ he will get in even without it. But for just two values of v, 29 999 and 30 000, it is better for me to cooperate than to defect. If $v = 29 999$ my vote turns a defeat into a tie (with a one-in-two chance that the coin the Returning Officer spins will come down for us). If $v = 30 000$ my vote turns a tie into a certain victory.

If an election is a lumpy public good, so must be any public policy which is the consequence of an election. Consider again the story of Keir Hardie and the Northumberland miners. The Eight Hours' Bill was a lumpy good which could only be achieved by the election either of a Labour government or of a Liberal government which was willing to steal some of the Labour Party's policies. Thus the dilemma facing any miner considering whether to make a contribution to Keir Hardie's party was a contributor's dilemma, but not an nPDG.

Many other public goods have an element of lumpiness. National defence, lighthouses, and a viable whale stock are examples. There is a point at which one more voluntary donation is just enough to pay for the smallest, cheapest, lighthouse. More money will produce a bigger and better one, so the good is not a pure all-or-nothing one like the election result. But neither is it a pure continuous one like Californian air-cleanliness. A whale stock (an example taken from Taylor and Ward 1982, which is essential background reading for this section) is 'lumpy' because as the number of whales gradually declines it reaches a 'catastrophe point' where each surviving breeding male is too unlikely to meet a breeding female for the species to continue. If I am a whaler *and if* the whale stock is just above the catastrophe point, I ought to cooperate with the International Whaling Commission and voluntarily cease whaling.

However, there is a catch. If I am smarter than the other whalers, and if I see the catastrophe coming, I can precommit myself to defection. I can announce, 'I shall carry on catching whales irrespective of anything the rest of you decide.' In that event the others will be locked into cooperating when the catastrophe point arrives, and I shall have succeeded in free-riding. But we have met this precommitment game before. It is our old friend Chicken. Like any other CG it carries the risk that everybody will precommit at once and the whale stocks will be destroyed. (This is a plausible explanation for the destruction of harvestable Blue Whale stocks since 1945.) We saw in section 7.3 that the supergame of deciding what CG strategy to play is itself a CG, so there may be no easy escape.

A similar dilemma may arise when choices are non-binary: when I must decide not just whether to contribute but how much. For any given level of other people's contributions, there is some sum which would enable the good to be provided. If that sum is both less than my total wealth and more than my evaluation of the good, I can provide it; and if we are playing a one-off game, I should. But if it is a supergame, I can precommit myself to not paying. If so, there is a Chicken supergame lurking behind what appears at first sight to be a PDG.

7.9 Cooperation: A Summary

No doubt the main thing to emerge from this chapter is that cooperation in coordination problems is a more complicated subject than it looks. But a review of the main landmarks may make the terrain easier to navigate. There are three classes of coordination games of any analytical interest. In AG, coordination in the supergame is easy. Either there is no conflict between the parties at all, or there is conflict that can be resolved by splitting the difference over a series of plays. CGs and PDG look very similar – in the two-person case the only difference is the transposition of the second-worst and worst outcomes for each player. But their supergames are different. In CGs the classic problem is precommitment. In PDGs, a cooperative solution is possible given sufficiently low discount rates and sufficiently few invaders. In the n-person game, many situations that are freely labelled 'PDG' are not really so on closer inspection. Specifically, in free-rider games, if the good to be provided is continuous the game is probably a genuine nPDG; if it is lumpy, it contains a Chicken nesting in it. The reader should now be in a position to go through all the coordination problems in this book and put them in their correct pigeonholes – an exercise I recommend but shall not carry out here.

Appendix: The Stability of Tit-for-Tat

Temptation Ratios in the Two-Person Prisoners' Dilemma Supergame

The supergame is defined as an indefinite sequence of ordinary games, each with the matrix:

	Coop.	Def.
Coop.	R,R	S,T
Def.	T,S	P,P

where $T > R > P > S$ and $2R > T + S$.

Each player has a discount parameter w, which is his evaluation of the ratio of a payoff next time to that of the same payoff now. Alternatively, he has a discount rate of $(1 - w)$. For example, if you believe a pound in a year's time is worth the same to you as 80p now, you have an annual discount rate of 0.2, and a discount parameter of 0.8. For each player w must lie between 0 and 1 inclusive.

If the other player is playing TFT, you know that you will get R in every game if you cooperate conditionally; if you defect you will get T in the first game and P in every game thereafter. For all values of T, R, and P there must be some point in the future at which the graph of non-discounted payoffs R + R + R + R + R + R ... crosses that of T + P + P + P + P + P ... from below. But this is not necessarily true of discounted payoffs. The temptation ratio gives the critical value of w below which it pays an individual to play ALL D rather than TFT. In any pair it is the individual with the higher critical value of w who is crucial. The other either knows that this player will defect if the temptation ratio is below this (and thus will also defect in the first game) or does not know, but finds out after the first game.

Maynard Smith (1982, pp. 202–3) proves that the only strategies which can ever beat TFT in an indefinite sequence of games are ALL D and Negative (or Nasty) TFT (NTFT: defect in the first round; thereafter do what your opponent did in the previous round). A gap in the proof of the same proposition by Axelrod (1984, pp. 208–9) was spotted and made good by Williams (1985, pp. 22–3).

Thus the way to find out the critical value of w is to compare what two TFT players get against each other with what ALL D and NTFT get against TFT. Recalling that each payoff is w times the one before, we have:

TFT versus TFT: $R + wR + w^2R + w^3R \ldots$

For $0 \leq w < 1$, this series has a sum given by the formula for a convergent geometrical progression:

$$\frac{R}{1 - w}$$

ALL D versus TFT: $T + wP + w^2P + w^3P \ldots$

$$= T + w(P + wP + w^2P \ldots)$$

$$= T + \frac{wP}{1 - w}$$

NTFT versus TFT: $T + wS + w^2T + w^3S + w^4T + w^5S\ldots$

$$= (T + wS)(1 + w^2 + w^4 + w^6\ldots)$$

Call $w^2\ Q$

$$= (T + wS)(1 + Q + Q^2 + Q^3\ldots)$$

$$= \frac{T + wS}{1 - Q} = \frac{T + wS}{1 - w^2}$$

The rule then is: Play TFT if and only if

$$\frac{R}{1 - w} \geq \text{max. } T + \frac{wP}{1 - w}, \frac{T + wS}{1 - w^2}$$

Solving these inequalities for w,

$$\frac{R}{1 - w} \geq T + \frac{wP}{1 - w} \quad \Rightarrow \quad R \geq (1 - w)\,T + wP$$

$$\Rightarrow \quad w\,(T - P) \geq T - R$$

$$\Rightarrow \quad w \geq \frac{T - R}{T - P}$$

$$\frac{R}{1 - w} \geq \frac{T + wS}{1 - w^2} \quad \Rightarrow \quad R \geq \frac{T + wS}{1 + w}$$

$$\Rightarrow \quad (1 + w)\,R \geq T + wS$$

$$\Rightarrow \quad w\,(R - S) \geq T - R$$

$$\Rightarrow \quad w \geq \frac{T - R}{R - S}$$

[NB: $1 - w^2 = (1 - w)(1 + w)$]

The Collective Stability of TFT in the Compound Supergame

Axelrod (1984, p. 56) defines a strategy as '*collectively stable* if no strategy can invade it. . ... a new strategy is said to *invade* a native strategy if the newcomer gets a higher score with a native than a native gets with another native' (stress in original). But this definition ignores the fact that an 'invaded' native gets a lower score than a native gets with another native. Unless the population is of infinite size, this factor must be allowed for.

In a population of infinite size, the temptation ratios are as in the section above, that is, TFT is collectively stable if for every individual

$$w \geq \max. \; \frac{T - R}{T - P}, \frac{T - R}{R - S}$$

For a population of finite size, they can be calculated as follows. Assume that there are $(n + 1)$ individuals altogether, of whom k ('the invaders') play ALL D or NTFT as the case may be, and the rest play TFT. Invaders never play one another; they know that they can do better by attacking the host population. Therefore an invader playing ALL D gets

$$T + wP + w^2P + w^3P \ldots = T + \frac{wP}{1 - w}$$

with probability 1. When a non-invader meets an invader he gets

$$S + wP + w^2P + w^3P \ldots = S + \frac{wP}{1 - w}$$

This happens with probability k/n. When he meets another non-invader he gets

$$R + wR + w^2R + w^3R \ldots = \frac{R}{1 - w}$$

This happens with probability $\frac{n - k}{n}$.

Theory

So TFT is collectively stable for the invaded population if and only if

$$\frac{k}{n}\left(S + \frac{wP}{1-w}\right) + \frac{n-k}{n} \times \frac{R}{1-w} \geq T + \frac{wP}{1-w}$$

Solving for w by the same sort of manipulation as above, we get

$$w \geq \frac{n\,(T-R) + k(R-S)}{n\,(T-P) + k(P-S)} \qquad (1)$$

Repeating the process for an invader playing NTFT: invaders get

$$T + wS + w^2T + w^3S \ldots = \frac{T + ws}{1 - w^2}$$

with probability 1. The rest get

$$S + wT + w^2S + w^3T \ldots = \frac{S + wT}{1 - w^2}$$

with probability k/n and, as before, R/(1 − w) with probability (n − k)/n. TFT is then collectively stable if and only if

$$\frac{k}{n}\left(\frac{S + wT}{1 - w^2}\right) + \frac{n-k}{n} \times \frac{R}{1-w} \geq \frac{T + wS}{1 - w^2}$$

or, in terms of w,

$$w \geq \frac{n\,(T-R) + k(R-S)}{n\,(R-S) + k(T-R)} \qquad (2)$$

As n tends to infinity, equations (1) and (2) converge on to the original ratios (T − R)/(T − P) and (T − R)/(R − S) from above. Remember that the higher the critical temptation ratio, the poorer the outlook for cooperation.

The next step is to take the partial derivatives of the right-hand sides of equations (1) and (2) with respect to n and k. The partial derivative with respect to n shows what happens to the expressions when n increases, all other values remaining constant; the partial derivative with respect to k does the same for k. The expressions for the partial derivatives are cumbersome and there is no need to write them out because we are only interested in their signs, which can be deduced from the known relationships

$$0 \leq w < 1$$
$$T > R > P > S$$

and
$$2R > T + S$$

We find that the partial derivative wrt n of both expressions is negative, and the partial derivative wrt k of both expressions is positive. This means that as n increases, the value of w needed for TFT to be collectively stable declines; as k increases, the necessary value of w for TFT to be collectively stable increases. In plainer language: other things being equal, the larger the population, the better the prospects for cooperation; other things being equal, the more numerous the invaders, the worse the prospects for cooperation. The second half of that conclusion is common sense. The first is less obvious, and its meaning is discussed in the main text of chapter 7.

8

Paradoxes of Voting

8.1 A Good Voting System: Some Criteria to Start With

The decathlon scoring problem of section 1.3 showed that it is not as easy as it looks to describe a good procedure for decathlon scoring – or for voting. This chapter will consider various voting procedures in turn, but before we consider them we need some criteria by which to judge them. Three attractive properties for a voting system are that it should use ordering information when it is available, that it should pick a **Condorcet winner** when there is one, and that it should minimise the opportunity, or the need, for **strategic voting**.

8.1 Using Ordering Information

The more information a voting procedure can use, the better. Usually when voters have to choose among candidates, or parties, or options, they know more than just which one is their favourite. (From now on, to avoid repetition, I shall use 'options' to mean 'candidates, or parties, or options'.) In fact if the number of options is small (less than about seven, say – see Miller 1956), voters can normally rank each of them against each other. For any pair of options a voter can say one out of 'I prefer a to b', 'I prefer b to a', and 'I am indifferent between a and b'. Other things being equal, a voting system which uses this information is better than one which never collects it or which collects it but then throws it away. For the reasons given in section 1.3, we do not expect our voting procedure to deal in cardinal numbers, but only in orderings. Just as a rational individual is defined as one who can make transitive and complete orderings among the options, we might expect our good voting system to do the same.

8.1.2 *Picking a Condorcet Winner*

A Condorcet winner is defined as an option which can beat all others in pairwise voting. If there are only two options, one of them must be the Condorcet winner (unless they tie, which can only occur with an even number of voters), and simple majority voting is the best way to find it. If there are three or more, it is always possible that there is no Condorcet winner. Section 1.3.2 introduced you to the simplest and most famous case, Condorcet's original 'paradox of voting'. In that case, which was introduced as the Liverpool housing versus open space dilemma, each option beat one other and lost to one other in pairwise voting. However, when there are three options there is usually a Condorcet winner, and when there are more than three options, there often is one. We would like our good voting procedure(s) to pick the Condorcet winner if it exists. If it fails to do so, it will have picked an option that would have been beaten by at least one of the others if there had been a run-off. That offends our sense of fair play (at least it does mine).

8.1.3 *Strategic Voting*

A strategic vote is any vote which does not truly express a voter's ordering (or part of it), but which is cast in the hope of improving an option's chances. Some voting systems force voters to consider a strategic vote. For instance, in a plurality vote (as in the Anglo-Saxon 'first-past-the-post' system for most public elections), if my favourite candidate is thought to have little chance of winning I must decide between the 'sincere' choice of voting for him and my 'strategic' choice of voting for my second-best in order to keep out my worst. A pairwise procedure may also force voters to consider voting strategically. Consider the dilemma of Liverpool Tories if a vote were held on the principle of housing versus open space. (Refer to the diagram in secrtion 1.3.2. if you need to refresh your memory). Open Space is their middle option. Housing includes their best (private housing) and their worst (council housing). It is not at all clear whether they should vote for their second-best or for a package that includes both their best and their worst. Whatever they do they have to think strategically. The environmentalists in the NSPS case (section 4.4) faced a similar dilemma.

Other voting systems, although they do not *force* any voters to think strategically, may still give them the chance to do so. People have long suspected that it is possible to 'manipulate' elections held under systems such as Single Transferable Vote (STV) to improve the chances of some candidates at the expense of others. Proponents of STV deny this possibility (e.g. Knight 1974, p. 16; Lakeman 1982, pp. 51, 159) but, unfortunately, they are wrong.

8.2 Some Voting Systems and Their Defects

Let us now judge some voting systems against these criteria. As we do so, other criteria will gradually emerge as we are forced, step by step, to the conclusion that there is something 'wrong' with every procedure.

8.2.1 Plurality Voting

Plurality voting is the familiar 'first-past-the-post' or 'relative majority' rule. Each voter puts a cross against the name of one candidate; the one with the most crosses wins. If there are only two candidates all is well; the procedure selects the Condorcet winner and everybody should be happy. But if there are more than two candidates, all hell breaks loose. Relative majority fails all our tests abysmally. Obviously, it does not use ordering information at all, and so must come bottom of the class on that measure. It also forces any voter who believes that his most preferred candidate has little chance of election to consider voting strategically. It often fails to select a Condorcet winner, and may sometimes select a Condorcet loser, or 'dominated' outcome: that is, an outcome which loses the pairwise vote with every other.

To demonstrate the last point, we have to reconstruct the preference orderings of voters who have had no opportunity to express them. What follows is an attempt to do this for one British constituency at the General Election of 1983.

A Perverse Result under Plurality Voting:
UK General Election of 1983, Hyndburn Constituency

The result (%) was:

Con.	Lab.	Alliance	Ecology	Independent
42.2 (won)	42.2	14.6	0.6	0.4

Assume:

1 4% of voters ranked A and voted strategically for Labour
                  L
                  C

2 4% of voters ranked A and voted strategically Conservative
                  C
                  L

3 Alliance voters divided equally into A and A
                              C   L
                              L   C

4 All voters regarded Labour as the leftmost, the Alliance as the centre, and the Conservatives as the rightmost party. Therefore:

All left-wingers ranked L
                      A
                      C

All right-wingers ranked C
                       A
                       L

All other major-party voters ranked A or A
                                 C   L
                                 L   C

5 Ecology voters ranked Con. bottom; their rankings of the other major parties unknown.

6 Independent voters' rankings unknown.

Then orderings among the major parties are:

% of voters							
38.2	4.0	38.2	4.0	7.3	7.3	0.6	0.4
C	A	L	A	A	A	?	?
A	C	A	L	L	C	?	?
L	L	C	C	C	L	C	?

Making pairwise comparisons among the major parties, L beats C, A beats C, and A beats L. Thus A is the Condorcet winner and C is the Condorcet loser, or dominated option, among the major parties. But C wins the seat under plurality voting.

In Hyndburn, Lancashire, in June 1983, the Conservative candidate won under first-past-the-post with a majority of only 21 votes over Labour. The Alliance was known to be unlikely to win, so voters who ranked the Alliance first were forced to consider a strategic vote. I assume that a total of 8 per cent of the voters did so. (This is considerably below the proportions who regularly tell opinion pollsters that they would vote strategically.) Voters who ranked Labour or Conservative first had no reason to vote strategically as the constituency was known to be marginal between these two. I next assume that those who ranked the Alliance first split evenly as to which other main party they put second. Third, I assume that the distribution of opinion was 'single-peaked'. This assumption, which guarantees that there is a Condorcet winner, means that all voters perceive the parties as lying along some continuum – perhaps a left-right scale – so that those who put Labour first always put the Conservatives last and vice versa (for a full discussion of single-peakedness see Black 1958, pp. 14–32). Fourth, I make only one assumption about the 1 per cent of voters who voted for a minor candidate: that Ecology voters liked the Conservatives least of the main parties.

The arithmetic of these assumptions, as set out above, leads to a startling conclusion: the Alliance, which came third, was the Condorcet winner by a comfortable margin, while the Conservatives, who won, would have lost substantially to the Alliance and narrowly to Labour in pairwise votes. Of course the assumptions can be challenged. I do not know the true rankings of the voters of Hyndburn and neither does anybody else. The ones I suggest are based on general trends revealed by survey evidence, and the conclusion that the Alliance was Condorcet winner is quite robust: that is, it stands up under a wide range of assumptions other than mine. Even if my assumptions are utterly wrong, democrats should be concerned at the ever-present *possibility* of relative majority leading to the election of a highly unpopular candidate. The Professor of Logic at Oxford, in an otherwise unemotional textbook on voting procedures, declaims:

No body of people engaged in making decisions, and free to choose by what means they shall arrive at those decisions, has ever chosen to employ the relative majority procedure. That is reserved for elections in Britain, the United States, and some other countries, because the electors are not free to choose the method of election they are forced to employ, the choice being left to those who are elected by this method, and who may be afraid that they would not be elected by some other. (Dummett 1984, p. 171)

8.2.2 The 'Elimination' Family

There is a group of voting procedures which share a common feature. If no candidate has got enough votes, in a count of first preferences, to be elected, then the candidate with fewest first preferences is eliminated and his supporters' second preferences (if they express any) are then taken into account. The three best-known members of this family are Alternative Vote (AV), the French two-ballot procedure used from 1871 to 1939 and again from 1958 to 1986, and STV.

Under AV, the voters rank the candidates in order from 1 down as far as they wish to go. If any candidate has over half of the first preferences, he is elected. Otherwise, the candidate with fewest first preferences is eliminated, and his supporters' votes transferred. The process continues as long as necessary until somebody has over half of the votes. In France, the first ballot was open to anybody. If nobody got an absolute majority, another ballot was held. In presidential elections, only the two top candidates from the first ballot could enter the second. For parliamentary elections, there was no such rule, but candidates and voters often behaved as if there were (see e.g. Wright 1983, pp. 154–8). STV is a more complex system using multi-member constituencies – normally between three- and six-member. For an n-member seat in which k votes have been cast, a quota is calculated as $k/(n + 1)$ rounded up to the next integer.[1] First preferences are counted. Anybody with more votes than the quota is elected, and his surplus is redistributed.[2] When nobody else can be elected in this way, the lowest candidate is eliminated, as in AV, and the counts continue with transfers of surpluses where available and eliminations otherwise until all the seats are filled.

The elimination family is obviously better than relative majority in that it records information about orderings (although we shall shortly find out that it is used in a peculiar way). It is said that it makes strategic voting unnecessary because those who most like a relatively unpopular candidate can put him first knowing that if he is eliminated their votes are not 'wasted', but will be transferred to somebody else. However, in the two-ballot system there is an incentive to vote strategically in order that a certain pair of candidates should appear on the second ballot. As to AV and STV, even if nobody needs to consider a strategic vote, anybody who wishes to may do so. The order in which candidates are eliminated is vital to their rivals in all elimination systems, and therefore some voters may vote strategically in order to ensure that one candidate rather than another is eliminated. Furthermore, elimination systems may be no better than relative majority at selecting a Condorcet winner. STV is the best of the elimination systems. Nevertheless, table 8.1 shows that it has two grave drawbacks: arbitrary use of preference information and failure to select a Condorcet winner. In table 8.1 and all subsequent tables in this chapter, the columns represent preference orderings (best at the top, worst at the bottom) and the numbers at the head of each column represent the number of voters with that ordering.

Why can STV lead to the perverse result shown in table 8.1? Because the ordering information is used *arbitrarily*. Information on lower preferences comes into play only if higher preferences are elected with a surplus or eliminated. The idea behind this is that each vote should be counted once and only once, but it is thoroughly confused. By concentrating on fairness among voters, STV (like other elimination systems) loses sight of fairness among candidates. For instance, the fact that w is the candidate least liked by everybody other than his fervent supporters never registers in the choice process. The fact that x is elected in the first situation and z in the second is nothing to do with a change in voters' feelings about x vis-à-vis z. It is to do with a change between x and y, but the system responds in the wrong way to the change; x gains popularity but

Table 8.1 STV may be non-monotonic and fail to select a Condorcet winner

No. of voters	9	6	2	4	5
	w	x	y	y	z
	z	y	x	z	x
	x	z	z	x	y
	y	w	w	w	w

$k = 26$, $n = 2$; quota = $26/3$ to next integer = 9. On first count w reaches quota with no surplus, z is eliminated, and on second count x is elected with a surplus of 2. Now suppose that they now prefer x to y but there are no other changes anywhere in the electorate; w is elected at the first count as before, but now y is eliminated and at the second count z is elected with no surplus. The only change between the first situation and the second is that x has become more popular; however, x wins a seat in the first case but not in the second. The Condorcet winner in both situations is z, who fails to get elected in the first situation. The Condorcet loser is w, who is elected both times. The Borda scores (see below) are w: 27, x: 45 (47), y: 35 (33), and z: 49 (numbers in brackets represent the amended situation).
Source: Riker (1982), p. 50; adapted from Doron and Kronick (1977).

loses a seat. This failing of STV is called 'non-monotonicity'. It seriously undermines the case for STV, which European (but not American) electoral reformers almost all favour. It also shows that STV can be manipulated. A voter may strategically put a candidate who is not his favourite first, in order to help ensure that another candidate is eliminated, whose votes might then be transferred to a candidate the voter favours. It may be improbable that any voter should do this; but it is possible.

8.2.3 The Resolution-Amendment Procedure

Now consider a procedure that is almost always used in committee meetings and almost never in elections. All Anglo-Saxon manuals for chairmen (e.g. Citrine 1952; Robert 1971) recommend binary procedures for voting on resolutions. A resolution is proposed, and then an amendment to it. The amendment has to be disposed of first.

If it is carried, it becomes the substantive resolution, which is then voted on. If it is lost, the unamended resolution is voted on. Before this process is complete, notice may be given of further amendments, which are treated in the same way.

How does this procedure do on our criteria? It uses ordering information all right. It does not eliminate the need or the opportunity for strategic voting (see the 'Liverpool Tories' example in section 8.1.3). It has a better chance of selecting the Condorcet winner if one exists than anything we have discussed so far. If there are only three options it will always select the Condorcet winner. But if there are more than three, not every pair is voted on. (For instance, suppose notice of a second amendment is given before the first amendment is put. The first amendment is put and loses. Then the second amendment is put. But the two amendments are never compared with each other.) Hence it is always possible that the procedure will select a non-Condorcet winner because the successful option happens never to be pitted against the one which would have beaten it.

8.2.4 *Borda's (and Lewis Carroll's) Method of Marks*

Another family of procedures gives a number of points to each position on the scale, adds them up, and chooses the candidate with the highest score. If there are n candidates the best-known, and simplest, scheme gives n − 1 points to the candidate each voter places first, and one point fewer to each successive candidate finishing with 0 for the lowest-placed. This was first proposed by Jean-Charles de Borda in 1781 and is now called a 'Borda count'.

Ten years after writing *Alice in Wonderland*, Lewis Carroll independently rediscovered the theory of voting.[3] He wrote a series of pamphlets about voting procedures which he circulated around Oxford, but unfortunately nobody else could understand what he was talking about. Thus the theory of voting had another false start which might have been forgotten altogether but for the efforts of Black (1958) who not only rediscovered the theory for the second time but also rescued Carroll's work and reprinted it at the end of his book. Carroll at first opted for the Borda count, which he called 'the method of marks'.[4] However, he must have been mortified to find that, as soon as he and his colleagues applied it to select a candidate for a job, it failed to find the Condorcet winner (see Black 1958, pp. 201–2). Thereafter Carroll sought to find some way of combining the Condorcet and Borda principles, but always applying the Condorcet principle first.

When the Borda and Condorcet principles conflict, it is not obvious which ought to give way. Carroll produced a case in which the Borda winner (a in table 8.2) seems to have a much better claim than the Condorcet winner (b).

Table 8.2 A conflict between the Condorcet and Borda principles: Lewis Carroll's example

No. of voters	3	3	3	2
	b	b	a	a
	a	a	c	d
	c	d	d	c
	d	c	b	b

Borda scores: a: 27, b: 18, c: 11, d: 10; b is the Condorcet winner.
Source: Dodgson (1958), p. 216.

Borda counts are also vulnerable to manipulation, for instance by voters placing the candidate they expect to make the strongest challenge to their favourite at the foot of their list. When somebody pointed this out to Borda, he retorted, 'My scheme is only intended for honest men' (quoted in Black 1958, p. 182). However, on one of our three original criteria, the Borda count comes out well ahead of anything else considered so far. It uses ranking information fully and systematically; plurality voting does not use it at all, and elimination and resolution-amendment schemes use it only selectively.

Table 8.3a An inconsistency in the Borda procedure

No. of voters	3	2	2
	w	x	y
	x	y	z
	y	z	w
	z	w	x

Borda count: w: 11, x: 12, y: 13, z: 6. There is no Condorcet winner.

Nevertheless, there is a problem with the Borda scheme which is perhaps more worrying than either its manipulability or its failure to pick Condorcet winners. Consider the orderings shown in table 8.3a.

In this table option z is dominated. Every single voter prefers y to it. So it might seem reasonable to drop z from the list of options to be considered. This produces table 8.3b.

Table 8.3b An inconsistency in the Borda procedure (ii)

No. of voters	3	2	2
	w	x	y
	x	y	w
	y	w	x

Borda count: w: 8, x: 7, y: 6. There is no Condorcet winner.
Source: Dummett (1984), pp. 142–3.

This is very odd. We might expect that dropping an option that was not in contention would make no difference. In fact it reverses the order of the other three. In slightly more formal language, the winner (y) in the set «w,x,y,z» fails to win in a proper subset of which it is a member, namely «w,x,y».

We have considered only a tiny proportion of the voting procedures which ingenious people have thought up. By now you may have suspected that if we were to go on in this way, we would merely make similar objections to every system in turn. If so, you are quite right. Two general theorems say that no voting procedure whatever – past, present, or future, known or unknown, simple or complicated – can satisfy some apparently undemanding requirements.

8.3 On Believing Six Impossible Things Before Breakfast: Two Theorems

Like Lewis Carroll's White Queen, we may find that we have to learn to believe some impossible things if we are to continue to search for a perfect voting system. Both of the theorems in this section are 'impossibility' results: they prove that it is logically impossible to have a system which satisfies several criteria at once. As it is logically impossible, there is no point in looking further. No amount of thinking will produce a scheme so ingenious that it gets round the obstacles. If you want to score, you will have to move the goalposts.

8.3.1 Arrow's Theorem

The first and most famous impossibility result was produced by Kenneth Arrow, then a graduate student in economics at Columbia University, in 1951.[5] Asked by a logician working on game theory and international relations whether there was any meaningful sense in which nations could be said to have preferences, Arrow replied that economists had techniques for adding up each individual's welfare to an aggregate called social welfare. However, on sitting down to write an account of them, he discovered that they were faulty (see Arrow 1984, pp. 3–5). Note that the question and the answer are subtly different. The question is 'Does any voting system get us reliably from the preference orderings of each citizen to the preference ordering of a nation?' The answer is 'No procedure which adds up individuals' preference orderings and calls the result "a social ordering" can satisfy some modest requirements.' Arrow's answer covers much more than the question he had been asked. For instance, it covers markets and all other forms of economic aggregation; for that matter it covers choice by an oracle or choice by lot. But for politics students its main importance is that it covers all voting procedures. The schemes we have looked at so far all fail to produce a satisfactory winner. Arrow's Theorem shows not that no procedure will pick a satisfactory winner (from a particular subset of the conceivable options) but that none will pick a satisfactory ordering (of all the conceivable options). This is a more general finding. It undermines confidence in the idea that the winner, by any procedure, could not be beaten by some other option.

In this section the theorem is stated and explained, but not proved. (There is a proof in the appendix which it does not require advanced mathematics to follow, only a cool head and some concentration; but you do not have to understand the proof in order to understand the meaning of the theorem.)

Arrow's Theorem: If there are at least three options and a finite number of voters, then no social welfare function (SWF) can simultaneously satisfy Universal Domain (Condition U), the weak Pareto condition (Condition P), independence from irrelevant alternatives (Condition I), and non-dictatorship (Condition D).

An *SWF* is any procedure for deriving a social ordering of the options from the orderings of each individual. The term thus includes all voting procedures. Both individual and social orderings are assumed to be *complete* and *transitive*. An ordering is complete if it can say of every possible pair of options either that one is better than the other or that they are equally good. An ordering is transitive if, assuming that it chooses x over y and y over z, it chooses x over z.

Condition U requires the SWF to cope with every possible individual ordering. Suppose the resolution-amendment procedure was extended to ensure that every option was compared with every other. This would be fine if there existed a Condorcet winner. However, with some combinations of individual orderings, there is no Condorcet winner, and the procedure would break down and be unable to make a choice. Thus this procedure fails Condition U.

Condition P requires that if every individual prefers x to y, the social ordering should prefer x to y. This is such a weak condition that many people's first reaction is, 'Of course, how trivial! Nobody would ever be so crazy as to propose a system which violated such an elementary demand.' So consider table 8.4.

Table 8.4   The resolution-amendment procedure may violate
Condition P (Plott's example)

No. of voters	1	1	1
	y	x	w
	x	w	z
	w	z	y
	z	y	x

First x is paired with w and wins. Then y is paired with x and wins. Then z is paired with y and wins. But w would have been unanimously preferred to z.
Source: Plott (1976), cited from Barry and Hardin (1982) p. 234.

Condition I requires that the social ranking of any two options depends only on the individual rankings of these two and is unaffected by individual rankings of either of the two against other 'irrelevant' options. This is the hardest condition to explain and justify. But consider two of our examples. First, the STV example (section 8.2.2 and table 8.1). Before the two key voters change their minds, the procedure picks x over z. Afterwards, it picks z over x. Two things have gone wrong. First, x has become more popular but less successful (non-monotonicity). But second, nobody changed his ranking of x vis-à-vis z. The key voters changed their minds about x vis-à-vis y. But that, Arrow and his followers maintain, is irrelevant to the preference ordering of x and z.

Now consider a modification of the Borda count example (section 8.2.4 and table 8.3). When asked to rank w, x, y, and z, the procedure puts y first, x second, and w third. But when asked to rank just w, x, and y – the same w, x, and y – the procedure puts w first, x second, and y third. But z could be anything. For example, he might be a candidate who had died between nomination day and polling day. Suppose that in some districts the electoral registration rules demand the removal of such persons from the ballot and in other electoral districts they forbid it. A Borda procedure would produce opposite results in the two cases, although the voters' preferences among the feasible candidates w, x, and y, were identical.

Condition D simply requires that there is no dictator – that is, no individual whose preferences automatically become society's irrespective of anybody else's.

Since all voting systems must break at least one of Arrow's conditions, it is to some extent a matter of taste which system anybody regards as 'best'. For instance, you may decide that condition I matters less than the others, and go for a voting procedure that violates I but respects U, P, and D. Or you may be content to see U violated and toss a coin when the voting procedure is unable to choose among the options in a cycle. Another way round the theorem is to put restrictions on choices or preference orderings. For instance, if only two parties were ever allowed to enter elections, and if there was always an odd number of voters, a simple majority vote between the parties would select the Condorcet winner. Arrow's Theorem bites only if there are at least three options. Again, if all voters can arrange the options along some common spectrum such that every option which anybody thinks the worst is at one or other end of the spectrum, as in the assumption of a left-right spectrum made in section 8.2.1, there is bound to be a Condorcet winner.[6] But a rule which banned every candidate from an election except two, or one which disallowed any particular individual preference orderings, would be obviously undemocratic. So these ways of slipping past Arrow's Theorem do not lessen its importance for democratic theory.

8.3.2 *The Gibbard–Satterthwaite Theorem*

It has long been suspected that every electoral system could be manipulated in one way or another. For instance, as long ago as 1910 a Royal Commission on Electoral Systems (Cd 5163, paras 75–6) dismissed the claim of advocates of STV that 'the order in which candidates are eliminated can make no difference.' From the first appearance of Arrow's Theorem, some people began to speculate that it could be used to show that every voting system was liable to manipulation. The speculation was proved, independently, by Allan Gibbard (1973) and Mark Satterthwaite (1975). The Gibbard-Satterthwaite Theorem is too hard to prove in a book such as this. But the intuitive idea is as follows. A voting procedure would be strategy-proof if it satisfied the following conditions. For all individual preference profiles it would ensure that whenever an option became more popular its chances of success would at least get no less; and it would ensure that the result could not be manipulated by adding or withdrawing options. But this turns out to be the same as saying that such a procedure must satisfy Conditions U, P, and I in Arrow's Theorem. Therefore if there are more than two options any strategy-proof voting procedure might throw up a dictator. Therefore there is no voting procedure which is non-dictatorial and strategy-proof.

Some people draw completely nihilistic conclusions from Arrow and Gibbard–Satterthwaite, insisting that they invalidate all value judgments about voting systems. This is a mistake. First, Arrow's Theorem is strictly about orderings, not voting procedures, and people often jump from believing in the 'impossibility' of the first to that of the second. Second, although there is no best voting procedure, there are better and worse. Some systems, such as first-past-the-post, are so bad that there are many ways of improving them without hitting the bounds set by Arrow. Some procedures are more strategy-proof than others, although nobody as far as I know has tried to measure this empirically (which would be very hard). It is therefore worth discussing electoral reform in the light of the two impossibility results.

8.4 Sense and Nonsense in Electoral Reform

8.4.1 Committees

Committees most often vote while carrying out one of two tasks: choosing among courses of action and choosing among candidates for a job. They almost always use a resolution-and-amendment procedure in the first task but there is no universally used procedure in the second. A committee designing a procedure from scratch ought first to ask itself which matters more, the Condorcet or the Borda criterion. On the Condorcet criterion, the 'best' option is that which no other can defeat in a straight vote. On the Borda criterion, the 'best' option is that with the highest ranking overall. They are both appealing criteria; yet they sometimes point to different options. A committee which ranks the Condorcet criterion higher ought to apply it first. If there turns out to be no Condorcet winner, it could then use the Borda criterion to break the tie (see Black 1958, p. 66). If it ranks the Borda criterion higher it ought to conduct a straightforward Borda count. It will have to live with the fact that the successful option may not be the Condorcet winner.

How does this advice translate into practice? A 'Condorcet-first' committee could extend the conventional resolution-amendment procedure to ensure that each option was voted on against each other. If there are n options, this entails $\{n(n-1)\}/2$ votes. This number may be quite large (10 for 5 options, 21 for 7 options, 45 for 10 options, for instance) and may preclude actually voting on each pair. Therefore it is probably better to insist that each voter list his preferences among all the options in order. It is then easy to read off both the Condorcet winner (if one exists) and the Borda winner once all the lists are written down. (If you are not convinced, practise on tables 8.1 to 8.4. It is a good deal easier than counting the votes in an STV election.)

Some practical modifications have been suggested. How does one deal with indifference? In a Borda count, the obvious procedure is that tied candidates score the average of the scores they would achieve if they were not tied. Suppose I prefer a to b and b to c, d, and e but have no preference among the last three; a gets 4 points and b gets 3. If I ranked the other three, they would get 2, 1 and 0 respectively – a total of 3. Therefore, as I am indifferent amongst them, they should score 1 each. It might be objected that this is too generous to candidates at the bottom of a voter's list. Especially if there are many candidates, the voter may wish to say 'I prefer a to b, b to c, and c to d. As to candidates e to z, I do not want to discriminate between them, but I know that I do not want any of them.' The best way round this is a modification suggested by both Carroll and Dummett (both of whom had observed votes on filling fellowships in Oxford colleges): treat 'no election' as if it is a candidate. The effect of this is that it enables each voter to set a line below which no candidate is acceptable. If this line is a 'candidate', it may win the Borda count and/or be the Condorcet winner, in which case the post is not filled.

8.4.2 Elections

In moving on to elections, we have to consider a number of further complications. The first is that the electorate is not normally filling a single post (except in a direct presidential election, as in the USA or France). There is a two-stage election: the electorate chooses representatives, and the representatives choose a government. Normally, candidates will belong to a party, and the party or coalition of parties which wins the most seats will form the government. It is therefore important not just that the candidate elected in each subdivision of the country is in some sense representative of the electorate, but also that the sum of all the candidates elected is. These two may be very different. For instance, suppose the UK retained its single-member constituencies but elected MPs by AV. (It very nearly did make this change in 1930.) Going by the average of the opinion polls in 1985–6, the SDP/Liberal Alliance would be the Condorcet winner in most constituencies and would win a Borda count in almost all. In some circumstances this could lead to an Alliance landslide under AV. From the point of view of a single constituency such a result would look 'fair', but from the point of view of the national electorate it would be ridiculous. Equally ridiculous results arise from first-past-the-post single-member constituency elections. Therefore any electoral systems which seeks a 'fair' representation of preferences nationwide must abandon or supplement single-member con-stituencies. There are various ways of doing this; the best are STV, the West German two-vote procedure and a variant of it called the 'Additional Member System' (see Hansard Society 1976). The Hansard Society proposed that three-quarters of MPs should be

elected by relative majority in single-member constituencies as at
present; the rest should be chosen from amongst the 'best losers' in
individual seats in such a way as to give each party a total
representation proportionate to its share of first-preference votes
(see Bogdanor 1984, pp. 68–71). This system will not do as it
stands. Like ordinary relative majority voting, it uses no information
about ordering and forces many voters to consider voting
strategically. But it could be modified by asking voters to rank the
candidates, not just choose one. The system could then select either
the Condorcet or the Borda winner in each constituency (whichever
Parliament, when it thought about these issues properly for the first
time ever, decided was the truer 'winner') and then use the
additional seats to give each party its proportionate share of first
preferences. As the balancing element might be large, the proportion
of MPs elected directly for constituencies might have to be lower
than three-quarters.

This system would be a rather messy compromise, and it might be
objected that it put too much stress on first preferences. A more
radical reform would involve abandoning constituency representation, asking each voter to rank all the parties, and giving them
seats in proportion to the Borda scores. This would overcome
the drawbacks of STV and the Hansard Society scheme, but would
be vulnerable to strategic creation and destruction of 'parties' in
order to bring about the sort of result displayed in table 8.3a and b.
It would also put the choice of candidates in the hands of parties
rather than voters, and break the link between the MP and his
constituency. These two points, unlike the theory of voting, are
extensively discussed in every book about PR (e.g. Lakeman 1982;
Bogdanor 1984) and I need not pursue them. Instead, consider two
further problems. First, remember that an election chooses a
candidate, or a governing party. It does not choose policies. There is
a relationship between the policies candidates offer and their
chances of success, but chapter 3 showed that it is not a
straightforward one. In particular, the government has to choose a
policy not just on one issue but on every one at once. That is what
was labelled 'the insoluble problem of full-line supply' in section
3.3. It is overwhelmingly likely that there is no Condorcet winner
among all possible *platforms* – a platform being a set of policies, one
for each issue, on every issue on which a decision has to be taken.
Thus if a voting procedure is regarded as a way of making a social
choice among the platforms – the original problem that Arrow was

asked to solve – it is very unlikely that any procedure will produce a stable outcome. This is discussed further in chapter 9.

Second, proportionality of seats is not proportionality of power. This should be obvious from chapter 6. The Irish Party held 12 per cent of the seats in the parliaments of 1910, but had a disproportionately large say. The Labour Party held 6 per cent of the seats and had no say at all. As it happened, the Irish Party was pivotal and the Labour Party was not. Even if the electoral system had secured the 'fair' share of the seats to each and every party, it would be unable to prevent those who were pivotal from having too much power and those who were not from having too little.

Thus electoral reform is a more complicated subject than it looks. None the less, anybody who has the ability and the patience to follow a logical argument ought to be capable of understanding the complications. It is distressing that politicians do not, and scarcely less distressing that most writers on electoral reform (on both sides) do not either. At least this chapter should teach the reader to distrust panaceas.

Appendix: A Proof of Arrow's Theorem (based on Sen 1982, pp. 329–35)

Some Notation

P means 'is preferred to', e.g. xPy means 'x is preferred to y'.

I means 'ties with' or 'is exactly as good as', e.g. xIy means 'x is exactly as good as y'. (The I stands for Indifference.)

R means 'is at least as good as', e.g. xRy means 'x is at least as good as y' and implies that either xPy or xIy must be true.

Subscripts under the P, I, or R indicate the group whose preferences are described, e.g. xP_My means 'Group M prefers x to y'.

If there is no subscript, the reference is to the whole society, i.e. aPb means 'society prefers a to b'.

Preferences are set out in columns, thus:

L	M	N
x	x	y
y z	y	z
	z	x

means 'Group L prefers x to y and z and is indifferent between y and z. Group M prefers x to y and y to z. Group N prefers y to z and z to x.'

=> means 'implies', e.g. xPy and yPz => xPz means 'If x is socially preferred to y and y to z, then x is socially preferred to z'.

<=> means 'implies and is implied by'. e.g. xRy <=> not yPx means 'If x is at least as good as y, then y is not preferred to x; and if y is not preferred to x, then x is at least as good as y.' (Don't worry if this sounds crazy or trivial or both. We shall meet a non-trivial example soon.)

The objects denoted by lower-case letters (a, b, x, y etc.) can be regarded as options, or candidates. As political scientists are most interested in the impact of Arrow on democratic theory, including voting theory, it is helpful to visualise them as candidates in an election, or policy choices in a referendum.

Some Initial Definitions

Completeness: For any x, y, either xRy or yRx or both. that is, a social choice procedure must be able to rank all possible pairs of choices or candidates.

Transitivity: xPy and yPz => xPz
xPy and yIz => xPz
xRy and yRz => xRz

that is, if x is preferred to y and y to z, then x is preferred to z. If x is preferred to y and society is indifferent between y and z, then x is preferred to z. If x is at least as good as y and y is at least as good as z, then x is at least as good as z.

Universal domain (Condition U): the social choice procedure can cope with every possible configuration of individual preferences.

The Pareto Condition (Condition P): xP_iy for all i => xPy, that is, if every individual in a society prefers x to y, the social choice procedure should pick x over y.

The Independence Condition (Condition I): the social ranking of any pair of options depends only on the individual rankings of that pair and is not affected by individual rankings of either member of the pair vis-à-vis others.

Non-dictatorship (Condition D): there is no individual whose preferences always become society's irrespective of everyone else's preferences.

(Note the distinction between **P** and **I** (in bold letters), which are labels for the Pareto and Independence conditions, and P and I in ordinary capitals, which denote the relationships of preference and indifference.)

SWF (Social Welfare Function): a procedure for deriving a social ordering of the options from the orderings of each individual. All electoral systems, for example, are SWFs, but so are many other procedures such as drawing lots and following the commands of an oracle.

Arrow's Theorem

If there are at least three people and at least three options, no SWF can guarantee to satisfy Conditions **U, P, I,** and **D.** The proof works by assuming that conditions **U,P,** and **I,** apply and showing that they may jointly produce a dictator. Condition **U** is used in the proof throughout, because different preference orderings are chosen in each part. Condition **U** says that any preference ordering, including all those used in the proof, must be admissible. Conditions **P** and **I** are brought in at a number of points as indicated below. The full proof goes in four parts.

Suppose there are two groups of people M and N, four options a, b, x, and y, and three sets of circumstances ∝, β, and γ. (Think of M and N as the members of a committee to choose somebody for a job, a, b, x, and y as possible candidates, and ∝, β, and γ as circumstances in which different selections of the candidates are available for appointment.)

Suppose the following applies:

		Circumstance			
∝		β		γ	
M	N	M	N	M	N
x	y	a	b	a	y
y	x	b	a	x	b
				y	a
				b	x

and that xPy in ∝ (i.e. group M gets its way in circumstance ∝).

Theorem 1: xPy <=> aPb
Proof: xPy in $\propto$ => xPy in γ (Condition I)
                aPx and yPb in γ (Condition P)
Hence in γ aPxPyPb => aPb (Transitivity)
Therefore in β aPb (Condition I).

The argument can be exactly reversed to show that aPb in β implies xPy in $\propto$, therefore it is proved that xPy both implies and is implied by aPb.

Define 'almost decisive' as 'guaranteed to win even if everybody else is opposed'. Theorem 1 has shown that if a group (here M) is almost decisive over one pair of options, it is almost decisive over every pair.

Theorem 2: if a group is almost decisive over some pair, it is decisive over that pair. 'Decisive' means 'wins whether or not opposed'. (It may seem very odd to have to prove that if a group wins when it is opposed, it also wins when it is not opposed. But it must be proved; it can't just be assumed.)
Proof: suppose that M and N have the following rankings

M	N			
x	z	or z	or	z
z	x y		y	x
y			x	y

and that M is almost decisive over x and y.

xPz (by Theorem 1, as M is almost decisive over x and y, it is almost decisive over x and z)
zPy (Condition P)
Hence xPy (Transitivity) irrespective of the order in which the members of N rank x and y.

Theorems 1 and 2 jointly imply that if any group M is almost decisive over some pair of options, it is decisive over all pairs.

Theorem 3: in any decisive group with more than one member there is a subgroup that is decisive without the support of the rest.

Proof: let M divide into M^1 and M^2 with the following preferences:

M^1	M^2	N
x	y	z
y	z	x
z	x	y

yPz (Decisiveness of M)

Either yPx or xRy (Completeness – these two possibilities are exhaustive).

If yPx, M^2 is almost decisive over x and y.

Hence by Theorems 1 and 2 it is decisive over all pairs.

If xRy,

$$xRy \text{ and } yPz \Rightarrow xPz \text{ (Transitivity)}$$

Hence M^1 is almost decisive over x and z; hence by Theorems 1 and 2 it is decisive over all pairs.

Thus some subgroup of M is bound to be decisive.

Theorem 4 (Arrow's Theorem): There is no SWF satisfying Conditions U, P, I, and D.

Proof: the set of all members of society is decisive (Condition P).

But this set can always be partitioned in such a way that one of the subsets is decisive (by Theorem 3) unless the decisive subgroup has only one member, which violates Condition D.

QED.

9

Conclusion: Unfinished Business

9.1 The Aims of this Conclusion

The title of this chapter may seem self-contradictory, but it is both a summary of what has been said and a pointer to possible future directions. There are two senses in which some of the business of public choice is unfinished. First, in some areas the theory is still fluid and its implications even more so. This applies, for instance, to the n-person collective action supergames of chapter 7. Second, this is not the sort of book that tells you what to think. As I have already said, I have views on all sorts of great questions, from nuclear disarmament to capitalism versus socialism. But a book like this is not the place to say what they are, still less to persuade readers to share them. It is the place to show how public-choice thinking can help to clarify the issues involved. Where you go from there is up to you. The two main parts of this chapter each look at one of the two problems we started with, pick out some unsettled issues, and break off with a string of unanswered questions.

9.2 Collective Action Problems

We began with four distinct ways of allocating scarce goods: altruism, anarchy, the market, and government. We have also suggested a three-way division of collective action problems into AGs, CG, and PDGs. Assurance coordination games can usually be solved cooperatively without a government. Chicken games are harder to solve, and their cooperative solution requires government more often; but not always. The Cuban Missile Crisis was solved without government intervention. It was a world crisis, and there is no world government. In fact it was solved anarchically. So is virtually any international crisis which is ever solved at all. There are some institutions which claim to have power over nation-states. The EEC is one, the Commonwealth another, the United Nations a third, and the International Whaling Commission a fourth. But these normally have only as much power as the governments of their member states are prepared to let them have. So if they can ever coerce nation states, that is best regarded as an example of anarchy, not of government.

Prisoners' Dilemmas are usually regarded as the toughest coordination problems, and are often thought of as insoluble without government intervention. One problem with this approach is that getting the government to intervene may itself be a Prisoner's Dilemma, although it may be a milder form of coordination problem. This emerges from the discussion of entrepreneurs (chapter 2), lobbies (chapter 4) and supergames in general (chapter 7). It is difficult to summarise this discussion because what counts as a true n-person Prisoners' Dilemma supergame is not settled. Some writers regard the whaling supergame of section 7.8 as a true Prisoners' Dilemma, others (including me) see it as Chicken. However, 'temptation ratios' for Chicken have not been worked out.

Another unresolved issue is the relationship between group size and the possibility of cooperation. Olson argues that small groups are more likely to solve their collective action problems cooperatively than large ones. In fact, as we saw in section 4.2.2, he uses two separate arguments which are hard to reconcile with each other. Most writers, both rigorous and popular, agree that 'small is beautiful'. E.F. Schumacher (1974), who invented the phrase, believed that 'people can be themselves only in small comprehensible groups' (p. 62) and argued that pollution control was impossible 'if the patterns of production and consumption continue to be of a scale . . . which . . . do[es] not fit into the laws of the universe' (p. 248). The idea is old (going back at least to Rousseau) and influential, but not carefully argued. Three counter-arguments can be put. The normative argument 'Small isn't necessarily beautiful, cooperation isn't necessarily desirable' is considered in the next section. There are two positive arguments for claiming that in some circumstances the prospects for cooperation improve with increasing group size. The first is the one we put in section 7.5. If a group has evolved customs of reciprocal altruism – TFT or something similar – then individuals on the frontier suffer when they meet cheats trying to invade the group. The larger the group, the lower may be the proportion of its members who are on the frontier. Therefore, in Axelrod games (compound nPDs), the opposite to Olson's conclusion may be true: the larger the group, the less vulnerable it is to invasion.

Chamberlin (1974) attacks Olson from a different quarter. He starts by stressing a distinction made, but not consistently used, by Olson – that between inclusive and exclusive public goods. An inclusive (also called 'non-rival') good is one that is not subject to crowding. The products of lobbying are examples of inclusive goods. The Miners' Eight Hours' Act is worth the same to every miner, no matter how many more people become miners. By contrast, an exclusive ('rival') good (public access to the national parks, for instance) is less valuable to each citizen for every new citizen who comes along. The more people there are, the more crowded the good is, and therefore the less it is worth to each (possible) contributor. Chamberlin argues that with *inclusive* goods the existence of other contributors does not necessarily induce me to stop contributing. As the number of other contributors goes up, the amount of the good I get for nothing also goes up. This shifts my 'budget line': that is, I have more to spend altogether. With most goods, this can be expected to lead to a drop in the proportion of my income that I spend on that good, but not to an absolute drop in the quantity of the good I buy. There would be an absolute drop only if the good is what economists call an 'inferior good'. Nylon shirts are an example (from Begg et al. 1984, p. 84). If nylon shirts become cheaper, I have, in effect, more money to spend on everything (including nylon shirts). With normal goods, this would induce me to spend some of my gains on the good which had become cheaper. But nylon shirts are nasty and sweaty. As I get richer I trade up to polyester shirts. So the consequence of nylon shirts becoming cheaper is that I actually buy fewer of them.

Chamberlin assumes that most collective goods are not inferior. The assumption is probably reasonable. Hardin (1982, p. 87; cf. Crenson 1971, pp. 12–17) even suggests that some are superior: that is, the richer I get, the higher the proportion of my income I spend on them. For direct evidence, consider the Live Aid concerts for Ethiopia in 1985. If Olson were correct, the more the media reported to have been paid to Live Aid, the less each individual would be motivated to give. The truth seems to have been the opposite. So Ethiopian famine relief was a superior collective good.

Chamberlin's argument merely applies the tools of standard microeconomics to Olson. But it shares with Olson the assumption that there is no strategic interaction between the players. That begs the question, as we argued in section 4.2.2. Nevertheless, it does provide a ground for arguing that the more (potential) contributors there are, the more chance there is of the collective good being provided.

9.3 Collective Action: Some Open Questions

In this section we consider four questions to which there is no right answer; but answers (on either side) which show understanding of public choice are better than those which do not.

9.3.1 Is Altruism a Good Thing?

It may seem odd that this question is even asked. The answer seems to be Yes, of course. But behind this lies a real dilemma: if altruism is good, is it good to encourage it by deliberately restricting the scope for non-altruistic provision of goods? Consider Titmuss on blood. One reason why plenty of blood is donated in the UK is that everybody knows there is no market in blood ('you cant get blood from supermarkets and chaine stores'). If there were a market for blood, it is arguable that less would be donated. Therefore Titmuss argues that it is desirable to encourage altruism by banning the market provision of blood. Titmuss was a radical socialist. But radical socialists do not seem to apply Titmuss's argument to other commodities, and those who do seem unwilling to apply it to blood. For instance, if neither the state nor the market provided old people's homes, infirm old people would have to be cared for by their relatives. There would at least arguably be more altruism about, but would the result be a better society than one in which the state and/or the market made some provision? Or is there no analogy between the two cases?

9.3.2 Is Anarchy a Good Thing?

Michael Taylor (1976, 1982) is not only an analyst of the possibilities of anarchistic cooperation; he is also an anarchist. He puts two main arguments for anarchism. One is that many of the things that are actually done by governments could be done by anarchistic cooperation. That argument is certainly valid. The other is that life in a small anarchistic community is in itself better than life in a large industrial society. Anarchists and near-anarchists believe that people are nicer to one another when they have to resolve their differences face to face all the time than when they have large anonymous institutions to do so. Opponents of this view say that small is not necessarily beautiful – a small community can just as easily be ignorant and prejudiced as kindly and open-minded. Most people have complex and sometimes contradictory views about this. For instance, Marx and Engels (in their youth at any rate) envisaged communist society as an anarchic utopia in which I can 'hunt in the morning, fish in the afternoon, breed cattle in the evening, criticise after dinner, just as I like without ever becoming a hunter, a fisherman, a herdsman, or a critic' (from *The German Ideology* 1846, as quoted in McLellan 1971, p. 36). But they also praised the bourgeois revolution for 'rescu[ing] a considerable part of the population from the idiocy of rural life' (in the *Communist Manifesto* 1848, quoted from Marx and Engels 1968, p. 39). This argument has been going on for three centuries or so and I do not propose to settle it here. But you should try to decide what makes small beautiful and what makes small suffocating.

9.3.3 Is The Market a Good Thing?

Modern advocates of the market put great store by the Pareto principle and general equilibrium. The Pareto principle states that if at least one person feels better off and nobody feels worse off as the result of some change, then society after the change is better than society before. Thus free trade in general is desirable, because parties would not consent to any trade unless each expected to be at least as well off after the trade as before; therefore, according to Robert Nozick (1974, p. 163), there can be no justification for forbidding 'capitalist acts between consenting adults'. A Pareto optimum is the situation where no further trades can take place without at least one person being made worse off. The **Pareto frontier** is the line linking all possible Pareto optima. General equilibrium theory states that if there are no spillovers (negative externalities) then only unfettered market competition in all markets will take society to a point on the Pareto frontier.

A technical objection to this argument is that if one market is imperfect (perhaps because there are externalities which it fails to regulate) then it no longer follows that perfect competition in every other market gets closer to the Pareto frontier than anything else: the second-best may look nothing like the best (see e.g. Begg et al. 1984, pp. 331–40). There are a number of moral objections. One is that exchange is not wholly voluntary. If I am poor and you are rich, and you offer me a job, I may have to accept worse terms than if I were rich and you were poor. Another is that free-marketeers assume that the existing system of entitlements is just. But I may be rich simply because I inherited great wealth. You may be poor simply because you were born with cerebral palsy. If the state taxes me to pay for your medical care, and if I object to being taxed, then the tax is not a move towards the Pareto frontier from the starting-point. But perhaps we should not rule out the possibility of such moves. Public-choice economists have elevated the Pareto principle to a godlike status. Their ostensible reason is that any comparison of Pareto-incomparable situations involves a value judgment, and they do not want to make value judgments. Unfortunately, some of them slide into the value judgment that redistribution is wrong – that the *only* social changes which are justified are moves towards the Pareto frontier. This is an extreme conservative viewpoint. It assumes that there is no need to argue about people's initial endowments: that it is fair (or at least not unfair) that one person should be born wealthy and another born with cerebral palsy.

This illustrates the best and the worst of public choice. The best is that you can start with very meagre assumptions and finish with unexpected conclusions. The standard economists' assumptions are: that there is no accounting for tastes, but that whatever an individual wants, he prefers more of it to less; that the more he already has of any good, the less he will want yet more of that good in preference to some other good; that he is procedurally rational in making consistent and transitive choices; that goods or options can be placed in order, but not normally compared cardinally. On these deliberately weak foundations both general equilibrium theory and Arrovian social choice theory are built. It is a most impressive intellectual achievement. But the meagreness of the assumptions can be a curse as well as a blessing. Public choice should not cut itself off from questions like 'Should the able-bodied be taxed for the benefit of the disabled, and if so how heavily?'; still less should it assert without arguing that the answer is No. It can and should enrich the debate.

9.3.4 Is Cooperation a Good Thing?

Many people feel that cooperation is morally superior to competition. 'To cooperate' means 'to work with'; 'to compete' means 'to enter into or be put in rivalry with'. Cooperation often needs no more justification than its dictionary definition.

However perhaps it depends on the purpose of cooperation. For instance, the fact that the cooperative outcome to the Prisoners' Dilemma supergame is sometimes stable is morally neutral. In some PDGs, most people approve of the cooperative outcome; in others, most people approve of the non-cooperative outcome. The game was originally named after a story about two prisoners who were trying to avoid being convicted of a crime they had committed. The cooperative outcome of that game leads to a miscarriage of justice. Other PDGs can have undesirable outcomes. If a lobby overcomes its internal collective action problem (arrives at a cooperative nPDG outcome), it can persuade the government to fix a tariff that benefits the members of the lobby but harms most citizens (Olson 1982, *passim*). A cartel whose members solve their nPDG cooperatively can keep prices high; one whose members fail to solve it collapses and prices come down to the perfect-competition level.

In fact, the relation between the market and cooperation is highly ambiguous. In the two cases just cited, if the market is to work, cooperation must fail. But in the case of fair versus unfair trading (the 'market for lemons' of section 7.5) if the market is to work, cooperation must succeed. Likewise, government and cooperation do not always harmonise, nor indeed anarchy and cooperation. So is it best to regard cooperation as a valuable thing in its own right, or as a neutral procedure which may be put to good or bad ends? The only possible answer is 'It depends'.

9.4 The Problem of Aggregating Preferences

The problem of aggregating preferences was raised in section 1.3 and discussed in detail in chapter 8. It, too, contains unsettled points and issues on which the reader must make value judgments. To put these points in perspective, let us restate and summarise the problem.

There are enormously many different ways in which a country can be run. Whoever runs the country has to take decisions on every issue which is decided by government. Voters have preferences, not just on each issue taken one at a time, but on 'states of the nation'. Take a ludicrously oversimplified example. In the 1985 Queen's Speech, the British Government announced that it would legislate to allow more trading on Sundays, to tighten the law on laboratory experiments involving animals, and to privatise British Gas. Suppose that each bill was incapable of being amended, and had to be passed or rejected exactly as proposed. These three bills, with only two possible positions on each, give eight possible states of the nation. For instance, Sunday Act plus Animal Act plus Gas Act, Sunday Act plus Animal Act plus no Gas Act, Sunday Act plus no Animal Act plus Gas Act . . . . (generally, when there are m policy areas, with n possible positions on each, there are n^m states of the nation). If voters have 'strong orderings' – that is, if they are not indifferent between any pair of the options – there are 8! ('eight factorial' = $8 \times 7 \times 6 \times 5 \times 4 \times 3 \times 2 \times 1 = 40\,320$) possible different preference orderings. If voters are allowed to be indifferent between one or more pairs of options, the number of orderings is far higher still. In the general case, there are $n^m!$ strong orderings. In any real country, this is a number so astronomical that merely to print it would probably take up most of this book. It follows that amalgamating the voters' preference orderings to society's choice is not easy. In chapter 8 we showed that there was no such thing as a 'true and fair amalgamation', to borrow Riker's (1982) phrase. If there is a cycle at the top, there is no procedure which can uncontroversially select the 'socially preferred' outcome. We have still not considered how much of a problem cycling is in real-world assemblies. This is one of the unsettled issues. To discuss it, we need to pick up the problem of voting on a 'platform' last discussed in section 1.3.

9.4.1 Logrolling, Cycles and Disequilibrium – Unresolved Issues

Usually, votes in committees and legislatures take issues one at a time. After disposing of one bill, Parliament will consider and vote on the next. But the problem of social choice is immeasurably more complicated because 'states of the nation' involve considering all the issues at once. In section 1.3 we gave a simple hypothetical example of a paradox which can arise when committees vote on all the issues at once – for instance, when after voting on the policies in a manifesto one at a time, the committee has to vote on accepting the manifesto as a whole. The outcome may well leave most members in the minority on most of the issues. Furthermore, logrolling among ever-shifting coalitions could lead to outcomes that are a very long way away from maximising the number of times that each member is on the majority side.

There is no room here for a full discussion of logrolling (for which see Brams 1975, pp. 125–56; Laver 1979, pp. 89–101). But one feature deserves notice. Logrolling entails strategic voting, sometimes on a heroic scale. People form logrolling coalitions by offering to vote against propositions they actually favour. Those excluded then try to form alternative coalitions by offering to vote against propositions *they* favour. Those now excluded try to get back into a winning coalition by offering yet other strategic votes. The process is almost bound to produce cycles *even if members' true preferences are not cyclical.* If you are not convinced of this, look again at the very simple example in table 1.1 and ask yourself where you expect the bargaining to stop. Or get together a number of friends and play Laver's (1979, pp. 89–101) game, 'Rolling Logs'.

Logrolling may thus produce disequilibrium where none existed before. At other times, there may be an underlying disequilibrium which existing voting procedures have failed to reveal, but which persistent losers have an interest in discovering. This is Riker's (1982, 1984) historical theme. His account of the origins of the American Civil War was summarised in section 6.1. Restated in terms of voting theory, his argument looks like this: The 'state of the nation' which won persistent majority support under Andrew Jackson and his successors was in a cycle with a state in which slavery was forcibly restricted. Opponents of the dominant Democrats kept looking for an issue on which they could beat the incumbents, and at the third or fourth try they found it, with (as it turned out) catastrophic consequences for everybody. It was always likely that there would be such an issue, and it was always in the interests of persistent losers to search for it. Therefore, Riker argues, large societies are almost always in disequilibrium. Even when a set of policies has steady popular support, there is some other set 'out there' which would beat it if it could be found.

Riker bolsters his argument by referring to some sweeping recent theorems in formal choice theory. Richard McKelvey (1976, 1979) has shown that unless opinion is symmetrical about some median point (so that every voter on one side of the median can be paired off with one on the other) there is not only a cycle, but a global cycle, involving all the choices. Norman Schofield (1978, 1983) puts the same point in terms of game theory. Multidimensional voting games typically have an empty core (where the 'core' is the set of equilibrium strategies from which it pays no player to depart). These are difficult mathematical arguments, but you can understand the spirit of them by looking again at the logrolling game of section 1.3. There is no equilibrium in this game. No player has a strategy which is supreme against all strategies of the others. Hence even perfectly rational and perfectly well informed players are not certain to arrive at any particular outcome.

Riker uses these results to draw a conservative normative conclusion: that democracy cannot possibly live up to many of the claims made for it, and that only what he calls 'liberalism' (which turns out to be democracy restricted by the sort of checks and balances provided in the US Constitution) is supportable. This is examined in the next subsection. But not all scholars agree. If there is no median, there is no equilibrium; that is undisputed. But perhaps there generally is a median.

There will be a median if opinion is 'single-peaked' on all the ideological dimensions and if those at the median position in one dimension are at the median in all. Suppose, for instance that there are two dimensions to politics in Ruritania: a left-right dimension and a Protestant-agnostic-Catholic one. Every citizen can place both himself and the politicians on both scales, and knows that he likes a politician, or a policy, more the closer it is to his own degree of leftness, or Protestantism. Also, if 'agnostic' is at the middle of the religious line (Protestants prefer agnostic policies to Catholic ones and vice versa), then religious agnostics are also political centrists. Furthermore there is a symmetry among the non-centrists such that every left-wing Protestant is balanced by a right-wing Catholic, and every right-wing Protestant is balanced by a left-wing Catholic. Conditions such as these guarantee the existence of an equilibrium. How common are they?

Before survey research, commentators used to assume that all voters had the same ideological map; in Britain and France, for instance, it was assumed that the map was a left-right one. From the 1940s to the 1960s, survey researchers showed this that assumption was wrong. They painted a picture of an ignorant and un-ideological electorate voting largely out of habit. Recent work (for representative samples see Nie et al. 1979; Scarbrough 1984) has redressed the balance to some extent. Voters are more ideological than the 1960s' picture of them. But that does not in general mean that they organise their ideologies in ways which fit the restrictive conditions for equilibrium. Nevertheless, some scholars believe that 'democratic voting is characterized by forces that keep outcomes reasonably close to the center of voter opinion' (Enelow and Hinich 1984, p. 223). This is more likely to be true in homogeneous societies. For a society to be homogeneous in this sense it is not necessary for everybody to agree. It is necessary for almost everybody to agree on the dimensions underlying politics in such a way that nobody puts the middle options last. Opinions still differ on whether there really are many such societies.

9.4.2 *Disequilibrium and Riker's Attack on Populism*

Riker believes that the technical problems we have been discussing dispose for ever of the case for what he calls populist democracy, or the doctrine that the 'will of the people' ought to be sovereign. 'What the people want cannot be social policy simply because we do not and cannot know what the people want' (Riker 1982, pp. 238). The only alternative is what he calls liberalism, which is a form of democracy with entrenched rules to prevent the 'tyranny of the majority'. Liberalism cannot claim that it chooses the 'right' outcome, because there is usually no such thing; it can only claim that it gives the electorate the chance to reject an unacceptable politician or party every so often.

Riker's views echo those of the best-known conservative democratic theorist of the previous generation, Joseph Schumpeter (see Schumpeter 1954, chapters 20–3). The echoes are so strong that it is odd there is no reference at all to Schumpeter (that I can find) in Riker's work. Both writers see populism as a road to tyranny on which innocent and optimistic democrats set foot. For both, the rot started with Rousseau; for Schumpeter it culminated with Stalin, for Riker, with Margaret Thatcher (Riker 1982, pp. 247–8). Both make the same central claim: that the 'will of the people' sought by all participationist democratic theorists is a will o' the wisp.

There have been many attacks on Schumpeter, none wholly convincing (but see Bachrach 1969; Pateman 1970). So far, the only analysis of Riker's argument I have seen is Weale (1984). Weale points out that checks-and-balances liberalism is not the only alternative to populism; if voting paradoxes rule out populism, why not go further? Why not say that they rule out any sort of representative government at all, leaving room only for anarchic self-government in self-selected groups, with people migrating around until they find a congenial group? Second, checks and balances put some outcomes in a privileged position. If the Senate and the House cannot agree, for instance, nothing happens. But this biases the decision in favour of those who wanted nothing to happen. They need not be a majority. Riker's argument starts with the observation that if there were only two choices, majority rule would be uniquely just because it would minimise the number of dissatisfied people and give an uncontroversial 'true and fair amalgamation' of their preferences. His recommendations of a twin-chamber assembly, central-local division of powers, and judicial review all give a privileged position to the status quo (as was classically pointed out by Dahl 1956, chapters 1 and 5). But this is inconsistent with his starting-point.

Like Schumpeter, Riker also ignores part of the participationist, 'populist' case for democracy. Rousseau and J.S. Mill, who had nothing else in common, extolled democracy for its educational and character-building qualities. If people are forced to decide for themselves, the participationist argument runs, they will act in a more mature way than if they have decisions made for them. That claim has not been proved, but it has not been disproved either. Thus Riker's normative claims are important but challengeable, and that argument on them has scarcely begun.

9.4.3 Does Arrow's Theorem Really Matter?

Some years ago, Charles Plott vividly summarised the impact of Arrow's Theorem on political theory.

The subject began with what seemed to be a minor problem with majority rule. 'It is just a mathematical curiosity', said some. . . . But intrigued and curious about this little hole, researchers, not deterred by the possibly irrelevant, began digging in the ground nearby. . . . What they now appear to have been uncovering is a gigantic cavern into which fall almost all our ideas about social actions. . . . Some are still edging along the sides of the cavern following the difficult paths that remain from the optimistic route, while others have already accepted a position at the bottom of the hole and are trying to construct some stairs which might lead out. (Plott 1976; quoted from version in Barry and Hardin 1982, pp. 231–2, 236)

There are three main ways to deny that democratic theory is in the bottom of an enormous hole. One is to say that, even though it is reasonable to demand that individual choices should be transitive, it is unreasonable to demand that social choices should be. 'Social choice' is a misnomer. Societies do not choose; individuals do. If we say, for instance, 'Britain claims sovereignty over the Falklands', we mean, of course, that a minister in the present British government has made this claim in some forum or other. And if societies are not individuals, it is perhaps wrong to expect them to have qualities which we extol in individuals, such as consistency (see e.g. Buchanan 1954).

The second line is to attack the reasonableness of Arrow's Condition I ('independence of irrelevant alternatives'). We saw in chapter 8 how the Borda count procedure violates Condition I by producing a different result when 'non-feasible' candidates − say people who have died since nomination day − are put on or taken off the list. Sugden (1981, pp. 144–5) and Dummett (1984, pp. 142–3) argue that candidates of this sort are not truly irrelevant. If the effect of introducing 'irrelevant' x to a list is to move y from below z to above z, maybe this shows that those who prefer y to z prefer him/her/it very strongly indeed, and introducing x has enabled this intensity to be revealed. Maybe; but this use of intensity information is arbitrary. It uses some pieces, but ignores others. No voting procedure we have considered uses intensity information. Nor should it, because intensity information is always liable to be misrepresented. If I say I want to go to the football a million times more than I want to go to the art gallery, you can retort that you want to go to the art gallery a million million times more than you want to go to the football game. An intensity-based social choice procedure would have to say that society preferred the art gallery by a margin of a million to one.

The third way to consider 'getting round' Arrow (and Gibbard–Satterthwaite) is to query the importance of the dictatorship condition. A social choice procedure which threw up a dictator who knew in advance that his preferences dictated society's would obviously be undesirable; but what about one where it could only be seen after a particular decision, or series of decisions, had been made, that somebody had been a 'dictator'? A dictator who does not know he is a dictator is obviously less dangerous than one who does.

9.5 Final Remarks

Public choice is an exciting field, and an expanding one. I have tried to show, without using any mathematical arguments in the main text of this book at all, that it can throw new light on old problems which are at the heart of politics and sociology. Once you have acquired the knack of looking for collective action problems, you see them everywhere – in government, in lobbies, in leisure activities, in the family. Three major areas of world-wide concern and importance are the politics of arms control, of the environment, and of free trade and protection. All of these involve participants in collective action problems. All of them may involve tragic dilemmas. The Cuban missile crisis could have led to a nuclear holocaust. Resource exhaustion in the Sahara and in the world's fish stocks are perhaps examples of an nPDG that has been aptly called the 'Tragedy of the Commons'. Efforts by producer-groups all over the world to protect their positions in their domestic economy may lead to everybody being impoverished. Public choice can analyse the origins of such tragedies, and perhaps even suggest how to avoid them.

Likewise, once you have a feel for the problems of social choice, you see all around you that some questions which most people think are simple are really complicated, and that ideas which are 'obviously' right are actually wrong. This applies both in practical matters (electoral reform, committee arrangements) and in discussing the classic claims of democratic theory.

A little knowledge – of public choice, as of anything else – can be a dangerous thing. All too often, people who have just met the two-person one-shot Prisoners' Dilemma immediately jump to the conclusion that it explains every collective action dilemma from free riding to nuclear war. And people who have just met Arrow's Theorem, or heard about it in a pub, often make grandiose claims to the effect that there is no point in discussing democracy, or voting, at all because of its devastating effect. It is important, but not *that* devastating. General equilibrium theory says that if there are no spillovers in any market, unfettered laissez-faire achieves a Pareto optimum. But there are spillovers, and therefore the general model does not necesarily apply to any real-world economy. This does not lessen the intrinsic interest of the general model, but it should warn policy-makers to be humble before drawing drastic conclusions from it. Analogously, the general equilibrium model of voting shows that if opinion is exactly symmetrical, democracy will lead to the median policy being chosen. This is also a discovery of great intrinsic interest, but it has to be applied cautiously in a world where some groups of voters have single-peaked preferences and others have not, and where one voting procedure will work in one place and another in another.

The next step is to be humble, and careful, and work out which collective action dilemma applies, or which of Arrow's (and related) constraints are binding in each real-world situation. You do not need to be a mathematician to do so; you can get a long way just by thinking coolly and carefully. One of the exciting things about public choice, indeed, is that it is an area where it is still possible to make real intellectual advances using only high-school mathematics (Axelrod's *Evolution of Co-operation* is a good example). If your appetite has been whetted, the Further Reading section contains some suggestions for where to go next.

Suggestions for Further Reading

If you want to go further in public choice there are two ways to do it. One is to understand the underlying theory more fully and deeply. In this you can go as far as you wish or as your mathematics will take you. (In the suggestions below books with which a student with O-level but less than university maths should feel comfortable are marked *; those which require more than that are marked **.) The other is to read the (relatively few) works which apply the theory and think up further applications for yourself. There is still plenty of scope for innovation.

A few books involve both theory and applications. Two excellent examples, each only a little more demanding than this book, are Barry and Hardin (1982) and Colman (1982). Barry and Hardin's book is in two parts, the first on collective action problems and the second on social choice problems. In each section they reproduce some of the seminal original and interpretative papers with a very helpful linking commentary. Colman covers much the same ground, but has considerable detail on psychological experiments in which groups of students play Prisoners' Dilemma, Chicken, and other classic games.

Two useful surveys of the field written for economists are *Mueller (1979) and *Sugden (1981). A lively introduction is Schelling (1978 – * for chapter 7 only). To go further, read **Shubik (1982) – a magisterial survey of game theory by one of its pioneers. Much of Shubik's book is fully accessible to non-mathematicians, including his discussion of simple but deep games such as the Dollar Auction and the Three-person Duel. Shubik's work does not fully supersede **Luce and Raiffa (1957). Everybody, mathematician or not, should read *Black (1958) if only for the story of Black's rediscovery of Lewis Carroll and for the text of Carroll's pamphlets. Another original and inimitable work is *Farquharson (1969). **Sen (1970) expounds Arrow and extends it in ways not discussed here, but 'Sen's liberal paradox' has generated more discussion in social choice than anything except Arrow. The book is written with mathematical and non-mathematical expositions in tandem.

Four important books bridge the gap between public choice and traditional political theory, each in a different way. They are Axelrod (1984), Buchanan (1975), *Margolis (1982), and Riker (1982). Brams (1983) even applies public choice to theology.

Now for applications. On **entrepreneurs** read *Frohlich et al. (1971) and Frohlich and Oppenheimer (1978). Many writers have tried to chart politicians' manipulation of the economy; I think only Tufte (1978) and, up to a point, *Kiewiet (1983) succeed. On **voters**: Downs (1957), Page (1978), and Fiorina (1981). There is no British study of voters from an explicitly public-choice perspective, but Himmelweit et al. (1981), Sarlvik and Crewe (1983), Robertson (1984) Dunleavy and Husbands (1985), and Heath et al. (1985) all have relevant material. On extending Downs' **spatial competition** model: *Page (1977) and **Enelow and Hinich (1984). I have explained in chapters 6 and 9 why I think this is a blind alley, but interested readers should judge for themselves. On **interest groups**: Olson (1965, 1982) set the terms of the debate. Mueller (1983) is a symposium on Olson (1982). The best case studies are Moe (1980) and Hardin (1982). Again, no explictly public-choice material on Britain, but see Richardson and Jordan (1979). On **bureaucracy** *Niskanen (1971) is a much better and less partisan book than summaries of and references to it may lead you to believe. The same is not true of Borcherding (1977). There are clear and good reviews by Jackson (*1982 and 1985). On **coalitions** the main theories are set out by Riker (1962) and Axelrod (1970). The literature is fiercely (but I believe misguidedly) attacked by Barry (1980). Taylor and Laver (1973) and de Swaan and Mokken (1980) attempt to test rival hypotheses. Weale (1984) reviews the whole of Riker's work. It is fascinating to trace the evolution of **the evolution of cooperation** through **Taylor (1976) and *Maynard Smith (1982) to Axelrod (1984). An excellent introduction to biological applications of game theory is Dawkins (1978). Scientific applications of the Axelrod model are proliferating; you may track them down by looking up Axelrod in the *Science Citation Index* and the *Social Science Citation Index*. The only books to apply **social choice theory** in the area of **electoral reform** are *Dummett (1984) and *Brams and Fishburn (1982). For what it is worth, I am not enamoured of the pet schemes of either book; but unlike other electoral reformers, their authors know what they are talking about.

Postscript. While this book was in press, *Robert Sugden, *The Economics of Rights, Co-operation and Welfare* (Oxford: Basil Blackwell 1986) was published. It covers the ground of Chapter 7 at a more advanced level than this book and more elegantly than anything previously published.

Glossary of Technical Terms

Assurance game: a collective action game in which each player prefers to cooperate if the other(s) cooperate and to defect if the other(s) defect; coordination among the players is sufficient to achieve the cooperative outcome.

Cardinal: relating to the natural numbers. Thus if A, B and C are in a straight line, A is a mile from B and B is two miles from C, it is possible to say that A is three miles from C. Cf. **ordinal**.

Chicken game: a collective action game in which each player orders the outcomes (1) I defect, you cooperate; (2) we both cooperate; (3) I cooperate, you defect; (4) we both defect.

Collective action problem: any situation where all players are better off if they all cooperate than if they all defect, but where it is not necessarily in each player's individual interest to cooperate.

Condorcet winner: an option which beats every other in an exhaustive series of pairwise contests.

Cournot equilibrium solution: an oligopoly equilibrium in which each firm sets its profit-maximising output given the output decisions of the other oligopolists, but does not collude with them to raise prices or cut production.

Cycle: a number of options related in such a way that A is preferred to B which is preferred to C which is preferred to (D . . . which is preferred to) A.

Dominant strategy: in a game, one which is at least as good as any other against every possible strategy by the other player(s) and better than any other against at least one strategy by the other(s).

Equilibrium: a state from which no player has an individual incentive to depart.

Externality: any cost or benefit which an individual imposes on others but does not have to take into account in deciding what to do.

Full-line supply: a situation where the items in a package must be taken together or not at all.

Indifference: equal desire for both (all) of two or more options.

Market failure: a situation where an unregulated market fails to reach a Pareto optimum, e.g. because of externalities.

Maximand: that which an individual is trying to maximise.

Monotonic: (of a function, or the corresponding line on a graph) that is either always increasing or decreasing; (of a voting procedure): having the property that an option cannot be hurt as a consequence of changes in voters' opinions in its favour.

Oligopoly: an industry in which there are sufficiently few producers (each called an oligopolist) that each one could recognise that his actions and the others' are interdependent.

Order of Preference: a list of options ranked in order of preference.

Ordinal: relating only to an ordering. Thus a statement that A is my first preference, B my second and C my third gives no information about the distances between them. Cf. **cardinal**.

Pareto criterion: the criterion according to which situation A is judged better than situation B if, and only if, nobody is made worse off and at least one person is made better off by the move from B to A.

Pareto frontier: the set of all Pareto optima.

Pareto optimum: a situation in which nobody can be made better off without at least one person being made worse off.

Pareto-superior: state of affairs A is superior to B if the move from B to A satisfies the Pareto criterion, and B is Pareto-inferior to A. Any two states which cannot be compared in this way (because a move from one to the other makes some people feel better off and others worse off) are called **Pareto-non-comparable**.

Payoff: the utility a player gets from a given outcome in a game.

Prisoners' Dilemma game: a collective action game in which each player orders the outcomes (1) I defect, you cooperate; (2) we both cooperate; (3) we both defect; (4) I cooperate, you defect.

Private good: a good which is individually produced and consumed, whose consumption by one person prevents it from being consumed by another, and on which it is hence impossible to free ride.

Public good: a good which is jointly produced and consumed, not subject to crowding, and from which it is impossible to exclude free-riders.

Rationality: the ability to compile a complete, consistent and transitive preference ordering, and to choose actions accordingly.

Single-peakedness: in a graph where options are listed on the horizontal axis and preferences measured on the vertical axis in descending order from best to worst, the situation in which each preference ordering has only one peak; loosely, the situation in which everybody agrees that the options lie on a single dimension. (see figures 8.1a and in the notes to chapter 8).

Strategic voting: casting a vote not in accordance with one's preference ordering, in the hope of improving the chances of an option one favours.

Transitivity: the property that if a stands in some relationship to b and b stands in the same relationship to c, then a stands in the same relationship to c. Thus if I prefer a to b, b to c, and a to c, my preference relationships are transitive.

Zero-sum (or constant-sum) game: a game in which the sum of payoffs to all the players is the same for every outcome. Therefore what one player gains, another must lose.

$>$: is greater than
$<$: is less than
$\geq$: is not less than
$\leq$: is not greater than
$\Rightarrow$: implies, entails. Thus 'A $\Rightarrow$ B' means 'If A (is true) then B (is true)'.
$\Leftrightarrow$: implies and is implied by. Thus 'A $\Leftrightarrow$ B' means 'A (is true) if and only if B (is true)', and is equivalent to 'A $\Rightarrow$ B and B $\Rightarrow$ A'.

Notes

Chapter 2 Entrepreneurs

1. The so-called Coase theorem (Coase 1960) states that the economically efficient solution to a pollution dilemma is either for the polluter to pay the victims a sum equal to the losses they have sustained or for the victims to bribe the polluter not to pollute by paying him what it is worth to them to have an unpolluted environment. Property rights and ethical considerations ('which was there first?') are swept aside as irrelevant. The Coase theorem is of little practical value. It does not explain how the payments (in either direction) are to be enforced; and it ignores the possibility of threats and other strategic manipulation. For instance, I may threaten to build a blood- and bone-boiling factory next door to you and then graciously agree not to, after you and all the neighbours have clubbed together to pay me not to. That would be an easier and less smelly way to make money than actually boiling blood and bones. See also Farrell (1986).

Chapter 3 Choosing Between Governments: the Voter as Consumer

1. Figures in this paragraph are from *NOP Political Social Economic Review* (London: National Opinion Polls Ltd, bimonthly), nos 14, p. 6, 18, p. 6, 19, p. 24 and 27, p. 5, reporting a total of six sets of salience questions from NOP's regular Omnibus Poll. Similar salience data are reported in *Gallup Political Index* and in Webb and Whybrow 1982, pp. 64–9. For the position in the 1960s and early 1970s see McLean 1982a, pp. 38–9.

2. Sources for this paragraph are as for note 1, plus *NOP Political Social Economic Review* no. 42, 1983, p. 21; *Public Opinion* June-July 1983, p. 24.

Chapter 4   Lobbying: the Role of Interest Groups

1. However, you can read *Which?* in a public library. Hence people may free ride on a privately-provided public good by using a publicly-provided public good. Judging by the condition of the current issues of *Which?* in Birmingham Central Public Library, they frequently do.

2. Circuit Judge Wald, US Court of Appeals, District of Columbia Circuit, in *Sierra Club* v. *Costle* 15 ERC 2137–237 at p. 2225, 1981. 'Intent' in the last line may be a misprint for 'interest'.

3. Interview, Jim Banks (Counsel, NRDC), Washington, DC, September 1984. This interview and Mitchell (1979) are the sources for this paragraph.

4. See Mitchell (1979), p. 124 and Hardin (1982), pp. 115–16. The evidence drawn on is Moe's (1980) survey of five Minnesota lobbies, three of them small trade associations and two of them large farm associations. When asked 'What effect do *your own* dues and contributions (and *only* your own) have on the association's success or failure in achieving its lobbying goals?' the proportions giving each answer (a big effect/some effect/no effect) were virtually identical between members of the 89-strong printers' association and members of the 58 000-strong farm associations. But it cannot possibly be true that the contribution of the 89th printer adds the same amount to the lobby's effectiveness as that of the 58 000th farmer. Therefore Hardin concludes, unlike Moe, that the sizeable numbers in each group who think that their own contributions make at least some difference are simply wrong.

5. The main sources for this paragraph are interviews with counsel and staffers for utilities, Washington, DC, and Richmond, Va, September 1984. See also Haskell (1982), pp. 34–7.

6. However, these promises appear in a section headed 'Railways', so perhaps they are producer-group demands after all: the demand

from producers of railway services that producers of road services should not have an unfair advantage over them.

Chapter 5   Bureaucracy

1. It is often objected that functionalist explanation is unscientific and value-laden: unscientific because it offers no hypotheses which can be tested by attempted falsification, and value-laden because it smuggles in an implicit conservative judgment – 'if it exists, it exists for some reason. It must be functional for somebody. Therefore it must have some good in it.' These issues are outside the scope of this book, but see e.g. Barry (1970), pp. 169–73.

2. On the face of it, hospital doctors in the UK are well paid, but this ignores the fact that their contracts force them to do enormous amounts of overtime, which, unlike in any other occupation, is paid at an hourly rate below, not above, the rate for the ordinary working day. At present, 120-hour working weeks are not unknown (there are 168 hours in a week) and one of the medical unions is pressing for an absolute limit of 80 hours on the maximum working week for hospital doctors. (For comparison, it is illegal for any coach driver in the EEC to drive for more than 48 hours in any period of 7 days.) At 1985 rates, a 30-year old hospital doctor may be paid about £15 000 a year for a contract that requires him to be on call for 40 per cent of the week over and above the regular working day. This overtime is paid at the rate of 40 per cent of the normal hourly rate. If the hourly rate is recalculated on the assumption that the overtime rate was the more normal 150 per cent, it works out at £2.73, or £5683 per annum.

3. Speech by John Banham, Controller, Audit Commission, to Institute of Housing, reported in *the Guardian*, 28 June 1985. He reportedly described the Commission's findings as 'a fact which went down like a lead balloon in Marsham Street' [the headquarters of the Department of the Environment, the bureau which oversees English local government].

Chapter 6   Winning Elections and Winning Power: The Theory of Political Coalitions

1. The set of all the coalitions can be divided into two halves, one half containing the first member and the other not. Then each half can be divided into two halves, one half containing the second member and the other not, and so on for each of the other members. Hence there are 2^n coalitions. If no coalitions are blocking, then each winning coalition is by definition partnered by one losing coalition. Therefore, half of all coalitions, or 2^{n-1}, are winning.

2. Details of what went on at the Conference began to leak out within two years (Ensor 1936 p. 422 n. 2), and were fully available by 1932. In preparing this section, I consulted all the recognised authorities, namely Ensor (1936), Halevy (1961), Jenkins (1968), Blewett (1972) and Murray (1980). None of these except Jenkins devotes more than a few paragraphs at most to the Conference, although it occupied the country's leading politicians for nearly half of 1910. Blewett actually says (p. 165), 'This unique event in British political history is of little concern here' in the middle of the longest scholarly narrative of the crisis of 1909–11. Is it because it is so hard to fit within received notions of party battles that it has received so little attention? And is it significant that the first historian to consider it seriously later became the first leader of the SDP?

3. It has been argued that the Edwardian crisis was really a 'crisis of Conservatism' and that the Conservatives were struggling to find a way of breaking up the dominant Liberal-Irish coalition (Pugh 1982, p. 106). If so, the Orange episode, like the earlier Conservative flirtation with Tariff Reform, could be seen in the same light as Riker sees the attempts to break up the Jacksonian coalition: persistent losers trying to find a new issue on which to divide party politics to improve their chances of winning. The Orange episode nearly led to a civil war, too.

Chapter 7   How People (and Animals) Cooperate

1. There are far more than three distinct two-person non-zero-sum games: in fact there are 78 with strict orderings (i.e. where there are no tied preferences as in Figures 7.1 and 7.2) and over 200 including

tied preferences (Rapoport and Guyer, 1966). But only a few are interesting coordination problems. Chicken is one of the 78 and Prisoners' Dilemma is another. Assurance games include several of the 78 and several of the games including tied preferences.

2. The word 'indefinite' is needed to sidestep the so-called 'last game' or 'Surprise Examination' paradox. If a game is known to be the last, both players will defect because they cannot be punished afterwards. So the outcome of the last game can be predicted in advance. But then the second-last game becomes the 'last'; therefore both players will defect in the second-last. And the same applies to the third-last, and the fourth-last . . . and the first (see Luce and Raiffa 1957, pp. 97–102). One interpretation of the discount parameter w is as the probability that the parties will meet again. If it is 0, the game is the last, and both parties will defect. This approach avoids the paradox, which has kept philosophers busy for decades.

Chapter 8   Paradoxes of Voting

1. $k/(n + 1)$ rounded up to the next integer is the lowest number such that no more than n individuals at most can each have that number of first preference votes.

2. By a complex procedure which is irrelevant to this discussion, but see e.g. Williams and McLean 1981; Dummett 1984, pp. 269–73. I am less keen on STV now than when I coauthored 'Why Electoral Reform?' for the reasons set out in section 8.2.2.

3. Carroll described his work as 'whether new or not I cannot say'. Black (1958, pp. 193–4) found that the Oxford copies of Borda's and Condorcet's works, which Carroll would surely have consulted if he had read them, were in their original uncut condition in the 1950s (the Borda volume still is). This is as near as possible to proof that Carroll rediscovered the theory independently and had not read either Borda or Condorcet.

4. Strictly, Carroll gives the name 'method of marks' to a procedure where each voter is given a fixed number of points to be distributed

among the candidates as he pleases. However, he quickly (?too quickly) dismisses this procedure on the grounds that it is vulnerable to manipulation:

Each elector would feel that it was *possible* for each other elector to assign the entire number of marks to his favorite candidate, giving to all the other candidates zero: and he would conclude that, in order to give his *own* favorite candidate any chance of success, he must do the same for him. This Method is therefore liable, in practice, to coincide with 'the Method of a Simple [relative] Majority', which has been already, . . . as I think, proved to be unsound'. (Dodgson (Lewis Carroll), pp. 214–22, quoted at p. 218; stress in original)

Carroll therefore immediately moves on to a Borda count, modified by including 'no election' as one of the options, and it is this which is often, though slightly incorrectly, called 'Carroll's method of marks'.

5. But his 1951 formulation contained a slight mistake, so citations in this book are to the second edition, Arrow (1963).

6. This condition ('single-peakedness') is defined in the glossary. It is easier to grasp in pictures than in words. See Figure 8.1a and b.

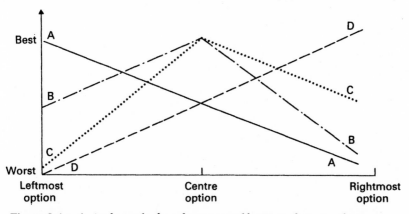

Figure 8.1a *A single-peaked preference profile. Here there are three options and four voters: A a leftist; B and C centrists; and D a rightist. All of their preference profiles can be drawn on the diagram in such a way that each has only one peak. This occurs when the options are arranged on the horizontal axis from the leftmost to the rightmost.*

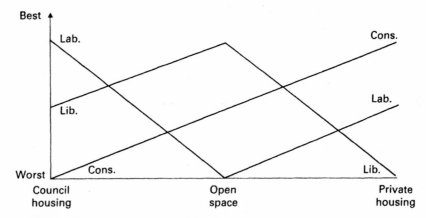

Figure 8.1b *A non-single-peaked preference profile. Here there are three options and three voters, but one of the voters (Labour) has a double-peaked preference profile. In whichever order the options are arranged along the horizontal axis, one voter does not have single-peaked preferences.*

References

Ackerman, B. and Hassler, W. 1983 *Clean Coal, Dirty Air: or how the Clean Air Act became a multibillion dollar bail-out for high-sulfur coal producers and what should be done about it* New Haven: Yale UP

Akerlof, G. 1970 'The market for "lemons": quality uncertainty and the market mechanism' *Q. J. Econ.* 84 pp. 488–500

Albrow, M. 1970 *Bureaucracy* London: Pall Mall

Allison, G. 1971 *The Essence of Decision: explaining the Cuban missile crisis* Boston: Little Brown

Arrow, K. J. 1951 *Social Choice and Individual Values* New York: Wiley (2nd edn 1963)

Arrow, K. J. 1972 'Gifts and Exchanges', *Phil. and Public Affairs* 1 pp. 343–62

Arrow, K. J. 1984 *Collected Papers of Kenneth J. Arrow vol I: Social Choice and Justice* Oxford: Blackwell

Association of District Councils 1985 *Circular 1985/86* London: ADC

Audit Commission for Local Authorities in England and Wales 1985 *Review* April. London: Audit Commission

Axelrod, R. 1970 *Conflict of Interest: a theory of divergent goals with applications to politics* Chicago: Markham

Axelrod, R. 1980a 'Effective choice in the Prisoner's Dilemma' *J. Conflict Resolution* 17 pp. 3–25

Axelrod, R. 1980b 'More effective choice in the Prisoner's Dilemma' *J. Conflict Resolution* 17 pp. 379–403

Axelrod, R. and Hamilton W. D. 1981 'The Evolution of Co-operation' *Science* 211 pp. 1390–6

Axelrod, R. 1984 *The Evolution of Co-operation* New York: Basic Books

Bachrach, P. 1969 *The Theory of Democratic Elitism* London: University of London Press

Barry, B. M. 1970 *Sociologists, Economists and Democracy* London: Collier-Macmillan

Barry, B. M. 1980 'Is it better to be powerful or lucky?' *Pol. Studies*, pp. 183–94 and 338–52

Barry, B. M. and Hardin, R. (eds) 1982 *Rational Man and Irrational Society?: an introduction and sourcebook* Beverly Hills, Calif.: Sage

Begg, D. Fischer, S. and Dornbusch, R. 1984 *Economics* Maidenhead: McGraw-Hill

Bentley, A. F. 1967 *The Process of Government* reprinted edn Cambridge, Mass.: Belknap Press (Originally published in 1908)

Bish, G. 1979 'Drafting the Manifesto' in K. Coates (ed.) *What Went Wrong: explaining the fall of the Labour government* Nottingham: Spokesman Books, pp. 187–206

Black, D. 1958 *The Theory of Committees and Elections* Cambridge: Cambridge UP

Blewett, N. 1972 *The Peers, the Parties and the People: the British general elections of 1910* London: Macmillan

Bogdanor, V. 1984 *What is Proportional Representation?* Oxford: Martin Robertson

Borcherding, T. E. (ed.) 1977 *Budgets and Bureaucrats: sources of government growth* Durham, NC: Duke UP

Brams, S. J. 1975 *Game Theory and Politics* New York: The Free Press

Brams, S. J. 1983 *Superior Beings: if they exist, how would we know?* New York: Springer-Verlag

Brams, S. J. and Fishburn, P. C. 1982 *Approval Voting* Boston: Birkhauser

Breton, A. 1974 *The Economic Theory of Representative Government* London: Macmillan

Buchanan, J. M. 1954 'Individual choice in voting and the market' *J. Pol. Econ.* **62** pp. 334–43

Buchanan, J. M. 1975 *The Limits of Liberty: between anarchy and Leviathan* Chicago: Chicago UP

Butler, D. and Kavanagh, D. 1980 *The British General Election of 1979* London: Macmillan

Butler, D. and Kavanagh, D. 1984 *The British General Election of 1983* London: Macmillan

Butler, D. and Sloman, A. 1980 *British Political Facts 1900–1979* London: Macmillan

Butler, D. and Stokes, D. 1974 *Political Change in Britain* 2nd edn London: Macmillan

Byrne, P. and Lovenduski, J. 1984 'Two New Protest Groups: the Peace and Women's Movements' in H. Drucker, P. Dunleavy, A. Gamble and G. Peele (ed,) *Developments in British Politics* London: Macmillan, revised edn, pp. 222–37

Carey, J. *Sunday Times*, 5 June 1983

Chamberlin, J. 1974 'Provision of collective goods as a function of group size' *Amer. Pol. Sci. R.* **68**, pp. 707–15

Chapman, L. 1979 *Your Disobedient Servant* 2nd edn Harmondsworth: Penguin Books

Citrine, W. (Lord) 1952 *ABC of Chairmanship* London: National Council of Labour Colleges Publishing Society

Coase, R. H. 1960 'The problem of social cost' *J. Law & Econs.* 3 pp. 1–44

Colman, A. 1982 *Game Theory and Experimental Games* Oxford: Pergamon Press

Converse, P. E. 1964 'The nature of belief systems in mass publics' in D. E. Apter (ed.), *Ideology and Discontent* New York: Free Press, pp. 206–61

Crenson, M. 1971 *The Un-politics of Air Pollution: a study of non-decisionmaking in the cities* Baltimore: Johns Hopkins UP

Crewe, I. 1981 'Why the Conservatives Won' in H. R. Penniman (ed.), *Britain at the Polls 1979* Washington, DC: American Enterprise Institute, pp. 263–305

Crewe, I. and Sarlvik, B. 1983 *Decade of Dealignment: the Conservative victory of 1979 and electoral trends in the 1970s* Cambridge: Cambridge UP

Crozier, M. 1964 *The Bureaucratic Phenomenon* London: Tavistock Publications

Cyert, R. M. and March, J. G. 1963 *A Behavioral Theory of the Firm* Englewood Cliffs, NJ: Prentice-Hall

Dahl, R. A. 1956 *A Preface to Democratic Theory* Chicago: Chicago UP

Davis, O. A., Dempster, M. A. H. and Wildavsky, A. 1974 'Towards a Predictive Theory of Government Expenditure: US Domestic Appropriations' *Br. J. Pol. S.* 4, pp. 419–52

Dawkins, R. 1978 *The Selfish Gene* reset edn London: Paladin

Dawkins, R. 1981 'In defence of selfish genes' *Philosophy* **56**, pp. 556–73

Dodgson, C. L. 1958 (Lewis Carroll) *A Discussion of the Various methods of Procedure in Conducting Elections* Oxford; privately printed 1873, reprinted by Black

Doron, G. and Kronick, R. 1977 'Single Transferable Vote: an example of a perverse social choice function' *Amer. J. Pol. Sci.* 21 pp. 303–11

Downs, A. 1957 *An Economic Theory of Democracy* New York: Harper & Row

Downs, A. 1960 'Why the government budget is too small in a democracy' *World Politics* 12 pp. 541–64

Downs, A. 1967 *Inside Bureaucracy* Boston, Mass.: Little, Brown

Dummett, M. 1984 *Voting Procedures* Oxford: Clarendon Press

Dunleavy, P. 1980 'The political implications of sectoral cleavages and the growth of state employment' *Pol. Studies* 28 pp. 364–83 and 527–49

Dunleavy, P. and Ward, H. 1981 'Exogenous voter preferences and parties with state power: some internal problems of economic theories of party competition' *Br. J. Pol. Sci.* 11 pp. 351–80

Dunleavy, P. and Husbands, C. 1985 *British Democracy at the Crossroads* London: Allen & Unwin

Dupeux, G. 1952 'Le problème des abstentions dans le département de Loir-et-Cher au début de la IIIe République' *Revue Française de Sci. Politique* 2 pp. 71–86

Enelow, J. M. and Hinich, M. J. 1984 *The Spatial Theory of Voting: an introduction* Cambridge: Cambridge UP

Ensor, R. C. K. 1936 *England 1870–1914* Oxford: Clarendon Press

Elster, J. 1985 *Making Sense of Marx* Cambridge: Cambridge UP

Farquharson, R. 1969 *Theory of Voting* Oxford: Blackwell

Farrell, J. 1986 'Rights and Efficiency', Waltham, Mass.: GTE Laboratories Inc. Economics Working Paper 86–1

Fenno, R. F. 1978 *Home Style: House members in their districts* Boston: Little, Brown

Fiorina, M. 1981 *Retrospective Voting in American National Elections* New Haven, Conn.: Yale UP

Frey, B. 1983 *Democratic Economic Policy* Oxford: Martin Robertson

Frohlich, N. and Oppenheimer, J. A. 1978 *Modern Political Economy* Englewood Cliffs, NJ: Prentice-Hall

Frohlich, N. Oppenheimer, J. and Young, O. 1971 *Political Leadership and Collective Goods* Princeton: Princeton UP

Gerth, H. H. and Mills, C. W. 1948 *From Max Weber: essays in sociology* London: Routledge

Gibbard, A. 1973 'Manipulation of voting schemes: a general result' *Econometrica* 41 pp. 587–601

Gregory, C. A. 1982 *Gifts and Commodities* London: Academic Press

Halevy, E. 1961 *The Rule of Democracy 1905–1914 (History of the English People in the Nineteenth Century vol. 6)* one-vol. paperback edn London: Ernest Benn

Hamburger, H. 1973 'N-person Prisoner's Dilemma' *J. Mathematical Sociology* 3 pp. 27–48

Hamilton, W. D. 1972 'Altruism and related phenomena, mainly in social insects' *Annual Review of Ecology and Systematics* 3 pp. 193–232

Hansard Society 1976 *Report of the Hansard Society Commission on Electoral Reform* London: Hansard Society

Hardin, R. 1982 *Collective Action* Baltimore: Johns Hopkins UP

Haskell, E. 1982 *The Politics of Clean Air: EPA standards for coal-burning power plants* New York: Praeger

Heath, A. 1976 *Rational Choice and Social Exchange* Cambridge: Cambridge UP

Heath, A., Jowell, R. and Curtice, J. 1985 *How Britain Votes* Oxford: Pergamon Press

Heclo, H. and Wildavsky, A. 1974 *The Private Government of Public Money* London: Macmillan

Himmelweit, H., Humphreys, P., Jaeger, M. and Katz, M. 1981 *How Voters Decide* London: Academic Press

Hofstadter, D. R. 1983 'Computer tournaments of the Prisoner's Dilemma suggest how cooperation evolves' *Scientific Amer.* 248 May pp. 14–20

Hood, C. and Dunsire, A. 1981 *Bureaumetrics: the quantitative comparison of British central government agencies* Farnborough, Hants: Gower

Hughes, H. Memo to R. Maheu, 1960, reproduced on cover of *Sunday Times Magazine*, 31 March 1985

Inglehart, R. 1977 *The Silent Revolution: changing values and political styles among western publics* Princeton: Princeton UP

Ingram, H. 1978 'The political rationality of innovation: the Clean Air Act Amendments of 1970' in A. F. Friedlaender (ed.), *Approaches to Controlling Air Pollution* Cambridge, Mass.: MIT Press pp. 13–65

Jackson, P. M. 1982 *The Political Economy of Bureaucracy* Deddington: Philip Allan

Jackson, P. M. 1985 'Economy, Democracy and Bureaucracy' in

R. C. O. Matthews (ed.), *Economy and Democracy* London: Macmillan pp. 168–203

Jenkins, R. 1968 *Mr Balfour's Poodle: an account of the struggle between the House of Lords and the government of Mr Asquith* reset edn London: Collins (Originally published in 1954)

Jones, T. 1971 *Whitehall Diary vol. III: Ireland 1918–25* (ed. K Middlemas) London: Oxford UP

Kellner, P. 1983 'Labour pays the price of too much unity' *New Statesman* 3 June p. 7

Kiewiet, D. R. 1983 *Macroeconomics and Micropolitics: the electoral effects of economic issues* Chicago: Chicago UP

Knight, J. 1974 *Northern Ireland: the elections of 1973* London: The Arthur McDougall Fund

Koutsoyiannis, A. 1979 *Modern Microeconomics* 2nd edn London: Macmillan

Lakeman, E. 1982 *Power to Elect* London: Heinemann

Lane, J. E. (ed.), 1985 *State and Market: the politics of the public and the private* London: Sage

Laver, M. 1979 *Playing Politics* Harmondsworth: Penguin

Laver, M. 1980 'Political solutions to the collective action problem' *Pol. Studies* 28 pp. 195–209

Laver, M. 1983 *Invitation to Politics* Oxford: Martin Robertson,

Lee, R. B. 1979 *The Kung San: men, women and work in a foraging society* Cambridge: Cambridge UP

Longford, Lord (previously F. Pakenham) 1967 *Peace by Ordeal: the negotiation of the Anglo-Irish Treaty 1921* London: New English Library (Originally published in 1935)

Luce, R. D. and Raiffa, H. 1957 *Games and Decisions* New York: Wiley

McGuire, T. G. 1981 'Budget-maximizing governmental agencies: an empirical test' *Public Choice* 36 pp. 313–22

Mackie, J. L. 1978 'The Law of the Jungle: moral alternatives and principles of evolution' *Philosophy* 53 pp. 455–64

MacKay, A. F. 1980 *Arrow's Theorem: the paradox of social choice* New Haven, Conn.: Yale UP

McKelvey, R. D. 1976 'Intransitivities in multidimensional voting models and some implications for agenda control' *J. Econ. Theory* 12 pp. 472–82

McKelvey, R. D. 1979 'General conditions for global intransitivities in formal voting models' *Econometrica* 47 pp. 1085–111

McLean, I. S. 1975 *Keir Hardie* London: Allen Lane

McLean, I. S. 1982a *Dealing in Votes* Oxford: Martin Robertson

McLean, I. S. 1982b 'Tit-for-tat and ethical computers' *Politics* 2 pp. 31–5

McLean, I. S. 1983 *The Legend of Red Clydeside* Edinburgh: John Donald

McLean, I. S. 1984 'Vote power, money power, and economic rationality: a case study in pollution control' available on request

McLean, I. S. 1986 'Should blood be for sale?' *New Society* 6 June

McLellan, D. 1971 *The Thought of Karl Marx* London: Macmillan

Malbin, M J (ed.), 1984 *Money and Politics in the United States: financing elections in the 1980s* Washington, DC: American Enterprise Institute

Margolis, H. 1982 *Selfishness, Altruism and Rationality: a theory of social choice* Cambridge: Cambridge UP

Marx, K. and Engels, F. 1968 *Selected Works* London: Lawrence & Wishart

Mauss, M. 1954 *The Gift* (transl. I Cunnison) London: Cohen & West

Maynard Smith, J. 1974 'The theory of games and the evolution of animal conflict' *J. Theor. Biol.* 47 pp. 209–21

Maynard Smith, J. 1982 *Evolution and the Theory of Games* Cambridge: Cambridge UP

van Mierlo, H. 1985 'Improvement of Public Provision of Goods and Services' in Lane pp. 53–69

Miller, G. A. 1956 'The magic number seven plus or minus two: some limits in our capacity for processing information' *Psych. R.* 63 pp. 81–97

Mitchell, A. 1983 *Four Years in the Death of the Labour Party* London: Methuen

Mitchell, R. C. 1979 'National environmental lobbies and the apparent illogic of collective action' in C. S. Russell (ed.), *Collective Decision Making: applications from public choice theory* Baltimore: Resources for the Future pp. 87–136

Moe, T. M. 1980 *The Organisation of Interests* Chicago: University of Chicago Press

Morgan, K. 1975 *Keir Hardie* London: Weidenfeld & Nicolson

Morison, S. E. Commager, H. S. and Leuchtenburg, W. E. 1969 *The Growth of the American Republic* vol. II New York: Oxford UP

Mueller, D. 1979 *Public Choice* Cambridge: Cambridge UP

Mueller, D (ed.), 1983 *The Political Economy of Growth* New Haven: Yale UP

Murray, B. K. 1980 *The People's Budget 1909–10: Lloyd George and Liberal politics* Oxford: Clarendon Press

Namier (Sir) L. 1957 *The Structure of Politics at the Accession of George III* 2nd edn London: Macmillan

von Neumann, J. and Morgenstern, O. 1947 *Theory of Games and Economic Behavior* 2nd edn Princeton: Princeton UP

Nie, N. Verba, S. and Petrocik, J. 1979 *The Changing American Voter* 2nd edn Cambridge, Mass: Harvard UP

Niskanen, W. A. 1971 *Bureaucracy and Representative Government* Chicago: Aldine

Nozick, R. 1974 *Anarchy, State and Utopia* Oxford: Blackwell

Offe, C. and Wiesenthal, H. 1980 'Two logics of collective action: theoretical notes on social class and organizational form' *Political Power and Social Theory* 1 pp. 67–115

Olson, M. 1971 *The Logic of Collective Action: public goods and the theory of groups* 2nd edn Cambridge, Mass.: Harvard UP (First published 1965)

Olson, M. 1982 *The Rise and Decline of Nations: economic growth, stagflation and social rigidities* New Haven, Conn: Yale UP

Ostrogorski, M. 1902 *Democracy and the Organisation of Political Parties* vol.I London: Macmillan

Page, B. I. 1977 'Elections and social choice: the state of the evidence' *Amer. J. Pol. Sci.* 21 pp. 639–68

Page, B. I. 1978 *Choices and Echoes in Presidential Elections* Chicago: Chicago UP

Palmer, J. L. and Sawhill I. V. (eds.), 1984 *The Reagan Record* Cambridge, Mass.: Ballinger

Parkinson, C. N. 1958 *Parkinson's Law and Other Studies in Administration* London: John Murray

Pateman, C. 1970 *Participation and Democratic Theory* Cambridge: Cambridge UP

Pincus, J. J. 1975 'Pressure groups and the pattern of tariffs' *J. Political Economy* 83 pp. 757–78

Plott, C. 1976 'Axiomatic social choice theory' *Amer. J. Pol. Sci.* 20 pp. 511–96

Ponting, C. 1985 *The Right to Know: the inside story of the Belgrano affair* London: Sphere

Pugh, M. 1982 *The Making of Modern British Politics 1867–1939* Oxford: Blackwell

Rapoport, A. and Guyer, M. J. 1966 'A taxonomy of 2 × 2 games' *General Systems* 11 pp. 203–14

Richardson, J. and Jordan, G. 1979 *Governing under Pressure: the policy process in a post-parliamentary democracy* Oxford: Martin Robertson

Riker, W. H. 1962 *The Theory of Political Coalitions* New Haven, Conn.: Yale UP

Riker, W. H. 1982 *Liberalism against Populism: a confrontation between the theory of democracy and the theory of social choice* San Francisco: W. H. Freeman

Riker, W. H. 1984 'The heresthetics of constitution-making: the Presidency in 1787, with comments on determinism and rational choice', *Amer. Pol. Sci. R.* 78 pp. 1–16

Robert, H. M. 1971 *Robert's Rules of Order* revised edn New York: Morrow

Robertson, D. B. 1976 *A Theory of Party Competition* London: Wiley

Robertson, D. B. 1984 *Class and the British Electorate* Oxford: Blackwell

Rose, R. 1984 *Do Parties Make a Difference?* 2nd edn London: Macmillan

Sabato, L. 1984 *PAC Power: inside the world of Political Action Committees* New York: Norton

Sarlvik, B. and Crewe, I. 1983 *Decade of Dealignment* Cambridge: Cambridge UP

Satterthwaite, M. A. 1975 'Strategy-proofness and Arrow's conditions: existence and correspondence theorems for voting procedures and social welfare functions' *J. Econ. Theory* 10 pp. 187–217

Scarbrough, E. 1984 *Political Ideology and Voting* Oxford: Clarendon Press

Schelling, T. C. 1960 *The Strategy of Conflict* Cambridge, Mass.: Harvard UP

Schelling, T. C. 1973 'Hockey helmets, concealed weapons, and daylight saving: a study of binary choices with externalities' *J. Conflict Resolution* 17 pp. 381–428

Schelling, T. C. 1978 *Micromotives and Macrobehavior* New York: W W Norton

Schofield, N. 1978 'Instability of simple dynamic games' *Rev. Econ. Studies* 45 pp. 575–94

Schofield, N. 1983 'Generic instability of majority rule', *Rev. Econ. Studies* 50 pp. 695–705

Schumacher, E. F. 1974 *Small is Beautiful: a study of economics as if people mattered* London: Abacus

Schumpeter, J. A. 1954 *Capitalism, Socialism and Democracy* 4th British edn London: Allen & Unwin

Sen, A. K. 1970 *Collective Choice and Social Welfare* Edinburgh: Oliver & Boyd

Sen, A. K. 1982 *Choice, Welfare, and Measurement* Oxford: Blackwell

Shapley, L. S. and Shubik, M. 1954 'A method for evaluating the distribution of power in a committee system' *Amer. Pol. Sci. R.* 48 pp. 787–92

Shubik, M. 1982 *Game Theory in the Social Sciences: concepts and solutions* Cambridge, Mass.: MIT Press

Singer, P. 1973 'Altruism and commerce: a defence of Titmuss against Arrow' *Phil. and Public Affairs* 2 pp. 312–20

Smyth, J. 1972 'The Prisoner's Dilemma II' *Mind* 81 pp. 427–31

Spann, R. M. 1977 'Public versus private provision of governmental services' in Borcherding pp. 71–89

Stokes, D. 1966 'Spatial models of party competition' in A Campbell, P. Converse, W. Miller and D. Stokes, (eds.) *Elections and the Political Order* New York: Wiley pp. 161–79

Sugden, R. 1981 *The Political Economy of Public Choice: an introduction to welfare economics* Oxford: Martin Robertson

de Swaan, A. 1973 *Coalition Theories and Cabinet Formations: a study of formal theories of cabinet formation applied to nine European parliaments after 1918* Amsterdam: Elsevier

de Swaan, A. and Mokken, R. 1980 'Testing coalition theories: the combined evidence' in L Lewin and E Vedung (eds.), *Politics as Rational Action* Dordrecht: Reidel, pp. 199–215

Taylor, M. and Laver, M. 1973 'Government coalitions in western Europe', *European J. Pol. Research* 1 pp. 205–48

Taylor, M. 1976 *Anarchy and Cooperation* London: Wiley

Taylor, M. 1982 *Community, Anarchy and Liberty* Cambridge: Cambridge UP

Taylor, M. and Ward, H. 1982 'Chickens, whales and lumpy goods: alternative models of public-goods provision' *Pol. Studies* 30 pp. 350–70

Tiebout, C. 1956 'A pure theory of local government expenditure' *J. Pol. Economy* 64 pp. 416–24

Tingsten, H. 1937 *Political Behavior: studies in election statistics* London: P. S. King & Son

Titmuss, R. 1970 *The Gift Relationship: from human blood to social policy* London: Allen & Unwin

Trivers, R. L. 1971 'The evolution of reciprocal altruism' *Q. Rev. Biol.* **46** pp. 35–57

Tufte, E. 1978 *Political Control of the Economy* Princeton, NJ: Princeton UP

Ward, H. 1982 'A reply to Iain McLean's paper' *Politics* **2** pp. 35–6

Weale, A. 1984 'Social choice versus populism? an interpretation of Riker's political theory' *B. J. Pol. Sci.* **14** pp. 369–85

Webb, N. and Whybrow, R. 1982 *The Gallup Report on 1981* London: Sphere Books

Wildavsky, A. 1964 *The Politics of the Budgetary Process* Boston: Little, Brown

Wilkinson, G. S. 1984 'Reciprocal food sharing in the vampire bat' *Nature* **308** pp. 181–4

Williams, M. E. 1985 'The Prisoner's Dilemma and the Invisible Hand', PPE thesis, Oxford University

Williams, M. E. and McLean, I. S. 1985 'Axelrod's *Evolution of Cooperation*: a critique', paper presented to Institute for Research in the Social Services Conference on Public Choice, York

Williams, P. M. and McLean, I. S. 1981 *Why Electoral Reform?* London: SDP

Wilson, J.Q. 1973 *Political Organizations* New York: Basic Books

Wright, V. 1983 *The Government and Politics of France* 2nd edn London: Hutchinson

Index

Callaghan, James, 41–2, 59
campaign finance, 30
Campaign for Nuclear Disarmament, 78
Campbell-Bannerman, Sir Henry, 114–15
canvassers, 47
cardinality, 2, 154, 182, 195
Carroll, Lewis, 10, 21, 26, 162–4, 170, 193, 202–3
catalytic converters, 21, 145–6
Chamberlin, John, 179–80
Chapman, Leslie, 90, 92
charisma, 82
Chemical Industry Association, 68
Chicken, 20, 48–9, 67, 73, 111, 126, 129–31, 137, 148, 177, 202; defined, 195; precommitment in, 67, 75, 133–4, 147; supergames, 133–4, 147
Churchill, Winston, 117
Civil Service (UK) 99; *see also* bureaucracy
civil rights (US), 66–7
Civil War, American, 106–7, 185
clean air, 2, 11, 34, 143, 198; as issue in US politics since 1970, 34–9, 53–5, 71–7
Clean Air Act Amendments (1970), 36–8, 74; (1977), 74
coal industry (UK), 31–2, 68, 78–9; (US) 38–9, 72–7
coalitions, 26, 201; blocking, losing, and winning, defined, 109; 'distributional', 65; governing, 103–21; minimal winning, defined, 111; minimal connected winning, 112–13
Coase theorem, 198
collective action problem(s), 9–10, 11, 97, 126, 177–83; application to lobby groups, 62–5, 77; defined, 195; *see also* Assurance Games, Chicken, Prisoners' Dilemma
collectively stable strategy, 137, 138, 142, 151–3
Colman, Andrew, 192
committees, election procedures for, 169–70

common law, 82
compound games, 126, 137, 138
Comptroller and Auditor-General, 90, 91–2
computers, home, 18–19
Concorde fallacy, 4
Condorcet, Marquis de, 21, 26, 155
Condorcet's paradox, *see* cycles; paradox of voting
Condorcet winner, 154–5, 156, 158–60, 162, 166, 169, 170–1; defined, 185
Congressional Budget Office, 72
Conservative Party, 40, 50, 55, 57–8, 60–1, 99, 100, 105, 158; and coalition bargaining 1906–14, 108–20, 201
constant-sum game, *see* zero-sum game
Constitution of the USA, 30, 39–40, 106, 186
constitutional conference (1910), 118
consumer groups, 64, 75, 77–8
consumer sovereignty, 53–4
Consumers' Association, 64
consumption cleavage, 99
conventions, 12, 19, 34
convergence, Downsian, 49–51, 55–8
Converse, Philip, 54
cooperation, in collective action problems, 125–53, 183
core (of a game), 52, 186
council housing, 21, 26, 52, 57, 155; sale of, *see* privatisation
Cournot equilibrium, 67, 195
Crenson, M.A., 35–6, 72
Crozier, Michel, 84
Cuba Missile Crisis, 131, 177–8, 190
cycles, 26–7, 103, 106, 167, 184–90, 195

Dean, James, 131
decathlon scoring, 22–4, 154
Defense, Department of (US), 88
demand curve, 84–6, 100–2
Democratic Party, 106–7, 185
democratic theory, and social choice, 184–91